OBSERVING STUDENTS AND TEACHERS THROUGH OBJECTIVE STRATEGIES

Sharon L. McNeely
Northeastern Illinois University

Allyn and Bacon
Boston · London · Toronto · Sydney · Tokyo · Singapore

About the Author

Sharon L. McNeely is an educational psychologist. She received her Ph.D. from the University of Wisconsin-Madison, in 1986, having earlier obtained a bachelor's and a master's degree in special education from the same institution. Since then, she has been working as a professor at Northeastern Illinois University in Chicago, Illinois. She teaches with both pre-service and in-service teachers. She also consults with schools to try to develop programs which may be effective in meeting the needs of their particular students. She has been working with classroom observations for several years, and also has developed various kinds of peer coaching programs for teachers to help each other develop their observation and teaching skills.

Copyright © 1997 by Allyn & Bacon
A Viacom Company
160 Gould Street
Needham Heights, Massachusetts 02194

Internet: www.abacon.com
America Online: keyword: College Online

ISBN 0-205-26434-4

Printed in the United States of America

10 9 8 7 6 5 4 3 2 1   01 00 99 98 97 96

TABLE OF CONTENTS

PREFACE

You have probably already spent over 11,000 hours of your life in classrooms. You have had your share of inspiring teachers, exciting and boring learning experiences, exhilarating, and not so fun experiences with peers. Along the way, all of your senses have had some workouts. Especially *seeing* and *hearing* since many typical school experiences rely on those two senses.

As you progress through this book, you will have opportunities to expand on how you use these senses and use them differently. You will have opportunities to reflect on your use of them. Then, as you think about some of your experiences it may change some of your conceptualizations of children and their development, of teachers and the teaching-learning process, and of classrooms today.

Ask any veteran teacher about classrooms and kids today and you will probably be told that neither is anything like they were five years ago. Students face different development issues and changing curriculum as they learn in rooms full of challenges to their thinking. Many classrooms now have various media and technology that may or may not be helping students develop and learn. Both students and teachers must cope with new standards and mandates, multitudes of tests and assessments, and demands to produce more in less time. We also face societal issues of violence, changes in families and communities, and onslaughts of media coverage focused on what doesn't work about education. Yet, every weekday and even some weekends, millions of students go to school and are able to learn because of dedicated teachers.

This book is designed to challenge you, the reader, to put aside years of accumulated experiences and expectations and take a fresh look at schools, students and teachers. Look now from a perspective you may not have experienced before. Your challenge is to become *objective* observers of the classroom processes. To do so, you must set aside your beliefs, attitudes and opinions, and set a goal to embrace various theories and models found in contemporary psychology literature and see what the students, teachers and classrooms look like from those varying perspectives.

It is not the intent of this book to cover any single theory or model in depth. In writing this, I assume you have or will get that information from other primary sources and are already building your own thoughts about those perspectives. Rather, I have designed this book as a supplement to help you revisit key points of the teacher-learner process as you try to observe related classroom processes.

While the majority of readers for this text are probably pre-service teachers, in-service teachers, administrators, parents and others who visit and want to learn more about classrooms will also find this a useful book. Many of the ideas and forms in this book can build self-awareness, be used with peer assistance or peer coaching, meet various guidelines for formative evaluation, and can help collect objective information about students and teaching processes.

My hope is that you will learn to value objective observance to reflect about what you have seen and heard. My goal is that everyone who uses this book somehow benefits from it.

I hope that after you have had your interactions with this text, you will let me know what worked and what didn't work for you. I will include feedback in subsequent editions and future readers will benefit from your experiences.

I would also like to take time to thank many of the people who have helped in the development of this book. My students, teachers, and administrators have used various editions of the forms included in this book. Their patience, feedback, and creative ideas for new applications have been incorporated. My family, and Lisa Tomkins Rivera, and her family, have been supportive. Andrea Iorio and Nancy Forsyth of Allyn and Bacon have been inspirational. Finally, I would like to thank the faculty who I have had the pleasure to work with at Northeastern Illinois University. Their models and ideas have given me many things to think about as I developed this. This book is dedicated to the education students that I have had the pleasure to interact with, and to my family for their continued support. I hope that I will always continue to enjoy the ways that I learn from all of them each day!

Sharon McNeely

CHAPTER 1

INTRODUCTION

HOW TO USE THIS BOOK

Whether you are a pre-service teacher, a beginning teacher, an experienced teacher, an educational supervisor, an educational administrator, or a parent, chances are that you will be, if you haven't already, observing in a classroom. Observation is a very important skill that one develops over time. If you haven't done any observations lately, then, you will probably want to read each chapter carefully, and practice with the various forms. If you are familiar with the observation process, then the chapters in this book should serve as a good review for you, and help you clarify how to link theories to observations. If you are engaging in any supervisory or evaluative observations, then this book may be a good resource for you to reflect on the processes you use, and what you value in the classroom.

In the past several years, research in education has lead to an enormous growth in the field of educational psychology as a discipline base. With the help of research, educational psychologists have learned more about what constitutes effective teaching and learning process in the past five years than they have in the twenty years prior. With the rapid growth of understanding in the field, what we consider to be effective and appropriate in terms of the methods that teachers use, and the classroom activities that students engage in, has changed. Additionally, the resources that teachers and students have available to them has changed. Even students in impoverished school districts usually have access to computers, calculators, video equipment, and other technology. Additionally, changes in what schools include in their curriculum, how they assesses learning, how they are managed, and how they are set-up all have impacted classroom processes. Then, of course, there are the considerations of society today, the growing concerns of violence, the needs to meet the diversity of our students, changes in national and state laws and policies, and a plethora of other issues also are impacting the educational processes and redefining what we consider as effective education.

In a recent interview with a principal, I was surprised when I asked the principal what constituted effective teaching, and she said, "Whatever works, whatever gets students learning, whatever thoughts teachers have that they say everyone can learn." When I asked her to clarify that into terms that we could both agree on, into something we could both observe, she was unable to do that. I told her that I didn't want to put her on the spot, but, how could she know who was doing a good job teaching and who wasn't, who to hire and who to avoid? She told me that she had a list of behaviors the district provided, and she followed the list. She then pulled out a form and handed it to me. When I looked at it, it seemed like a simple checklist. She explained that it was one of two things she had to do to evaluate effectiveness. This form required a simple classroom visit, and was simple and efficient to use. The total number of checks after twenty minutes constituted a total score, and allowed for an effectiveness rating to be given.

The second evaluation, which was based on a model of clinical supervision required a pre-observation meeting to establish what was going on in the classroom, and what behavior would be observed. Then, there was the observation. This was followed by the post-observation meeting to talk about what was observed. The principal stressed to me that while this second observational process was not new in the field, it was new to the district, and she was excited about using this process because it really opening up the description as to what was effective, and helped teachers redefine professional behaviors for themselves. She added that she was relying on educational research to help her as she helped the teachers define professional behaviors.

What was surprising to me was that this principal was not able to easily articulate what she considered as effective practice. Yet, she was supervising and evaluating teachers. Additionally, while she stated she was using educational research to help her, she did not cite any current research, theories, or models on which she was basing her processes and decisions. I left wondering if she was aware of all of the observational methods that were available to her, and to her teachers.

In writing this, I tried to keep her and other administrators, teachers I have worked with, my pre-service students, student teachers and parents in mind. I wanted to provide each of them with basic information about classroom observation based on theories of development, learning, and building thinking skills and give them easy-to-use forms for application in the classroom. I hope that in reading this, you can relate to the case examples, think about the issues each case provides for observation, and think about ways to apply theory to classroom-related concerns. I also hope that you will find the observation forms easy to apply and modify based on your particular needs and concerns. With practice, the process of observing, and making decisions based on those observations, should become easier and easier. In the long run, ideally you should be able to use your own reflective thinking skills to expand on your observations and build your own forms based on emerging theories and models in the field. If this text is used correctly, then regardless of the theories that emerge over the years, you ought to be able to build a useful, meaningful observational process to consider its application in the classroom!

Each chapter in this book has some common features. Each starts out with learning objectives. The objectives are divided into two types, things that you should know, and hopefully understand, and things that you should be able to do as you apply your knowledge. Each chapter has cases, or builds on cases presented in prior chapters. These cases are developed based on real people. Their names and the names of the schools they are associated with have been changed. Each chapter presents educational theories, links the theory to practice and application in the classroom, and draws on those linkages to build observational forms. Each form is designed for classroom use. All of the forms have been tried and tested in various classrooms, and modified to try to meet general concerns. Specific practitioner concerns may, of course, require that you make other modifications. The use of the forms, and the thinking about the theories that they are linked to, is part of the process used in this book to build reflective skills. Whether you are observing yourself, someone else, or getting ready to observe, learning what to look for, how to look at it, and how to think about what you have seen are vital processes for self-awareness and professional growth. At the end of each section that reviews a theory or model, there is a small box with a few questions designed to build reflective thinking. Of course, the actual building will depend on your prior learning, current experiences, and the ways that you choose to interact with the text. Each chapter ends with questions that review the content of the chapter, and provide opportunities for you to continue to build your reflective processes. Again, where you are in your own concept development will determine, in part, the extent to which you benefit from the questions.

REMEMBER ETHICAL CONSIDERATIONS

Whether you are going to be a teacher, are a teacher, are an administrator, or a parent, there are ethical considerations that you should be aware of, and try to appropriately deal with when you are in a school classroom observing. Instead of quoting specific ethics of various education professional organizations, the major ethical considerations will be covered. I urge you to also get a copy of, know, and follow the ethical guidelines of your particular professional association.

First, you are a guest in the classroom. Each classroom exists because the public (for public schools) or a group of people (for private schools) have agreed that it was needed. Various regulating and legislating groups have had input as to what should be in the room, what should happen, how the classroom functions, etc. The classroom, though assigned to a teacher, and the school, though assigned to a principal, ultimately belongs to the people who pay for it. As a guest, you do not have the right to know all about everything that goes on in the room. In fact, you may be asked to leave a room at any time for a host of reasons, none of which need to be provided to you. Simply being asked should always be a sufficient reason for you to leave. The usual appropriate response then is to contact the host agent to determine if and when you may return to that room or that school. There are various reasons that someone may be asked to stop observing. It may be that there is a test given which did not allow for observation. It may be that a parent has asked that his or her child is not observed. It may be that the school is engaged in some kind of study and does not want to have the process interrupted. It may be that the school is having some sort of assembly or other event that they prefer is not witnessed. Of course, there is also the possibility that the observer was asked to leave because his/her behavior was considered unethical or inappropriate for the school. In this last instance, the observer should learn what the problem was, apologize, and speak with the observation supervisor.

Second, everyone has a right to privacy. Any information which is gathered and/or recorded by an observer is confidential. It should be treated as such. Your notes should not provide the real names of individuals, unless you are a professional in a professional situation (e.g., teacher-to-teacher, administrator-to-teacher observer). You should not provide the real name of the school or the classroom participants you have seen in any open discussions you have about the observation. In some cases, you may provide this information to your instructor, but that should be in a one-on-one meeting. It is in a small part of the supervisory role that anyone makes judgments about what is seen in the room, and needs to share this. Otherwise, the role of an observer is to observe and record information. If you do make judgments, you need to be careful that you are not judging based on limited information, and that your judgments are not shared openly. Yes, you can have opinions, but you need to recognize that you should not be violating privacy when you share your opinions.

Third, everyone has a right to informed consent. The teacher, the students, and the administration has a right to know what you will be doing in the classroom, and how you will use the information you obtain. Everyone has a right to refuse to participate, to refuse to be the object of the observation, and the right to refuse to respond to an observer's questions. When you go into a room to observe, the teacher and the students should know that you are there observing, and should be given the chance to approve your being in the room. In some schools, parents also must give permission for anyone to be in a room that their child is in. In these schools, parents must also be provided information about the observation, and must provide prior approval for the observation.

Fourth, everyone has a right to be protected from harm. The observer typically is not going into the classroom to conduct an experiment, or to harm the subjects of the observation. However, it is important that you think about this, and make sure that you are not going to engage in any behaviors which may harm anyone. This includes interacting with students when you are supposed to be observing, jumping in to try to help the teacher when you are supposed to be observing, or providing helpful hints or answers for students who are engaged in learning.

Fifth, the results of your observation should be appropriately shared. If you observe a teacher, the teacher has the right to request a copy of the information you obtained. If you are engaged in objective observation, the request should be easy to meet. If, however, you are engaged in some other kind of observation, you may be embarrassed, or worse, when trying to meet the request. If you are a preservice teacher, discuss the process your instructor would like you to use in sharing the information you obtain. In all circumstances, you should discuss with the teacher what information will be shared and how you will do that prior to beginning the observation.

ONE FINAL CONSIDERATION

There are hundreds of reasons why someone engages in observation. While the reason that one is observing is important, I cannot tell you if your reasons for observation are right or wrong. What I can ask is that you think about why you are intending on observing, and what you will bring to the classroom observation. No, this is not a present, this is you. What do you bring to the room? I hope that you bring with you a cheerful, pleasant, professional persona. I hope that you come to the school clean, properly attired in clothes that are similar to those of the professionals in the school, and ready to work. No one should have to loan you a pen, or paper. No one should have to ask you to wear appropriate clothes. No one should have to ask you to take off distracting jewelry or your hat! Think about when you were a child. If someone came into your room, what things made you pay attention to that person? These are things to avoid. What things made you generally think the person was "boring" and go back to your work? These are the things that you want to emulate for your observation! Please, respect the classroom and the people there, and treat them as you want to be treated in a similar situation!

CHAPTER 2

Introduction to Observation:
Thinking about
Observation as Part of Teaching

LEARNING OBJECTIVES:

After you read this chapter, you should know:
1. the difference between objectivity and subjectivity;
2. why classroom observers strive to be objective;
3. the various types of objective recording systems;
4. the difference between reliability and validity.

After you read this chapter, you should be able to:
1. think about how your schooling experiences may impact your classroom observations;
2. differentiate examples of various types of coding systems for objective observation;
3. write about yourself or someone else as a "case" for considering how to use objective observation.

THE CASES:

An Expert Teacher Considers Observation: The Case of Steve

Steve Whilder had been teaching math to seventh and eighth graders for fifteen years. It was the start of his sixteenth year. The first two weeks of school were done, and Steve was taking time to reflect and continue to plan for the year. He had spent the first two weeks getting his students established in their classes. His eighth graders were easy, they had been his students the year before. Although there were some new faces, the students knew each other, knew how to work in groups, and had been able to establish their judicial system of management fairly quickly. The seventh graders, were new to him, but not to the school. They were having some problems establishing the management system, but tended to interact together pretty well. They seemed to be more concerned about their learning then the eighth graders.

Sixteen years! During that time there had been several major changes in the school, school rules and regulations, and his students. First, the state had enacted revised standards and objectives for learning. Some of the curriculum had to be rewritten to teach things that previously were taught in high school. Now his eighth graders had to take, and pass, several tough achievement tests before they were allowed to graduate to high school. Steve realized that could put a lot of pressure on his students and make them more anxious or even more angry about testing than they already were. He remembered how last year some students got sick when it came time for tests, and some of his best students did poorly on multiple choice exams but could answer anything orally. Adding to that was the state mandate that teachers use more alternative assessments in their classrooms. So, while Steve had to help his students get ready for the state tests, which were traditional achievement tests, he also had to teach his students how to show they had learned things in other ways, such as writing, performing speeches, developing displays, etc.

Second, his school district had decided to change from the traditional kindergarten through eighth grade buildings, and have "learning centers." There was an early childhood center that now had pre-school through second grades. There was an elementary center that housed third through fifth grades, and the middle school center, that had sixth through eighth grades and the high school transition program for those students not yet quite ready for high school. Five years ago he and his students moved into the new middle school center, called Lincoln Middle, and his teaching "life" had been changing continuously since then.

Third, there were his students. When everyone moved to the new building, he thought the move, the building, all the changes had caused his students to be a bit harder to control, a bit less attentive, a tad less mature in their conduct than his earlier classes. However, those excuses wore thin quickly, and he soon began to believe that there were other things he needed to consider about his students' development.

The move to a middle school center had been followed by a change in the school's curricular processes. Everyone talked about how this was going to be a "true" middle school. His school had a series of inservices on middle school philosophy. That was followed by the teachers again rewriting a lot of the curriculum, and developing new ways to test the students' learning. Two years ago the school began using block schedules and teams. Steve's team had four main subject-area teachers. They met to plan the learning experiences everyday for a few minutes, and once a week for an extended period. So far, the team had worked individually with their group of students. However, this year, the team was beginning to use actual team-teaching, with two teachers in the same room sometimes, and the lessons coordinated across all the teachers, so that everyone was working on the same concepts at the same time.

Additionally, the school was going to use inclusion of the special education students in the regular curriculum. This meant Steve now had several students in his classes that previously would have been in the segregated special education room. The special education teacher was resourcing to his room, coming to help not only the special education students, but other students as well. While the special education teacher joined the team and was now involved in all curricular planning, Steve also had separate meetings with her to deal with the special aspects of his subject areas and meeting the needs of his students.

Finally, Steve had to think about his new team member, and mentee, Danielle Poke. This was Danielle's first year as a full-time teacher. She had graduated, with honors, from a local university. She had student taught in a middle school that was a bit further along in the process of becoming a middle school. She was teaching science. It was important for them to integrate their math and science lessons, as well as integrating science with the other subject areas, so they had to work well together. So far, Danielle had let Steve lead with all the ideas, and she had gone along with the plans when they met together and with the entire team. Steve wondered if this would continue, or if she had her own ideas and just wasn't comfortable sharing them.

Somehow they had to really become a working team, especially since this year the school wanted to add advisory periods to the scheduling at the start of the second quarter. The homeroom period was going to be extended, and all the teachers were going to provide supportive time with the students. Steve had a very vague idea how this was going to work, and yet he and Danielle were supposed to work with the other teachers to be preparing to implement this. Since he hadn't seen this in action, he had no idea what was going to happen. He had to find a way to get Danielle to take the lead on this, because she had been student teaching in a school that had an advisory program called advisor-advisee.

Steve had recently taken a graduate class on education. In the class, he had to observe some other teachers. He learned a lot from those experiences in other classrooms. He decided to observe himself, and Danielle, maybe a few advisee session at another school, and see what he could learn about his own teaching, helping his mentee, and helping his students.

A Novice Teacher Considers Observation: The Case of Danielle

Danielle Pretter had mixed emotions as she began her first year as a full-time teacher. She had loved student teaching in the Taft Middle School. She had learned so much about herself and her capabilities to teach. She had experienced almost everything that the other student teachers in her university group had. Taft was way ahead of her current job's implementation of middle school. She had been part of a real team. The school had used progressive progressions with the team of teachers starting with sixth grade and staying with those students for three years. They not only knew the students well, but daily made curricular plans to meet the needs of the students based on the desired outcomes for learning. She hadn't been assigned someone to mentor her, she hadn't needed that. Her cooperating teacher had said she was doing fine, and didn't need help. She couldn't understand why she needed a mentor now. She knew this year would be hard, but, what could be harder than student teaching?

Danielle wondered about her job at Lincoln. In the two full days of teacher meetings at the beginning of the school year, Lincoln's teachers were talking about how hard inclusion would be, and what they would do about advisory, and how they would team, and other issues that Danielle had experienced in action at Taft. Lincoln's teachers seemed so consumed with trying these new things that she wondered if they had thought about other critical issues such as discipline, and what to say to parents, and what classroom rules they would all use for the team.

The first two weeks had been relatively uneventful. She had worked to get her students to accept the rules that the school imposed, and to develop ways to function in the classroom. She was trying to learn about her students, and her team. She was also trying to learn about the curriculum, and how Lincoln's administration helped the process of teaming.

Danielle approached this mentor thing with Steve carefully. He obviously was excited about mentoring. Her cooperating teacher had told her not to make waves in her new job. So, while she tried to share Steve's enthusiasm, she wasn't sure what to support, because she didn't know what was normal in the school. She thought back to her sociology of the schools course where she had learned about school climate. It would take her awhile to figure out the climate at this school. Afterall, she couldn't just walk in and take a survey of her colleagues.

Danielle had no idea why Steve wanted to make tapes of her teaching. Was this his way to "get" her, or use her ideas so he didn't have to do his own work? Danielle was confused. She thought about her own pre-service education. She had been in classes and observed. She had seen what teachers did and what students did. What good did it do to watch tapes of yourself, or of someone else? She had already learned all about teaching. Now was time to do it!

Of course, Danielle knew that she wouldn't be perfect at first. Her university instructors had told her all about novice teachers. However, she thought that she was not your typical novice. She had already been using reflective journaling, and she knew she was on her way to becoming an expert; afterall, she had much broader concerns than those of her former classmates. In fact, at the first two meetings of the teacher education graduates, she had found herself giving advice to others who had a lot of day-to-day concerns.

Steve's push for observation reminded her of when she was in school. Every new idea had to be experimented with, new hypothesis developed, new methods tried. Danielle had tried everything at least once. Hadn't Steve? Hadn't he tried observation before, learned from it, and moved on? Was he going to be one of those teachers who had to try everything that came out on the market, no matter how redundant or boring? Would Steve grow out of this and come along with something else? Would Steve turn out to be a problem for her? How much did this mentoring thing mean to the school? She knew she wasn't supposed to make waves, but did she really have to agree to this so she kept her job?

It also occurred to Danielle that observing herself in the room could be wonderful for her career and for her students. The right tapes in the right hands could mean that Danielle had a good chance of being rehired for the second year. The tapes could support her claims of problem children or the need for special disciplinary procedures in working with parents. She started to think that maybe the tapes weren't such a bad idea, but, how would Steve use them?

> **Reflective Questions:**
> - In what ways are the concerns of Danielle different from your concerns? The same?
> - Why do you think that Danielle is considered a novice teacher?
> - If you were in Danielle's place, how might you use observation?

A Pre-Service Teacher Considers Observation: The Case of Fran

This was Fran DuMonde's first semester at the four-year university. Having transferred in credits from the local community college, Fran had just declared a major in education, and was taking the first education class. This introduction to the schools class required all students to do 20 hours of observation in the classroom. Fran had scheduled the hours through the university's student-school placement center. The local middle school principal had agreed to the visits, and she couldn't wait to see what the middle school here looked like.

Fran's professor explained that observation was an effective means to learn how schools and classrooms are organized, how teaching occurs, what teaching methods are used, how students interact in the classroom, how teachers and students communicate, how classes are managed, what behavior is acceptable for what grade levels, what work is assigned, and a variety of other things that could be helpful for teaching. Fran's professor also explained that teaching was an unique combination of art and science. Through observation, a student who was objective when observing and reflective could learn about not only the things that good teachers do that fit with the learning and developmental theories in education, but also about the art of how to apply theory in a manner that was effective for optimizing the learning processes of the students.

Fran had no idea what to observe in the schools. The professor for the course passed out Forms C2A , C2B, and C2C the first day of class, and said that these forms had to be completed before the students could do any other observation hours. Additionally, the students would have different assignments for observation. Fran wondered aloud how many different things could be observed in a classroom. The professor picked-up on that, and after a brainstorming session, over 100 different ideas had been listed by the students. Fran had never thought about many of these behaviors, and wondered how to begin to observe some of these in the classroom.

> **Reflective Questions:**
> - In what ways are the concerns of Fran different from your concerns? The same?
> - If you were in Fran's place, how might you use observation?
> - What are some of the behaviors you might try to observe in a classroom?

Reflecting on the Cases

By most standards, Steve is an **expert** teacher. His administrators, colleagues, and students all think that he does an excellent job instructing students. His students typically show gains of at least one year on standardized achievement tests. He has few discipline problems in his class, and parents generally say that they think he does a good job, with many of them specifically asking for their children to be put in the group that is taught by his team.

However, Steve is also an expert because of the way that he thinks and then acts in the classroom. Over the years, Steve learned not to react to a lot of the little things going on in his room. He learned that most classrooms have a lot of potential distractions going on at once. He had to choose what to pay close attention to, what to monitor, what to ignore. Some things required his immediate attention. Other things went far better if he didn't deal with them immediately, but rather dealt with them later, and made changes to that particular events were less likely to occur again in the future. In his pre-service learning, Steve had been told to start the school year out tough, not smile much, and not become friends with his students. It had been hard for Steve to learn to differentiate how to be friendly without being a friend, how to be warm and welcoming, without losing respect, and how to be a disciplinarian without constantly disciplining.

In fact, the first few years of teaching, when Steve was a **novice,** had not gone well. Many times Steve had wanted to quit, sometimes he had gone home and cried. He had felt like he was in battle, and he had been defeated. The kids would get to him, the pressures would get to him. He would spend hours at night developing a lesson, and it would bomb, or it would go well but the students had been behavior problems; he just never knew how it would go. Steve had expected all of his kids to like him, and to want to learn from him. He hadn't expected that some kids wouldn't even want to like him, and wouldn't like school. He would spend so much time disciplining, sometimes even yelling, he would not get some of his lessons done. His frustration was evident, and if it hadn't been for some of the expert teachers spending some time with him (in those days the school didn't have a mentor program), Steve says that he would have left teaching.

The expert teachers didn't tell Steve what to do. They instead gave him sage advice of how to teach, focusing on the big picture. In time, Steve found that the day-to-day things became easier to manage, and much less frustrating when he didn't personalize, when he thought about what behaviors on his part lead to specific behaviors on the students' part. This thinking lead him to stop reacting to a lot of the things that took his time and energy, and instead to focus on the learning objectives in a new way. That focus was on the "big" objectives, the end learning that he wanted in the students. His thinking lead him to whole new ways of thinking about teaching, and new learning experiences in his classroom. Steve had learned how to use cooperative learning in his student teaching. When he started teaching, he used it a lot. Now, he understood that cooperative learning was a strategy to use with particular objectives. Other objectives required other strategies. The expert teachers had given him suggestions that lead to his refining these strategies for himself. He now accepts his own style of teaching, instead of trying to mimic others, or teach as he had been taught.

When Steve had started teaching, most parents came to parent-teacher conferences. They listened attentively, and they usually agreed to try to help make their children learn. In becoming an expert teacher, Steve had learned to differentiate the responsibilities of parents from those of their children who were his students. It was not up to the parents to make their children learn. It was up to them to encourage learning and schooling in a positive, productive way. It was up to them to make a home for their children to feel secure, and to be taken care of physically, emotionally, socially, and spiritually. It was up to them to provide learning experiences that the schools could not. Steve now knew that neither he nor the parents could make the children learn anything! Children had to want to learn, and had to be willing to learn. His students had to be participants in the learning processes, not just recipients.

As Steve had become an expert teacher, he had learned to become more **objective** in his thinking. He tried to put aside his opinions, attitudes, and biases. He tried to remain neutral, and frame things from the view of professionals in the field. He worked hard to lose some of his **subjective** thinking. He didn't try to impose his views, attitudes, biases on everything he saw and did. He believed that his opinions were valuable, and he did rely on them, but, he was careful to make sure his opinions were built on solid evidence, not on feelings and vague impressions, or on hearsay from other teachers.

Advice from seasoned teachers had lead Steve to keep track of some of the behaviors of his students, and to think about his own behavior. However, it wasn't until he had been forced to do observations as part of his own education that he had really concentrated on how much he could learn from observation. Not only could he use it for his own teaching, but also he could use it to help him be a better mentor. His professor had repeatedly stressed to him to be objective. At first, Steve thought he would have no problems there. He could count behaviors. However, he soon learned that it wasn't just what he counted, but how he defined the behavior, what occurred around the behavior, and what the definition of the behavior did not include that was also important to him becoming objective. He laughed as he thought about his first proposals to his professor. What he wanted to observe was just that, what he wanted to see, not what we could objectively observe. He wished that the patience his professor showed in getting him to think about his thinking could be transferred to his own work with his mentee and his students.

Danielle and Fran have yet to have experienced teaching enough to really understand some of the issues they face, and some of the ways that their thinking is likely to change in the coming years. Danielle and Fran are both novices. Danielle has the advantage of now being in a classroom, and some of the concepts that were provided in her pre-service training to become a teacher have the chance to really be clarified and developed more fully. The problem is that Danielle has to be ready to accept that she is a novice, and be willing to learn from her interactions with others. She also has to be willing to ask for and accept advice from others, including Steve.

Fran has different thoughts concerning the observation. Fran has to decide if teaching is the correct career path, what age of students to teach, if the skills required in teaching are a good match for the abilities and skills Fran already has and/or wants to further develop. One of Fran's biggest challenges is to figure out what objective observations may help clarify if teaching is the best career for her.

PLANNING THE SCHOOL VISITS

Schools are most countries' largest businesses. They employ thousands of people, and "house" millions of youth. With a changing society, and some hard lessons about safety, school officials have become protective, and often selective as to who is in the school building, and who has access to the classrooms and the students. Many schools have locked their entrances, and require all guests to have clearance from the main office prior to visiting any classrooms. Some schools have to be careful so that non-custodial parents do not have access to their children in violation of court orders. Some schools have to be careful because of gangs who try to get into the schools or get students to engage in acts of violence. Some colleges of education carefully screen their students and try to make sure that people who have criminal histories are not part of their educational classes and having access to schools.

While most schools like to welcome guests, they also have a lot to be wary of when anyone wants access. With this in mind, you need to plan your visits so that you are a welcomed guest of the school. Form C2A is designed for use primarily when you are not already working in the school where you are planning to observe. Even if you are a "seasoned" professional, like Steve, you may find the form valuable when you plan to visit another school.

Form C2A has a variety of questions for you to answer prior to your contact with the school, as well as questions you may want to ask the school representative prior to actually being at the school. Some of the questions may not seem appropriate to your setting, or you may already have the answers. However, it does not hurt to ask and make sure. You may find that the principal, or whoever your contact at the school is, may have a series of questions for you. By completing the first part of Form C2A, you should be in a better position to answer the questions if they are presented to you.

If you don't know who to contact at the school, and you are arranging your observations directly, typically the best place to start is with a phone call to the school clerk. Ask the clerk to take a couple of minutes with you on the phone. Introduce yourself, and explain why you want to ask a few questions. Ask who in the school normally arranges for visits and observations in classrooms. Ask how and when to best reach that person. Find out the title of that person. If the contact is not the

My Name:_____ Date:_____

Part 1:

1. What do I know about the school?
2. What is my philosophy of education?
3. Why do I want to visit the school?
4. What do I hope to learn by being an observer?
5. Do I want to see one teacher or several?
6. Do I want to see one group or students or several?
7. What grade level(s) and subject(s) am I interested in observing?
8. What days and times do I have available?
9. How many hours do I plan on being there each time? In all?
10. Do I have any relatives, friends, colleagues, acquaintances at the school?
11. Do I have any special needs for the school/school official to be aware of?
12. Am I also going to visit another school?

Part 2:

1. What are your policies for visitors and observers?
2. Where is the school located?
3. Where do visitors park?
4. What door should I use?
5. Where is the place I should check in when I arrive?
6. What are the hours that classes are in session?
7. Are they any days the school will be closed or there will be special events that I am not to be there?
8. How is the school organized? Are there grades? Are there teams? Is there departmentalization? Are there combined grades? What grade levels does the school serve?
9. What are the arrangements for special education? Is inclusion used? Are there special education rooms?
10. Does the school have a dress code for teachers? For students? What is the typical dress for teachers? Are there any kinds of clothes or colors that I should avoid?
11. What are the typical student characteristics? Anything I should know before I come in?
12. What is the school motto?
13. What is the average number of students per room? Do the students stay with the same teacher all day? Do the students have recess? Where do the students eat lunch?
14. Is there a teacher break room or work room for observers to sit and write-up notes?
15. Are there any special things that I should know about the school that I have not asked about?

principal, you should also get the name of the principal. With more and more schools having technological access, you may also want to get a facsimile number, and an internet address. Many times it is easier to arrange a visit through FAXES or emails.

Form C2A has a place to ask the typical dress for the school personnel, the dress code at the school, and any colors and/or kinds of clothing to avoid. It is always a good idea that any observer try to dress as professionally as possible, but within the range of what is normal for the school. If most teachers wear suits, then the observer should wear a suit also. If most teachers wear "office clothes," so should the observer. The dress is important because as an observer you do not want to bring undue attention on yourself, or cause a distraction in the classroom.

When considering the clothing, the shoes your wear should be comfortable for walking easily and quietly around the building. Additionally, in most schools, it is a good idea to not wear any jewelry. Jewelry may be distracting to the students, or be a violation of school policies. The same way that you should avoid wearing jewelry, you also want to make sure that your general appearance is conservative, with your hair, nails, and any make-up kept to a minimum, so as to draw minimal attention to you, and allow you to blend into the surroundings. It is hard to be able to concentrate on your observation, and to try to be objective, if you are the center of attention in the classroom.

When you do have confirmation of your observation times, and have established how to dress, it is also important to plan your observations so that you can be objective. Throughout this book, objectivity is discussed in more detail, and various forms are provided to help you try to become an objective observer. However, to use these effectively, there are some other things you should know and activities you should engage in.

Reflective Questions:
- Given what you know about the schools you are in what are some other considerations for your observing?
- If you don't know much about the local school where you are observing, what are some other ways to get information which may be helpful for you?

DIFFERENTIATING OBJECTIVITY AND SUBJECTIVITY IN OBSERVING

Objective observation requires that the observer goes into the situation with a lack of pre-conceived notions about what will be seen, and why classroom events occur, and is able to record specific behavioral events. Even those who have not been in a classroom in years may have some ideas about classrooms. Memories of favorite or feared teachers, classrooms with their blackboards, desks, chairs, chalk, paper, and texts, all evoke feelings in the observer. A good observer is able to distinguish what was from what is, even if there are similarities.

Most classrooms today still have teachers, blackboards, desks, chairs, chalk, etc. However, what the teacher does, what the students do, and how the teaching-learning process occurs may be very different. The good observer thinks about, and tries to be aware of his/her own feelings and beliefs, and how those impact what is seen in the classroom. The observer knows what classroom stimuli lead to personal reactions.

As an observer, you will need to get in touch with your own feelings and attitudes about classrooms. Once you are aware of what you typically think and feel when you enter a school and a classroom, you will be able to use that knowledge to help you build and maintain your objectivity. The chances are that if you are teaching, or if you are going to become a teacher, you have good feelings about at least some classroom experiences. You probably have some fond memories of events or teachers which significantly influenced your life. Remembering these is good and helpful, but you need to remember that these are only part of your feelings. Getting in touch with them is not an easy task. If you are not currently affiliated with a school, you need to find a school, and a principal, where you will be warmly received. Being welcome is important because if you feel unwelcome, you will probably become tense, then you may feel concern for the process, and not be able to concentrate on your own needs. Additionally, the process of getting in touch with your feelings takes different amounts of time for different people. Even teachers who are in schools everyday and go through this process report wide ranges in how long it takes them to really become aware of their feelings.

There are times when taking your attitudes, feelings, and opinions into the classroom is valuable. When you are asked to use your feelings to judge something, to give your opinion about what you like and don't like, to express yourself, or share some part of you, being subjective is typically good. Being able to differentiate when to use your feelings and when to try to keep them in check is a skill that you build. With practice, you should be able to distinguish when to use your feelings and when to put them in check.

The Process of Getting in Touch With Your Subjectivity: Forms C2B & C2C

You should be planning your classroom visits, the processes you will use for observation, and what behaviors you will be observing before you visit. This same planning should take place for you to start getting in touch with your subjectivity. Sit down with Form C2B. Form C2B is not an objective observation form. It is a form that you probably will not share with anyone. It is for you to use to help you get in touch with your feelings and memories. Note that the form has three parts. The first part asks you to do some free-writing. The form is not intended that you only use the space provided for that writing, but rather, that you start writing. Most people who use the form continue on to at least a few other pages of writing, and may find themselves adding to their writing over time. The second part of the form asks you to respond to some specific questions. By asking you to reflect on each of these areas, you may find yourself having more to add to the first part of the form. The third part of the form again has you do free-writing, but this time you are asked to anticipate your feelings about being in school observing. Unlike parts one and two, where you are primarily remembering, in part three, you are projecting how your memories may impact you when you go into a school.

When you have completed Form C2B, you should review what you wrote, and think about what you may need to do if your memories and beliefs do come up when you are in school. While having a memory, and experiencing the feelings that go along with it, in and of itself is not typically bad, you need to be aware that a memory could lead you consciously, or subconsciously to bias your observations or lead to conclusions that are not supported by the classroom events.

The next step in the process of getting in touch with your subjectivity involves using Form C2C. You need to find a school that will welcome your visit. If you already teach in a school, you might want to try to a different school for this experience. Take Form C2C with you, and go to the school. Before you enter the school, stop for a moment and think about your feelings. Are you happy, anxious, curious? As you proceed in, make sure that you let the main office staff know you are there. Then, walk around, let your feelings lead you. Look at the halls, the displays, the classrooms. Go into the classroom that you arranged to visit, and look around. What are you feeling? What are you thinking about? What is similar to when you were in school? What is different? If you arranged to get to the school before students were there, and you made arrangements to stay, see what feelings you get when you are in the room with students. Use the time to focus on your feelings and thoughts before you try to observe classroom processes. Whether you were able to be by yourself in a classroom, in a classroom with students, or both, you should now be ready to complete Form C2C. Find a place in the school where you can fill out the form, or leave and then fill it out. However, try to complete it as soon as possible after the experience.

When you have completed Form C2B and Form C2C, you should be beginning a reflective thinking process that may continue for a long time to come. Hopefully, your reflections will lead you to develop awareness of some of your feelings, attitudes, and beliefs. From there, you will need to take charge of these, and work to become aware of when they are entering into the observations you make in the classroom.

Form C2B: My Memories and Feelings About School

Part 1: Free-write:

What comes to mind when I think of school? What are my best memories? What are my worse memories? What do I feel when I think about these things?

Part 2: Specific questions:

1. How many schools did I attend as I was growing up? Which was my favorite? Why?

2. What were the names of my teachers? What teachers don't I remember? Why do I remember some names and not others? What do I think and feel about the teachers that I remember?

3. Who was my favorite teacher? Why? What did I learn from this teacher?

4. Who was my least liked teacher? Why? What did I learn from this teacher?

5. What was my favorite school subject? Why?

6. What was my least liked school subject? Why?

7. What did I feel about the school office/disciplinarian? When was I sent for discipline? Why?

8. Why did I miss school? What happened when I missed school?

9. What interests did I have with my peers that the school met? What clubs did I participate in?

10. What after-school or out-of-school activities was I involved with?

11. The one word I would use to describe my feelings about school is:

Part 3: Free write:

What do I think I might feel when I am in school observing? What events may trigger feelings or memories? Are there any things that may impact my being a good observer?

Form C2C: While I Visit the School:

Part 1: Just before I enter the school:

What are my thoughts and feelings?

What are my predictions of what I will find when I look around?

Part 2: In the school:

What are my thoughts and feelings?

How is this school similar to the schools I went to?

How is this school different from the schools I went to?

Part 3: Now that I have spent some time looking around:

What do I expect of a good teacher at this school? Is this expectation different from what I would normally expect of a good teacher? If so, how, and why?

What do I expect of a teacher who is having problems? is this expectation different form what I would normally expect? If so, how, and why?

How do the classroom set-ups differ from what I expected?

What do I expect of a well-disciplined student at this school? Is this expectation different from what I would normally expect of a well-disciplined student? If so, how, and why?

What do I expect a teacher to do if a student does not behave appropriately in this school? Is this expectation different from what I would normally expect? If so, how, and why?

What are my other thoughts and feelings?

The Case Expert Teacher Reflects Using Form C2B and Form C2C

Steve credits his good sense of humor for ever getting him to start the process of completing Forms C2B and C2C. Afterall, he was in classrooms all year long for the past fifteen years. Plus, he had graduated from college and was now a graduate student. He didn't think he had anything to get in touch with! However, as he filled in Part 2 of Form C2B, and then found himself thinking about what he wrote, Steve started to ask himself some hard questions. Why did he put such glowing attributes on his male teachers? What lead him to say his worse experience in school was flunking a major test because he was ill and the teacher made him take it? Did his feelings enter into his teaching today? Did he treat male teachers, or male students differently? Did he overplay the importance of tests? Did he have instant sympathy for anyone who said they didn't feel well?

One of Steve's former colleagues was now a principal at an elementary school in another school district. Steve arranged a visit there. Steve's initial feelings were rather cynical. He reported that he worked hard not to laugh at the silliness of this. However, once he started wandering around the school alone, he found himself sitting in a classroom staring at a chalkboard that read, "Today we will review for the test on Friday." Steve found himself writing on Form C2C on the spot. He not only had a lot of memories come back, but he also connected to the knot in his stomach and the headache from the glint of the lighting. Was he stressing his students by putting so much emphasis on a test? Were they feeling stomach pains?

The other place that Steve found himself lingering was the gym. The school he was visiting was overcrowded, and the gym was now converted to classrooms. However, it still had the distinctive floor and walls. Steve acknowledged the pride he felt in the gym. He had done well here, when he was a student. Unfortunately, only his physical education teacher had appreciated his motor skills. Other teachers had vaguely praised him, if they even bothered. He remembered a couple teachers who had wondered aloud, much to his embarrassment, if he could learn to use his brains the way he used his muscles. Steve found himself feeling shaken. Did he ever put down a student in front of others? Did he ever berate one skill over another one? Did he miss praising the students' skills and successes, even if they weren't in his classroom? Was he even aware of some of the skills students brought to the class? Steve decided that he needed to think about these feelings some more, and engage in some objective observations to see if he ever did any of these things in his classroom.

The next step for Steve was to develop a strategy about how to think about the observations. Afterall, the observations are not designed for anyone to use to berate him- or herself or anyone else. They are designed to help provide information so that teachers can use theory and research with the observation to gain insights, to make decisions, and maybe to make changes in the future. Steve decided he needed to review what he knew about observing, and establish an observation plan.

The Case Novice Teacher Reflects on Using Forms C2A, C2B, and C2C

Initially Danielle skipped over Form C2A without filling it out. Afterall, she was already a teacher. However, when she thought about it, she really wasn't sure what she knew about Lincoln School. She sat down and tried to fill-out Form C2A without talking to anyone at the school. When she looked at all the blank spaces on her form, she decided that she needed more information. She felt rather embarrassed. How could she have taken a job at a school that she knew so little about? How could she have answered questions posed by students or parents if she didn't know these items? What would her peers think of her when she talked about her school with them? It became more obvious to Danielle that she didn't know everything she thought she did. She decided to spend some time with the school clerk, and maybe ask Steve some of these questions. She decided Form C2A would be completed!

Completing Forms C2B and C2C were also eye-openers for Danielle. She found Form C2B easy to complete. Her best day ever was when she won an award for spelling. The award, a certificate, was presented in a ceremony, and she still had the certificate. For years it had hung on her bedroom wall. Danielle didn't even remember what other awards had been given that day. She just remembered hers, and the feeling she had that she had been so special. Danielle's mom had taken off of work to come to the ceremony. Danielle remembered how she introduced her mom to her classmates and her teachers. Then, Danielle thought about how a teacher had told her mom, right in front of Danielle, that the mom ought to be at the school more often, and should pay more attention to Danielle. Danielle had felt a rush of tears. That teacher was wrong then to say that, to judge her mother. Even now, Danielle felt that the teacher had been wrong. She felt a surge of concern for her mother. Danielle thought about how important it was to encourage her students, and to encourage her parents. She hoped she would never judge a parent the way that her mother had been judged.

Danielle found herself wondering how to make this situation more objective. What did she need to know? She wondered how the teacher had come to the conclusion that her mother didn't pay enough attention to her daughter. Where would she develop that idea? Was it prejudice of some kind? Was there something in Danielle's school file? Was there something she wasn't considering about her mother? Had her mother missed any important school events, like report card pick-ups, or meetings with teachers? Did her mother have more information which may help her understand the situation? Would asking her mother questions lead to a discussion of the event? Would her mother be objective in recalling information? Danielle determined to think more about this. She also made the decision that she would have to try to keep feelings out of situations in which they didn't belong.

Going to the school and really thinking as she looked around brought out two more important realizations for Danielle. First, she found herself staring at the stairs. The stairs of Lincoln were nothing like the stairs at the schools she had attended. She remembered big steps that seemed to go up indefinitely. There seemed to be hundreds between each floor. She remembered how as a youngster the steps lead to where the older kids were, and she wasn't allowed to go there. As she got older, the steps lead to isolation from the younger kids. She started wondering how many times she had run up the steps to not have to be bothered with younger kids. Did she still think that way? Was that why she had always wanted to teach older kids?

Second, Danielle remembered her math teachers. They loved math. They tried to get their students to love math. They didn't let students have calculators. They demanded that the students know the number facts first. Danielle cringed. Number facts had always been something she worked extra hard to try to get. Her mother would spend hours with her trying to find ways to memorize things like how to combine fractions and how to figure out square roots. She could remember how upset she was when the teachers would make her recite the number facts, or do those number facts worksheets with a stop watch in hand. Yes, Danielle could spell, but dealing with number facts was a different thing! Danielle had learned that her own learning style was not conducive to learning number facts. She hadn't learned a strategy to change how she approached the task. Her early failures lead to frustration and more frugal attempts in the future. Like most other people, she had preferences for what to learn and how to learn it. She needed to remember that her students would all have different learning styles and learning strategies. She had learned that again and again in student teaching. Maybe, she thought, she ought to get to know their styles and preferences, what they found easy to learn and what was hard to learn, as soon as possible.

The Case Pre-Service Teacher Reflects on Using Forms C2A, C2B, and C2C

Fran enjoyed using Form C2A. With a phone call, Fran set-up an appointment at Lincoln School and spent a half hour with the assistant principal going through the form. The assistant made a copy Form C2A as they began. She said that these were questions that she wanted to ask anyone coming in to observe, and things she wanted to make sure to tell anyone who did come in. She decided everyone should know these things if they came to the school. With that, Fran relaxed a bit and was glad that Form C2A provided for conversation. The task of observing seemed less cumbersome!

Forms C2B and C2C were also copied by the assistant principal. She said that she had never seen forms like this, and was curious to try them out. She said that she learned new things every single day on the job. She wished she had time to write a book about her experiences as a teacher.

That perked-up Fran, who was somewhat interested in writing. Fran agreed to meet with the assistant principal again when the observation times were done, and they would compare their thoughts about what teaching involved on a day-to-day basis.

Walking around the school, Fran found the computer room. None of Fran's schools had had computer rooms. In high school, some of the rooms had computers. However, none of the teachers ever spent much time with the students on the computers. Were the teachers afraid of the computers? Did the teachers know how to use them? Most students in Fran's generation knew of and had access to computers regularly. They thought of the teachers as "old-fashioned" when they insisted on students doing work by hand or on typewriters when the work could be done on a computer. Fran remembered this and wondered how much computers influenced and were part of education in this school. Fran wondered if all schools had mandates to use computers or if there were still some schools that didn't have computers.

Fran also thought about art. Lincoln School didn't seem to have an art room. They had a fine arts center. Fran found that and thought of the differences between that and the art rooms in some high schools. This multi-purpose art center allowed students to engage in different activities more so than a typical art room. Art was Fran's draw to teaching. Fran's art teachers had been inspirational. They had recognized that Fran had talent. Mr. Denau had even told Fran that Fran's talent should not be wasted, and while creating artistic wonderments was fine, it would not pay the bills. Fran ought to teach art, which would allow for creative time, and still pay the bills. Yes, Fran had Mr. Denau to thank. his words had set-up Fran's course of action into college and education. There were no other options! Fran made a note to call and thank Mr. Denau for his help. Fran wondered if Mr. Denau would remember his inspirational words and if he would be proud that one of this students was following in his footsteps.

It was three weeks later, in the middle of doing an observation at Lincoln that it occurred to Fran that being a teacher meant following in the footsteps of all teachers, not just the one you most remember. Fran had been planning to teach as Mr. Denau had taught. Maybe, though, Fran should also think more about what other things teachers had taught, how they had acted, what they had said. Fran started to believe there was something to learn from every teacher, and quickly jotted that down on the side of the observation sheet.

Differentiation in Definitions of Objective Observation

In any educational area one is likely to find differences in how terms are defined and used. One of these areas is in the use of the term objective. Some instructors will use the term "objective" to refer to the idea of "a goal." Thus, for them, objective observation is the idea that one has a goal when one observes. Other instructors will use the term "objective" to refer to the idea of "being analytical". Thus, for them, objective observation is the idea that one observes things in an analytical manner, avoiding subjectivity. While both uses of the terms are correct, this double-meaning often leads to confusion. Is someone observing with a goal in mind, or in an analytical manner? In this text, we will be combining the definitions, and using the term "objective" to mean goal-directed and analytical. Thus, engaging in objective observation will require that the observer not only have a specific goal (or behavior) to observe, but also be able to observe this in an analytical, non-subjective manner.

There really is no perfect non-subjective observation. In the same way there is no perfectly defined goal when it comes to specifying what someone is observing. Rather, there are degrees of objectivity. As we get into linking theory and application, we will see that some theories lend themselves to more easily specifying goals, others to more easily avoiding subjectivity. For some theories, the goals will become more obtuse, and the degree of subjectivity will rise, making it more difficult to draw conclusions that could easily be supported by others.

Yes, one of the goals of engaging in objective observation should be that you can describe to others what occurred, and the others would be able to understand it. If the others were present, they would agree that the things you describe occurred just as you described them. In fact, if the objective observation is well-developed, we ought to be able to have a lot of people observing, and all leaving

with the same behaviors recorded in the same manner. While there would be lots of different opinions about why something occurred, everyone would agree on what did occur. That would make for a good objective observation, and provide valuable
information about when application of theories is occurring in the classroom processes. The observational information could then be used to draw conclusions (which are subjective) about how and to what extent a theory is being applied in a classroom.

Objective observation not only requires the observer to put aside preconceived notions, but also to be able to determine what is being sought in the observation, that is, what behavior is being observed. In determining the what, a variety of aspects of behavior need to be defined and operationalized.

The observer needs to be able to explain the "what" in terms that others would accept and agree with. Steve, our expert teacher, has asked the question if he is treating tests and testing situations as something to be dreaded. In exploring this idea, Steve decided that his statements to students about tests may be different from the other statements he makes. He initially defined the behavior he wanted to observe as his statements to students about tests.

The next step is to further refine the "what" behavior. Are statements only those the teacher makes directly to all students, or to a small group, or to one student? Are they only during class? Can they be comments the teacher makes in reaction to students' statements and questions, or should they only be teacher-initiated? Does a statement have to have the word "test" in it, or can a statement that mentions quizzes or other assessments also be considered? As Steve thought about this, he decided to refine his definition to be "any verbalizations that he made related to assessing student performance." Although Steve teaches math, he didn't add "in math" to his definition, because he realized that he may be making important verbalizations about assessments in general, and he didn't want to lose out on learning about how he treated this topic. Steve felt confident that this definition was still objective, and was one that most observers could use.

Operationalizing the Objective Observation

The next step is to operationalize the behavioral observation. This includes specifying the "what" into specific circumstances. Steve decided that he had to be realistic in his limits of observing his classroom teaching. He decided first of all that he could only consider statements he made in the classroom. There was no way he could set-up observations of himself in other situations. He also decided to limit his observations to his seventh grade class. It wasn't that his eighth graders weren't important, but he couldn't observe himself all day long. He had to make a choice. Steve knew that he had the seventh graders for two years. He felt that if he learned from this observation, he could make changes that could impact his teaching these students. He also knew that he had the seventh graders in the morning. That was important for him because he felt the mornings were generally harder for him, and his frustrations with testing may be more evident.

The operationalizing of the behavioral observation requires that the observer determine a method of observation. Most observers are going into see someone else, so they take a pencil, and some paper, usually with some form for collecting information already developed. Steve was not able to observe himself in the classroom unless he either videotaped or audiotaped his classroom. He thought about audiotaping. It was certainly easier and less obvious than videotaping. He could wear a pocket audiotape recorder that was voice activated and would turn on whenever he spoke. While that seemed less intrusive, he knew that he couldn't pick up any of the "details" he wanted from the audiotape. Steve decided he wanted to videotape the classroom instead. He knew the videotape would take some time for the students to get used to, and that it would take some space in the classroom to set-up. However, the videotape would allow him to distinguish the important detail as to the receiver(s) of his verbalizations. Steve knew that there was educational research that said that male and female students had different views of math by the time they were in seventh grade. He knew that in his own classroom sometimes some of the girls would not work as hard as some of the boys. He always tried to encourage everyone to do well, he hoped. However, he also knew that unless he considered the gender of the receiver of the message, he might miss out on some important information about how he dealt with assessments in his classroom. The videotape would let him pick-up the gender of the receiver of his verbalizations.

Operationalized the behavioral observation also requires that the observer determine the frequency, length, and schedule of observation. Is the observation going to be everyday for one hour over one week, or every Tuesday for the entire day over eight weeks? Will the observation be continuous, or only for set time events? Steve had to think about his videotaping. He couldn't do it for months at a time. He could, however, bring in a video camera for four weeks. He could then tape his seventh grade class for an hour every day. He could then take the tapes home and do his objective observations by watching the tapes. Steve knew it would take some time to get his seventh graders adjusted to the idea of the taping He also needed to tell administration, and he wanted to inform parents that he was going to videotape, and that the videos would not be used for anything but his own teaching. Given that these things take some time, he planned to start his observations in three weeks.

Steve thought that the next part of operationalizing the observation, determining the coding schedule and coding system, would be fairly easy. The coding schedule was the frequency of observation. Steve was going to continuously watch the one-hour tapes, so he was using a continuous schedule. Other observers may use other schedules, and may choose to observe for their defined behavior once every five minutes, once every thirty seconds, or on some other schedule that fits with the parameters of the defined behavior. Those who observe at set times typically look to see if the defined behavior is occurring; or they identify what behaviors (within a set definition of behaviors) are occurring, and note which ones occurred.

There are many different methods and systems for recording behaviors. The recording of the behaviors takes more time to develop, and will be based on the defined behavior. Typically, an observer chooses a system to record the behavior. The system is chosen based on the nature of the behavior that is being observed. It the behavior is something that one can simply say it happened, some sort of checkmark recording should suffice. If the behavior needs to be broken down into component parts, then checkmarks alone may not work. While recording may seem cumbersome at first, it actually can simplify the observational process, and yet provide important information for the observer. Before choosing a recording system, it is important to know some of your major options.

SYSTEMS FOR OBJECTIVELY RECORDING BEHAVIORS

Coding systems

Coding systems typically record the frequency of a behavior. They are typically the most objective (least subjective) of the recording systems because they require few judgments or inferences on the part of the observer. Different coding systems require different amounts of work by the observer, and also require different information is obtained. Counting systems, sign systems, and event systems are common ways to code information. Once the behavior is adequately defined, the observer can determine if a coding system will work, and if it will, which one is most likely to be adequate to gather the information.

A **counting system** is a type of coding system that allows the observer to count the number of time intervals in which a behavior occurs. When the observer is observing two or more different behaviors at the same time, this system will allow a tally to be made to indicate that the behavior occurred during the time interval that the observation took place. For instance, Fran was interested in the use of computers in the school, so during some of her observation hours, she focused on computer use. Having defined the behavior as "anytime a teacher or a student is directly touching or sitting in front of and looking at the computer," she decided to look at the behavior on three different one-hour visits. She decided that the classroom she was observing in had to have a computer, and the teacher had to indicate that the students did have opportunities to work on the computer. Fran set up her counting system as follows. She decided that she would code in one minute intervals, so if the behavior occurred during the minute, it was recorded as having occurred. Further, she decided to use the counting system to make the distinction between the teacher's and the students' use of the computer. She decided that she would use an "T" to code that the teacher had used the computer within the one minute interval, and to use a "S" to code that a student had used the computer within the one minute interval. Thus she set up Form C2D.

Form C2D Coding Counting System

School:_____ Room:_____ Teacher:_____

Grade Level_____ Subject Matter:_____ Number of Students:_____

Date:_____Start Time:_____ Finish Time:_____Total Observation Time:_____

Room Set-up/Special Information:_____

Definition of Observation:_____

Interval (time span =)	Count of: (behavior =)
1	
2	
3	
4	
5	
6	
7	
8	
9	
10	
11	
12	
13	
14	
15	

Upon arrival in the classroom where Fran was assigned to observe, she wanted to revise her counting system worksheet. There wasn't one computer in the room, there were four! Fran quickly added columns to her coding sheet to keep track of the use of the four computers over one minute intervals. Thus, Form C2D became Form C2D2. With this form, Fran was able to code the computers' use easily. Form C2D2-example shows the results of her coding efforts. Note that with this particular type of coding, Fran was able to see who used each computer within one minute intervals. She did not note which student used a computer, if more than one student was at a computer at a time, and if the student and the teacher were at the computer together or separately.

As you can see from Fran's example, the counting system allows for sampling of a specified behavior in a fairly easy manner, once the observer gets used to the coding system. The counting system also allows someone to easily analyze the information into statistical data, such as ratios and percents, although one has to be careful with interpretation of the data. In this case, Fran could say that computer #1 was used 95% of the time that was observed (20 minutes), computer # 2, 80% of the time, computer #3, 75% of the time, and computer #4, 90% of the time.

A **sign system** is a type of coding system that is similar to the counting system because it allows for observing patterns of use or interaction over time intervals. Sign systems are typically used when there are multiple behaviors that are to be observed over long periods of time, such a five minutes. The sign system records a behavior's occurrence only once within the set interval. Sign systems can be used to compare the same behavior over different time periods, and/or across different individuals.

Danielle, the novice teacher, was interested in learning if she ever made statements that were either judgmental about or embarrassing to students. While she hoped that she didn't she wasn't sure. She also was interested in her attempts to meet the learning styles of her students. Danielle struggled with defining these behaviors. She decided to define judgmental verbalizations as anything she said that directly criticized, or made inferences or judgments about a student. She decided to define embarrassing verbalizations as any statements which were meant for one student about his/her behavior, but were made in a public manner so that more than the intended receiver could hear the statement. She defined meeting the learning styles of her students as any specific changes in tasks or assignments to meet the needs of individuals or groups, and any times that students were grouped to engage in differential tasks. When she saw how Steve was using videotaping in his room, she decided to also videotape her room. She investigated the different coding systems, and decided that she could easily use a sign system to code these behaviors. She decided to take for two hours each day, the first hour of the morning, and the last hour of the afternoon, the times that her students were the most disruptive, and she was likely to be the most stressed. She also decided to use five minute intervals for her coding. Form C2E shows the sign system coding form that Danielle developed. Form C2E-example shows the form for Danielle coding one hour in a morning. Danielle coded her ten hours of videos. She decided that she was not engaging in any embarrassing behaviors. She had made some judgments. She was surprised because there were verbalizations related to learning styles (as she had defined them) a bit less than 50% of the time. Danielle spoke to Steve, and he agreed to let her use her coding system live in his room. Danielle hoped to compare the percentages of her references of learning styles to those of Steve's to see if they were similar.

Danielle found that using the sign system to try to code Steve's verbalizations related to learning styles was more difficult than when she coded from her videotapes. Her definition didn't fit as well with Steve's classroom set-up. Steve's classroom was set-up in small groups, and there were learning centers in his classroom. His students moved from center to center as they worked in groups or individually. As Steve spoke quietly to a small group or an individual, it was difficult to hear his verbalizations. Danielle had learned that although she could multiple behaviors using a long time interval, with little practice, she could not figure out the frequency of her behaviors, easily interpret the data she obtained, nor establish a the sequence of classroom events. Danielle decided that a different coding system may give her more information about meeting learning styles in the classroom.

Form C2D2: Revised Coding Form for Counting System for Four Items

School:_____ Room:_____ Teacher:_____

Grade Level____ Subject Matter:_____ Number of Students:_____

Date:_____Start Time:_____ Finish Time:_____Total Observation Time:_____

Room Set-up/Special Information:_____

Definition of Observation:_____

Interval (time span =)	Count of: (behavior =)			
	Computer #1	Computer #2	Computer #3	Computer #4
1				
2				
3				
4				
5				
6				
7				
8				
9				
10				
11				
12				
13				
14				
15				
16				
17				
18				
19				
20				

Form C2D2-example: **Revised** **Coding** **Form** **of** **Counting** **System** **for** **Four** **Items:**
Example **of** **Fran's** **Completed** **Sheet**

School:_____ Room:_____ Teacher:_____

Grade Level_____ Subject Matter:_____ Number of Students:_____

Date:_____Start Time:_____ Finish Time:_____Total Observation Time:_____

Room Set-up/Special Information:_____

Definition of Observation:_____

Interval (time span =)	Count of: (behavior =)			
	Computer #1	Computer #2	Computer #3	Computer #4
1			t	s
2	s	s	t	s
3	s	s	t,s	s
4	s	s	t,s	s
5	s	s	t,s	s,t
6	s	s	s	s,t
7	s	t,s	s	
8	s	t,s	s	
9	s	s	s	s,t
10	s	s	s	s,t
11	s	s	s	t
12	s		s	t
13	s		s	s
14	s		s	s
15	s	s	s	s
16	s	s		s
17	s	s		s
18	s	s		s
19	s	s		s
20	s	s		s

Form C2E: Sign System Coding for Specified Behaviors

School:_____ Room:_____ Teacher:_____

Grade Level_____ Subject Matter:_____ Number of Students:_____

Date:_____Start Time:_____ Finish Time:_____Total Observation Time:_____

Room Set-up/Special Information:_____

Definition of Observation:_____

Five-Minute					Intervals					Behaviors
1	2	3	4	5	6	7	8	9	10	
										T criticizes a student (S)
										T criticizes S in public
										T judges S
										T judges S in public
										T embarrasses S (public)
										T assigns/has small grp tasks
										T assigns/has individual task
										T uses different tasks/group
										T references S learning styles

Form C2E-example: Sign System Coding for Specified Behaviors (Danielle completed)

School:_____ Room:_____ Teacher:_____

Grade Level____ Subject Matter:_____ Number of Students:_____

Date:_____Start Time:_____ Finish Time:_____Total Observation Time:_____

Room Set-up/Special Information:_____

Definition of Observation:_____

Five-Minute					Intervals					Behaviors
1	2	3	4	5	6	7	8	9	10	
			x							T criticizes a student (S)
										T criticizes S in public
x				x						T judges S
					x	x				T judges S in public
										T embarrasses S (public)
	x	x	x		x	x				T assigns/has small grp tasks
x	x	x	x							T assigns/has individual task
			x	x	x	x	x	x		T uses different tasks/grp
	x	x		x		x	x			T references s learning styles

An **event system** is a coding system that allows for defined behaviors to be recorded as they occur. As no time intervals are involved, the actual number of times that a behavior occurs can be determined when this system is used. The simplest type of event system is a **frequency count** record. Frequency count data collection sheets are fairly easy to develop. Typically, the behavior is listed, and there is a place for slash marks to be made for each time the behavior occurs. Form C2F is an example of a frequency count form that Danielle developed to record Steve's verbalizations related to learning styles. She redefined the behavior as teacher verbalizations to affirm, praise, inform, provide assessment, explain, cue, and respond to a student. She also decided to code if the teacher's behavior was directed at an individual student or at a small group of students. Danielle found this form easy to use, and it gave her information about the frequency of the behaviors. She particularly liked this way to collect information because the data she collected could also be used to collect rank ordered data.

Form C2F: Example of an Event System Frequency Count

School:_____ Room:_____ Teacher:_____

Grade Level____ Subject Matter:_____ Number of Students:_____

Date:_____Start Time:_____ Finish Time:_____Total Observation Time:_____

Room Set-up/Special Information:_____

Definition of Observation:_____

Behavioral Event	Frequency of Event to Small Group	Frequency of Event to Individual Ss
Affirmation		
Praise		
Provides information		
Gives assessment		
Explains		
Cues		
Responds to a S		

Rank ordered observations are done when the number of occurrences of different events are collected. Then, the information is ranked, with the item with the most occurrences listed first, the item with the next most occurrences listed second, etc. Rank-ordered information is helpful in not only telling about the frequency of behaviors, but also in giving information about which behavior occurred most often, least often, etc. Frequency count forms and rank ordering may be easy to use, but this type of data collection does not provide any information about the sequence of the classroom events. Danielle found that even though she had been in the classroom observing and recording, she found that keeping track of the behaviors through her current methods did not provide her the opportunity to keep track of the sequence.

Danielle next tried to revise how she used the frequency count form. She tried to observe Steve's class again. This time, instead of using slash marks to simply note the behavioral occurrence, she started placing numbers in the columns, starting with the first occurrence being number 1, the second #2, etc. This allowed her to later look at the data and determine the order of the behaviors. This kind of observation is called a **frequency-sequence count**.

Steve found Danielle's frequency-sequence count form obtained some interesting data. He thought about the information that he had more verbalizations to individual students than to small groups. He was pleased that he praised students, but, surprised that he cued and informed students as often as he did. He decided that he could use some sort of event system coding to answer some of the other concerns he had. He asked Danielle to return to observe his verbalizations, but this time to add the exact sequence of events, so that he could later determine if his verbalizations were different when he was dealing with the students receiving special education services who were now

Form C2G: Symbol Coding Frequency-Sequence Event Recording

School:_____ Room:_____ Teacher:_____

Grade Level____ Subject Matter:_____ Number of Students:_____

Date:_____Start Time:_____ Finish Time:_____Total Observation Time:_____

Room Set-up/Special Information:_____

Definition of Observation:_____

Key:	Affirmation = A	Praise = +	Provides information = >	
	Gives assessment = ^	Explains = !	Cues = //	Responds to a S = <

Event #	Code:	Note: (to whom?)
1		
2		
3		
4		
5		
6		
7		
8		
9		
10		
11		
12		
13		
14		
15		
16		
17		
18		

included in his classroom, or when he was dealing with those students who were not receiving services. As Danielle was on his team, she knew which students fit into which category, and could do this coding. Danielle, who was curious about her own behaviors in this area, agreed to help Steve and code his behaviors so that she could practice and later code her own.

Danielle and Steve quickly learned that such coding required an entirely different form. The information that Steve wanted did require event recording, but, numbering across all these different categories and columns for any length of time was cumbersome and confusing. Instead, Danielle and Steve made a modification to a **sequence event recording system** used by Good and Brophy (1990). Using the Good and Brophy system as an example, they developed a set of symbols for the behaviors. Then, Danielle could move right down a sheet of paper placing in the appropriate system as an event occurred, and noting the receiver. The form they developed for this is Form C2G Danielle found that once she practiced using the key, this systems was easy to use, provided more information about the sequence of events (although it was still limited information), and allowed for clarification as to the receiver of the verbalizations. The problem was that this required much more work on the part of the observer if the observer was to really learn the code, and consistently use it over time. Additionally, this system gave no indication as to the duration of the events.

Duration recording

Duration recording involves the coding of the length of time that an event occurs. Duration recording is best done with a stop watch or watch with a large sweep second hand on it. Duration recording also requires clarification on the part of the observer. Once a behavior is defined for observation, duration recording usually involves the number of seconds, or the number of minutes that the behavior occurs. Duration recording is typically used in classrooms to keep track of a teacher's behavior, or one student's behavior. When Form C2H was used, Steve was surprised to learn that he was cueing two students who were receiving special education services more than other students. He decided that his videos would be a good source of information as to the duration of behaviors prior to Steve's cueing them. Steve revisited some of his videotapes, and he learned that the two students engaged in behaviors which were not similar to those of other students, one frequently taking other students' items and handling them, and the other one moving out of his group's area into other groups' areas. While Steve had already discovered this, and seen it in the classroom, he had not really stopped to think about the frequency and duration of these behaviors. Steve developed a simple form for keeping track of the duration of the two defined behaviors while also keeping track of the frequency of each one. Form C2I is the form Steve developed and subsequently started to use with some of his videos.

Steve coded less than three hours of his videos using the duration recording form when he came to the realization that the duration alone was not the only information he needed. He also needed it noted if either he, or a different student had cued or otherwise stopped the behavior(s), or if the student had stopped the behavior on his/her own. Martina was the student who he had observed taking other's possessions and handling them. She was labeled as having some emotional disorders. Roman was the student who was frequently moving about the room. Roman had been labeled as attention deficit disordered with hyperactivity several years ago. Although Roman was on medications which supposedly lowered his hyperactivity, it was clear that some days Roman had a harder time controlling his behavior than on other days. Both Roman and Martina were bright, and despite their problems, they tended to do well on various school-related learning tasks. Steve wondered if cueing these students to behave was really helping them, or not. Maybe, he hypothesized, if they weren't cued, they could learn to control these behaviors on their own, that is if they showed any signs of self-regulating their behaviors now.

Steve revised his coding form. He added columns for each student's behavior to note if the behavior was externally cued, and then ended, or was not cued. To make this clear, he added a coding system by coding in if he, or another student was seen or heard cueing the behavior to stop. Now, Steve could use Form C2I2 with his videotapes.

Form C2H: Duration recording (with frequency count)

School:_____ Room:_____ Teacher:_____

Grade Level____ Subject Matter:_____ Number of Students:_____

Date:_____Start Time:_____ Finish Time:_____Total Observation Time:_____

Room Set-up/Special Information:_____

Definition of Observation:_____

This recording is done in # of seconds the behavior occurs.

Event #	S1 hands	S2 moves
1		
2		
3		
4		
5		
6		
7		
8		
9		
10		
11		
12		
13		
14		

Form C2l: Duration recording, with frequency, and event noting

School:_____ Room:_____ Teacher:_____

Grade Level____ Subject Matter:_____ Number of Students:_____

Date:_____Start Time:_____ Finish Time:_____Total Observation Time:_____

Room Set-up/Special Information:_____

Definition of Observation:_____

This duration recording is done in # of seconds the behavior occurs.
The event noting key uses T for teacher and S for another student in the classroom.

Event #	S1 hands	Cue S1	S2 moves	Cue S2
1				
2				
3				
4				
5				
6				
7				
8				
9				
10				
11				
12				
13				
14				

Checklists

A well-defined, objective observation may be limited by listing items that the observer may then check as present, or having occurred. As Fran was learning about classrooms, her instructor gave her a management checklist to complete (see Form C2J). This form listed many teacher behaviors. Fran was told to observe in two different classrooms, or to observe the same teacher at different times and fill out the same form each time. Afterwards, Fran could reflect on the similarities and differences between the observations, and try to think about what behaviors of the teacher, and what behaviors of the students lead to effective classroom management. Form C2J-example is an example of two observations Fran made. Fran concluded that the teacher in the first observation was more effective in managing the classroom than the teacher in the second observation. What would you conclude?

Verbal accounts

Verbal accounts, if done correctly, may be fairly objective. However, generally, they are tricky or cumbersome to do, and require different work on the part of the observer. The most frequently used type of verbal account is a **verbatim recording.** When the observer engages in verbatim recording, everything that is said is recorded. Anyone who has spent five minutes in a typical classroom knows that this is a very difficult thing to do, many different people are saying different things at the same time. Some of the things are easier to hear than others. An observer who is attempting to do a verbatim recording typically will focus only on one individual in the classroom and write down everything that that person says. If the observer wants further clarification, the observer may add the time of the verbalization, where the speaker was in the room, etc. One of the problems with verbatim information is that the other verbalizations and classroom events are not recorded.

Steve believed that one of his students seemed to ask a lot of questions, often interrupting the lesson. He decided to do a verbatim recording of everything that the student said in one lesson. Watching his video, he wrote down everything that the student said. As Steve did this, he started to realize that he often verbally responded to the student's verbalizations. Watching another video, Steve did a verbatim recording of the student's verbalizations and his own verbalizations. Steve then analyzed what he had recorded, and found that in over half of the instances, he had engaged in verbal rounds with the student. Steve decided that he would try not to respond and see if that changed the student's verbalizations.

Another type of verbal account is an **interview**. For an interview to be objective, the questions which will be asked have to be carefully developed, and as non-judgmental as possible. Generally, questions may be close-ended, such as those that start with "Do..." to obtain a yes/no response; or they may be open-ended, such as those that start with "Tell me about..." Steve had the opportunity to interview a teacher at another school that had an advisor-advisee program. He decided he wanted to get as much information as possible about the program and how it worked. He carefully developed his questions. He decided that he did not know enough about the program to ask close-ended questions. Additionally, when he tried to write close-ended questions, he found that the questions sounded too judgmental for what he wanted. He wrote the following questions:

1. Tell me about how the advisor-advisee program works at your school.
2. Tell me about how the program was developed and set-up at your school.
3. Tell me about how the teachers were trained to implement the program.
4. Tell me about your day-to-day responsibilities for the program.
5. Tell me about the successes of the program.
6. Tell me about some of the concerns you have about the program.
7. Tell me about any specific problems that you encountered in running the program.
8. Tell me anything else you feel is important for me to know.

As he looked at the questions, Steve felt that none of them was too judgmental, and each could be expanded, depending upon how the teacher responded, if he felt he needed more information. Steve

Form C2J: Checklist of Classroom Management

School:_____ Room:_____ Teacher:_____

Grade Level____ Subject Matter:_____ Number of Students:_____

Date:_____ Start Time:_____ Finish Time:_____ Total Observation Time:_____

Room Set-up/Special Information:_____

Definition of Observation:_____

____ Teacher states his/her expectations for behavior.
____ Teacher explains what work is supposed to be done.
____ Teacher holds students' accountable for their behaviors.
____ Students follow teacher expectations for behavior.
____ Students do the required work.
____ Students are seen working on school-related tasks.
____ Students follow school rules.
____ Teacher tells students that they are important.
____ Students praise each other.
____ Teacher has students work in small groups.
____ Teacher has students work individually.
____ Students follow established routines.
____ Teacher shows respect for students and their property.
____ Students show respect for teachers.
____ Students show respect for each other and their property.
____ Students are allowed to talk with each other.
____ Students work together to get a group task done.
____ Students say they are responsible for their own learning.
____ Teacher has consequence for misbehavior.
____ Student misbehavior is given consequences.
____ Teacher tells students they should cooperate.
____ Teacher deals with interruptions.
____ Students return to tasks after interruptions.
____ Teachers gives directions.
____ Students follow directions.
____ Teacher sets noise level for tasks.
____ Students function at or below the set noise level for tasks.
____ Teacher has students participate in the classroom tasks and activities.
____ Students volunteer to participate in the classroom tasks and activities.
____ Teacher encourages students to be creative.
____ Teacher encourages the students to problem solve.
____ Teacher encourages the students to think about their behavior.
____ Students serve as resources for each other.
____ Students move from task to task without teacher oversight.
____ Students encourage each other to behave per classroom rules and expectations.

Form C2J-example: Checklist of Classroom Management completed for two teachers

School:_____ Room:_____ Teacher:_____

Grade Level_____ Subject Matter:_____ Number of Students:_____

Date:_____Start Time:_____ Finish Time:_____Total Observation Time:_____

Room Set-up/Special Information:_____

Definition of Observation:___Two Teachers classroom management_____

<table>
<tr><td>_x_</td><td>_x_</td><td>Teacher states his/her expectations for behavior.</td></tr>
<tr><td>_x_</td><td>_x_</td><td>Teacher explains what work is supposed to be done.</td></tr>
<tr><td>____</td><td>_x_</td><td>Teacher holds students' accountable for their behaviors.</td></tr>
<tr><td>____</td><td>_x_</td><td>Students follow teacher expectations for behavior.</td></tr>
<tr><td>_x_</td><td>_x_</td><td>Students do the required work.</td></tr>
<tr><td>____</td><td>_x_</td><td>Students are seen working on school-related tasks.</td></tr>
<tr><td>____</td><td>____</td><td>Students follow school rules.</td></tr>
<tr><td>____</td><td>_x_</td><td>Teacher tells students that they are important.</td></tr>
<tr><td>____</td><td>_x_</td><td>Students praise each other.</td></tr>
<tr><td>____</td><td>_x_</td><td>Teacher has students work in small groups.</td></tr>
<tr><td>____</td><td>____</td><td>Teacher has students work individually.</td></tr>
<tr><td>_x_</td><td>_x_</td><td>Students follow established routines.</td></tr>
<tr><td>____</td><td>_x_</td><td>Teacher shows respect for students and their property.</td></tr>
<tr><td>____</td><td>_x_</td><td>Students show respect for teachers.</td></tr>
<tr><td>____</td><td>_x_</td><td>Students show respect for each other and their property.</td></tr>
<tr><td>____</td><td>_x_</td><td>Students are allowed to talk with each other.</td></tr>
<tr><td>____</td><td>____</td><td>Students work together to get a group task done.</td></tr>
<tr><td>____</td><td>_x_</td><td>Students say they are responsible for their own learning.</td></tr>
<tr><td>_x_</td><td>_x_</td><td>Teacher has consequence for misbehavior.</td></tr>
<tr><td>_x_</td><td>____</td><td>Student misbehavior is given consequences.</td></tr>
<tr><td>____</td><td>____</td><td>Teacher tells students they should cooperate.</td></tr>
<tr><td>_x_</td><td>____</td><td>Teacher deals with interruptions.</td></tr>
<tr><td>____</td><td>____</td><td>Students return to tasks after interruptions.</td></tr>
<tr><td>_x_</td><td>_x_</td><td>Teachers gives directions.</td></tr>
<tr><td>____</td><td>_x_</td><td>Students follow directions.</td></tr>
<tr><td>____</td><td>_x_</td><td>Teacher sets noise level for tasks.</td></tr>
<tr><td>____</td><td>_x_</td><td>Students function at or below the set noise level for tasks.</td></tr>
<tr><td>____</td><td>_x_</td><td>Teacher has students participate in the classroom tasks and activities.</td></tr>
<tr><td>____</td><td>_x_</td><td>Students volunteer to participate in the classroom tasks and activities.</td></tr>
<tr><td>____</td><td>_x_</td><td>Teacher encourages students to be creative.</td></tr>
<tr><td>____</td><td>_x_</td><td>Teacher encourages the students to problem solve.</td></tr>
<tr><td>____</td><td>_x_</td><td>Teacher encourages the students to think about their behavior.</td></tr>
<tr><td>____</td><td>_x_</td><td>Students serve as resources for each other.</td></tr>
<tr><td>____</td><td>_x_</td><td>Students move from task to task without teacher oversight.</td></tr>
<tr><td>____</td><td>_x_</td><td>Students encourage each other to behave per classroom rules and expectations.</td></tr>
</table>

decided to take verbatim notes on what the teacher said, so that he could make sure he got all the information correct.

Anecdotal reports

Anecdotal reports are saved for last because they generally seem to be the least preferred when it comes to objective recording of information in the classroom. The reason is that by the nature of what the reporting involves, they tend to be subjective. Anecdotal reports may be limited to a particular incident, or may be limited to a particular time period. Either way, the observer writes down what is seen, what the observer believes happened. The most frequent use of anecdotal reports is usually related to an incident. For instance, Fran was concerned about discipline and classroom management. She decided to do incident reporting on the first five minutes of the class each day, to record what the teacher and how the students reacted. She tried to make sure that she recorded the events that happened. However, she often found that her opinions and judgments were creeping into the process. As Fran did this for two weeks, she learned to become more objective. Look at some of what she wrote for day one, as compared to day ten.

Day one: The teacher said, "let's get going." or some version of that six times. The students are busy milling around and are slow getting to their seats. The teacher starts to yell and then the students scurry to their seats. The teacher then yells to the students that if this happens again tomorrow they will sit detention one minute for each minute of class time that they are not in their seats.

Day ten: The teacher spoke in a voice just above a whisper. She said, "Class, we need to begin now. Please take your seats." Six students are still standing and moving around the room thirty seconds after the teacher's directive. The teacher repeats the statement, using the same voice level. Four students move to their desks, and are seated within twenty seconds of the second statement. The two students who are still not seated are standing talking to students who are seated. The teacher moves over near the students. One student asks the teacher a question, "What do you think of Sari's book? Her brother sure made a mess of the cover, didn't he?" The teacher tells the two students, by name, to take their seats. The students move to their desk within thirty seconds. Meanwhile, the teacher tells all students to open their cooperative workbooks and look at page 105. The teacher tells Sari that she shouldn't worry about the book right now, and that they will talk later.

Not only is Fran more objective by day ten, but she also is providing details that are more objective. She has clarified the voice level of the teacher, the number of students involved, the time periods involved, and the behaviors. Thus, she has learned to provide a more objective anecdotal report.

Reflective Questions:
- How might you use each type of data collection in your observations?
- Are there other ways of collecting data that you think might be objective? If so, what are they?

Issues of Reliability and Validity in Observation

For most people who are new to the observation process, distinguishing the defined behavior from other classroom behaviors is not always easy. With practice, and the right opportunities for observation, you should become fairly good at observing the defined behavior. However, even if you feel that you are good at observing, there are two issues which you may need to consider. One of those is the reliability of the observation. **Reliability** is the stability of the observation. There are different types of reliability that relate to the observation process. One type, **inter-rater** reliability, refers to two or more observers rating the same thing the same way. If both Fran and Danielle use the same observation form when they are observing Steve at the same time, will they walk out of the observation and report the same behavior? Will the form they used have the same records of check, frequencies, or sequences of events? If Fran and Danielle have the same or nearly the same observation record, then they are said to have inter-rater reliability.

Another type of reliability is **alternative** times reliability. If Fran used the same form to observe Steve on two different occasions, would she get the same information both times? Depending on the defined behavior, and the classroom processes, Fran may or may not expect to obtain the same information both times. If it is expected that the same behavior would be recorded each time, then this type of reliability may be important. However, if it would be expected that there may be different behavior on the different occasions, then this type of reliability may not be important.

Another type of reliability is **intra-rater** reliability. This refers to the observer's own stability in observing. An easy example of this would be Steve's coding of his videotapes. If Steve codes 30 minutes of one videotape using one form, he would be expected to get one set of information. If Steve later went back to code the same piece of videotape using the same form, we would expect that he would get the same set of information as he did the first time. If he did, then he would have good intra-rater reliability. If, however, Steve's second set of information was different from the first set, then he may not have good intra-rater reliability. Then, Steve should be concerned about why he had the differences. Did he redefine the behavior? Did he pay more attention during one viewing than another? Did he code the exact same segment of video? Was he interrupted or distracted during one of his viewings?

Validity is the idea that the form is measuring what it is reported to, or supposed to be measuring. When the form is designed to measure a particular construct or concept, we would expect the form to have good **construct** validity, that is that it would indeed measure the defined construct, and not some other concept or idea. If Fran is observing classroom management, and the form she is using has good construct validity, then we would expect that experts in classroom management would agree that the form adequately assesses classroom management and not something else, such as student motivation.

While there are other types of validity, and other types of reliability, these are the primary types which usually are of concern to classroom observers. Another concern is defining what constitutes acceptable, or good reliability or validity. Observers who are serious about establishing reliability and validity will need to do some basic statistical calculations. These days, most of these can be easily done using a statistical program on a calculator or on a computer. The statistic that is run is a *correlation*. The correlation compares how one set of scores compares to another set of scores. When the statistic is calculated, the resulting coefficient is called the correlation coefficient, which is usually a lower case letter r. The correlation coefficient can range in value from a +1.00 to a zero, to a -1.00. The closer the r is to +1.00, the stronger the correlation, that is, the more similar the set of scores. The closer the r is to -1.00, the stronger the correlation, but now, as one set of scores increases, another set of scores decreases. That is, with a negative correlation, the sets of scores are opposite. The close the r is to zero, the more dissimilar the sets of scores are from each other. In most cases, a correlation coefficient of +.70 or greater is acceptable, or considered good, for both reliability and validity. If the r is less than +.70, then, typically, we should question the reliability or validity (depending on what was calculated), to make sure that the form is appropriate, is being appropriately used, etc. A general rule to remember is that validity should be calculated first. If a form is not valid, it can not be reliable. Think of it this way, why would you want to use a form that is not measuring what you thought it was? Even if you had good reliability, without good validity, you would not know what you were measuring!

Reflective Questions:
- What are some other observation situations in which reliability and validity may be important?
- What are some other classroom situations in which reliability and validity may be important?

REVIEW QUESTIONS

1. What is the difference between objectivity and subjectivity?
2. Why should classroom observers strive to be objective?
3. What are the various types of objective recording systems?
4. What is the difference between reliability and validity?

DISCUSSION QUESTIONS

1. Do you think it is important as a teacher to know the experiences that your students have with schools and their processes? Why, or why not?
2. What are some ways that objective observation may interfere with collecting information about a classroom?
3. What do you think is a reasonable amount of time to observe in a classroom before you start to draw some conclusions about what you have seen?
4. Why do you think that it is important to engage in observation prior to trying to teach?

CHAPTER 3:
OBSERVING STUDENTS AND THEIR
INDIVIDUAL DIFFERENCES IN THE CLASSROOM

LEARNING OBJECTIVES:

After you read this chapter you should know:
1. How to observe differences in student motor development in the classroom.
2. How to observe differences in student cognitive development in the classroom.
3. How to observe differences in student personal/learning styles in the classroom.
4. How to observe differences in student psychosocial development in the classroom.
5. How to observe differences in student personality characteristics in the classroom.
6. How to observe differences in student language development in the classroom.
7. How to observe differences in student social development in the classroom.
8. How to observe differences in student moral development in the classroom.
9. How to observe differences in student environmental considerations and needs in the classroom.

After you read this chapter, you should be able to:
1. Identify and describe various behaviors and characteristics of students in the classroom.
2. Use the forms provided to observe for a variety of student individual differences in the classroom.
3. Develop your own forms to observe for a variety of student individual differences in the classroom.
4. Explain to others how to observe students in the classroom.

INTRODUCTION

Whenever we are interacting with students, whether it is as an observer, as a teacher, or as another student, we need to be mindful that each student is an unique individual. Each student brings his/her own experiences, schemas, ways of learning, ways of thinking, ways of interacting, expectations, beliefs, attitudes, etc., to the classroom. The more students in a room, the more differences that exist, and the more behaviors and characteristics that might be observed in the classroom.

What can we learn from observation of students in the classroom? In 1991, Shrock and Stepp published an article in which they described how they observed the social interactions of students when a microcomputer was introduced into the classroom. Based on their observations, they concluded that students showed varied abilities, with some students emerging as microcomputer "experts" who were able to handle the technology with ease. Additionally, they found that there were wide differences in peer interactions, with the microcomputers adding a dimension to those interactions.

In 1990, Beckstead and Goetz observed students who were labeled as having severe disabilities as they interacted in an integrated school setting with students who were not labeled. They looked at the variations in who initiated contact, if interactions were task-related or social-related, if students were on-task, if they actively participated, if they isolated themselves for any length of time, if they were aggressive, and who engaged in what classroom-oriented activities. By observing, they were able to consider the complex interactions within the classroom.

In 1991, McIntosh chose to observe the rates of classroom interactions of students who had learning disabilities, with those of non-labeled students. They found that the learning disabled students had lower rates of interactions with the teacher, with other students, and with classroom activities.

Findings were different in 1994, when Butera observed special education students who were included in regular education classes through the use of a system of coding the presence of 15 discrete kinds of behaviors every six seconds. In these classes, the social interactions with peers and with teachers were comparable among special education students and non-special education students.

Anderson and Roit (1994) used classroom observations and analysis of videotapes of classrooms to identify student reading comprehension and language development. Through development of these processes, they were able to consider 1) the flexibility of the use of the English language, 2) the use of less-imaginable basic vocabulary, 3) the use of elaborative responses, 4) the extent to which students engaged in natural conversations, 5) the considerations of larger contexts when comprehending, and 6) the determining of importance and unimportance of aspects of text.

Observation has also been used to compare students from different nations. For instance, Weisz (1995) watched students in American schools and their Thai age-mates. The conclusion from this direct behavior observation was that there were twice as many instances of off-task and problem behavior among American students. Of course, when one makes these comparisons, one needs to be careful as to how the behaviors are defined within each culture, the cultural relevance of the behaviors, and how the teachers are allowed to react to the behaviors within each culture.

If you engage in a search of the educational literature, you will find that there are thousands of studies which have used observational techniques to record various aspects of classroom processes. We cannot begin to discuss them all. Instead, the idea is to get you thinking about the possibilities as we consider the characteristics, development and individual differences among students. In doing so, we will review theories of development and individual differences that are typically found in teacher education programs, and focus on how these theories link to the observation processes. We will review key observation forms and processes you might use, as well as develop and explain some new forms and processes. As in the first chapter, we will use some case examples to help with the illustration of applying the theories to the observation processes.

THE CASES:

Revisiting One Pre-Service Teacher, Fran:

Fran (from Chapter 1) was surprised when she called the school to set-up her observations and was told that she would be observing in the same classrooms as another student, Alton. Alton, who was also in her teacher education program, had a different set of educational instructors than she did. Fran was excited by the opportunity to compare notes on the observations with Alton, and to compare what the instructors were requiring for the observations. However, she also was concerned that having two observers in the same classroom at the same time may be distracting to the students and to the teacher. Fran decided to make sure that she explained to the teacher that it was not her idea that both of them be there at the same time. She also decided to ask the teacher if she could introduce herself to the class, hoping that that might make the students and the teacher less concerned about what Fran was doing. Fran thought this might make her observation a bit more naturalistic.

When Fran got to the school for this set of observations, she explained to the teacher that she was there to see the classroom and watch the students. She showed the teacher the variety of forms that her instructor had requested that she complete, and assured the teacher that no verbatim statements that the teacher made would be recorded. She asked to introduce herself to the students, and proceeded to present as naturally as she could, her memorized statement. she said, "Hi, my name is Ms. Remk. I want to be a teacher. I am here to see what classrooms are like, and what teachers do. I am a student at the university, and my teacher assigned me a lot of work while I am here. So, while you do your work, I will be doing mine. I am sorry, but, I won't be able to answer your questions or talk with you while I am doing my work. If you want to talk with me, you will need to do that during lunch. I really appreciate your letting me do my work here. Thanks, in advance, for your help."

Fran found that making that statement lead to a few comments from some students about why anyone would want to be a teacher, and smiles from others. Then, as she settled in and began her work, they settled in and did theirs, rarely seeming to look her way. Fran also noted that Alton did not introduce himself to the class, and frequently had his observations interrupted by students coming to him with questions, or to make comments. Fran decided to make a small mark on her observation sheets whenever Alton was interrupted. If they later had to compare notes, it would help her to be able to note to Alton where their differences might be!

> **Reflective questions:**
> - What are things that you might want to include in your introduction to a class you are observing?
> - Why do you think it is important to tell the students you won't be able to answer their questions when you are observing?

A Post-Bachelor's Degree Student Considers Teaching: The Case of Alton

Alton was surprised, and somewhat scared when his university instructor told him that he had to be in the classrooms observing. Alton knew friends who had started teaching without any training, much less observation. When would he get into the classroom and get to teach? After all, wasn't that what his program was all about? Being enrolled in an alternative certification program at the university, he already had a bachelor's degree in business. He had worked in sales for a few years. He found it hard to pitch a product, especially if it did not meet the needs of the consumer. He constantly found himself asking questions of the customers, and then, reluctantly making suggestions for other products or services based on the customers' needs. His bosses suggested that sales weren't a good choice for him, and he soon found himself thinking about teaching.

Some of Alton's friends had started substitute teaching a few years ago. The state law allowed them to have a substitute certificate for several years without having a teaching certificate. Alton's friends had found that they could make an adequate living subbing, and were doing that daily for some of the large districts. In fact, they bragged that they had their choices of schools and jobs, and that was much better for them. They had begun subbing without any educational training, and kept saying that if they got in enough subbing time, the state may let them have a certificate to teach which would be limited, but, a start for waiving the requirements for education at the local university.

This, however, was not the information that the local university instructors gave Alton. They wouldn't waive courses needed based on short experiences in the field. In fact, they expected their students to be engaged in a lot of experiences in schools, but not subbing while taking classes. The university instructors repeatedly said that the best teachers were the ones with training before they taught, so that they wouldn't go in and necessarily teach the way that they had been taught! The instructors also repeatedly said that observation was one of the processes that students needed to learn as they learned to become reflective practitioners. Alton wanted to do things correctly, so, he patiently began the observation processes as his instructors required.

There was one concern that Alton had. He was not sure he wanted to be a teacher. In fact, he was not sure what he wanted to do. Sales did not work for him, although he continued to keep his sales job while he went to school to study something else. He did not know what, but something. Teaching seemed like a good choice. He could get that done quickly, with minimal additional expenses. He could still work and go to school until he student taught. He liked kids, and loved the idea that he would have each summer off. He knew teachers weren't paid very well, but he also knew teachers who had extra side jobs or coached for more money. He knew he would be a great coach for some sport, so, that would help!

Alton listened carefully as inservice teachers told him how they went to school during the summer so that they could keep their jobs, or they worked at the school, or they did both. Alton also met a couple of teachers from a year-round school. These teachers were convinced that many more school districts would be requiring their students to enter into year-round schooling, and thus year-round teaching He learned that many teachers also developed curriculum, worked on special projects or grants, or volunteered for other school projects during the summer. He started to wonder how many of his own teachers really never did have a summer "vacation" that was similar to that of the students. He also started to consider that maybe teaching would not mean summers off!

The university instructors also kept reminding all of the pre-service teachers that schools were under constant scrutiny these days. That meant that teachers had to be working hard to constantly prove themselves, and to meet new, tougher standards. Those that were coaches usually did have experience in the sport or activity that they were coaching. Alton decided that if he was going to be a teacher, he better take some physical education classes to help him prepare to do some extra coaching. He wondered if he would be able to observe in physical education classes at the local school.

A Parent and Non-Traditional Student Considers Teaching Options: The Case of Selma:

Selma was excited that the university advisor told her that it would take awhile, but she could go to school part time and eventually earn a degree. Selma's two children were now enrolled full-time in school. She had some free time during the day, and wanted to pursue her dream of being a teacher. She loved teaching younger children. She had taught at a religious school every week since she had been in high school. She was good at teaching. In fact, she had taught her own kids to read and write, and when they entered school, they were doing well.

Selma was now a citizen. However, she had been born and raised in another country where English was not the primary language spoken. Selma knew that if she was going to be a teacher, she should be very fluent in English. Although she was learning, she felt that she didn't know the rules of grammar for English well enough to verbally interact in the English-speaking community, much less teach it. She looked forward to continuing to learn English as she took her classes to become a certified teacher.

At the first parent-teacher conference, Selma shared her goal with her son's teacher. The teacher suggested that while Selma was taking some classes at the school, it might be helpful for her to do some volunteer work in the schools. She could see how teachers taught the language, what teacher's did, and also be connected with a school. Although this school had a policy that parents could not volunteer in the same room where they had a child, there were plenty of other classrooms for her to spend some time. The teacher continued by saying that it was a good way to later get a job. In fact, the last two people hired at the school as teachers had first been parent volunteers in the school. Selma agreed on the spot to go to talk to the principal about volunteering.

The principal immediately had additional suggestions for Selma. If Selma started working on her degree and accumulated some credits, she could also work in a teaching position. She could be an aide, or a teacher in a bilingual classroom. The principal told her how there was a need for teachers who were bilingual, and could teach in classrooms where other languages were spoken. In fact, if the school sought permission from the state, the school could hire her without a degree, and help provide money for her education. Selma was surprised, but pleased. She agreed to think about this avenue and talk it over with her university advisor.

Selma's university advisor cautioned her to gather a lot of information before she made a decision to teach without a degree. She told Selma that although this was acceptable to the state, few people finished their degrees while teaching full time. It was hard to go to school, teach, raise children. She should take things slowly for a semester or two, and then decided how much she wanted to add to her workload. The advisor also reminded her that the course work would be more difficult as she was still learning English. Selma had a lot to think about! She agreed with the advisor, and decided to start out doing 10 hours a week of volunteer work in her son's school.

Reflective Questions:
- What are some of the possible reasons that someone chooses to become a teacher? How do those compare with your own reasons?
- Imagine that you get to do it all over again, and go through elementary and high school. This time, you have complete control over who teaches you. Do you want a student teacher? Do you want someone to teach who has children in the same school? What do you want? What do your desires in a teacher say about your choices for quality education? What is important for your own teaching?

OBSERVING CHARACTERISTICS OF STUDENTS BASED ON MAJOR DEVELOPMENTAL AND INDIVIDUAL DIFFERENCES THEORIES IN THE CLASSROOMS

Although we cannot consider ways to observe every theory about how individuals learn, develop their characteristics and behaviors, and interact within the school setting, some of the more widely used theories, and those lend themselves to observational applications to teaching need to be considered. Determining which theories are most widely used, or lend themselves to observation is not easy. Although most of the major theories covered in texts of individual differences and human development will be considered, not all of them lend themselves to objective observation. Some require more subjectivity, interpretation, or analysis to be applied. Others require deeper development of the concept, and while they may be observed in classrooms where teachers have a great deal of experience and knowledge about the concept and the applications, they are not easily translated into methods of observation for novice observers, or for those lacking the deeper concept development. Therefore, you should not assume that if the concept is not covered in this chapter it is not important to consider in developing your understanding of the student in the classroom. Whenever you come across theories and concepts, it may be useful for you to reflect on how you develop those in the classroom, and how you might observe them as they apply to students.

PHYSICAL DEVELOPMENT: Body and Motor Skills

There are a variety of factors that come into play when one looks at body and motor skills development and individual differences. Genetic studies have shown the genetic linkages for many aspects of physical development. Like any of the other areas for individual differences, the environment also has an impact on development. There are many areas of physical development which could be the focus of an objective observation. The observer may be interested in the development of the senses of hearing, vision, taste, smell, and touch. The observer may be interested in how and of these senses are used. Another focus may be on the body size and shape or growth over time. The observer may be interested in the use of motor skills such as running, jumping, sitting, standing, writing, etc. The observer may focus on what the student eats, or how he/she eats if nutrition or nutritional skills are a concern. The observer may be interested in finding out if the student imitates others and then repeats that behavior in other circumstances.

Many times teachers focus their observations on other aspects of development of motor skills such as the number of times a student gets out of his/her seat, the number of times a student goes to sharpen a pencil, or goes to the bathroom, the number of times a student moves to the space of another student, or the incidents of attending behaviors. While the earlier observations are fairly easy to count, and could be enhanced by also recording the length of time involved, other students involved, etc., the incidents of attending behaviors are more difficult to objectively record and risk subjectivity when you start to enhance the descriptors.

Alton's instructor had told the class that as much as possible they should try to focus on observing and recording positive behaviors. The instructor said that it is easy to focus on negative behaviors, and sometimes as teachers one ends up thinking in negative terms about bad behaviors that disrupt the learning process. However, if the preservice teacher can learn to think in positive terms, maybe he/she will continue to try to do that when teaching. The instructor told about a teacher who had an extremely disruptive student in the classroom. Putting this into positive terms, the teacher had told that parent, "I admire the energy and enthusiasm your son brings to class every day. He is able to pay attention to and show concern for and about everyone, sometimes all at once. I am working to find a way to help him pay attention to less things for a longer period of time!"

Alton thought about one student in Mr. Wilder's homeroom. The student was out of his seat or assigned work area more than others, and when he was in his seating area, he seemed to pay attention less frequently. Alton knew that paying attention was a judgment, not an observable behavior. He thought about the 'positive teacher' and thought that he could count the instances in which the student was engaged in the learning by looking at the number of times the student raised his hand, asked questions, followed teacher directions, etc. He could also count the number of seconds that the student sat in his seat, had his books or materials in front of him, or was writing. As Alton thought about this, he realized that the motor skills that he was interested in observing were also indicators of cognitive skills. If Alton was going to keep this focused on motor skills, he could do a drawing of where the student moved in the room and then note how long he was there. Alton decided to use a classroom schematic to chart the behavior of this student. The results of his efforts are found in C3A.

Reflective Questions:
- Based on what you know about physical development and motor skills, how would you expand or change Alton's form?
- Based on what you know about physical development, what other objective observations might you develop?

COGNITIVE DEVELOPMENT: Piaget's Theory

Practitioners vary in their beliefs that Piaget's (1928) theory of cognitive development is relevant and appropriate for considering the ways that children develop their thinking skills over the years. While few practitioners still hold to the strict age/stage categories that Piaget proposed, many still believe that there are some characteristic behaviors of children that fit into the theory's model, and can be observed in the classroom. As you review the major stages, various tools that Piaget tested these with may come to mind, such as masses of clay and various glass water containers.

Sensorimotor   *Birth - 2 years*
   reflexive schemes, primary circular reactions, secondary circular reactions, coordination of secondary circular reactions, tertiary circular reactions, mental representations

Pre-operational   *2 - 7 years*
   egocentrism, animistic thinking, perception-bound thought, centration, momentary states, irriversibility, transductive reasoning, lack of hierarchical classification

Concrete   *7 - 11 years*
   conservation, spatial operations, decentration, seriation, reversibility, transitive inference, hierarchical classification

Formal operational   *12+ years*
   hypothetico-deductive reasoning, propositional thought

Form C3A-example: Classroom Schematic that Shows Student Movement

School: Lincoln Middle _____ Room:_____ Teacher:____SW_____

Grade Level _7__ Subject Matter:___math and science_____ Number of Students: _27__

Date:___9/20_____Start Time:___10am_ Finish Time:__10:40am Total Observation Time: _40 min____

Room Set-up/Special Information:____None_____

Definition of Observation:_Position of MS1, and amount of time in that position_____

Key:	*X* is a position MS1 stays in for more than 5 seconds.
	The # before *X* is the position number (1 = first, 2 = second, etc.)
	The # after *X* is the number of seconds in that position.

Boards

Door

Demonstration Table	Work/Demo Table

B o a r d s

Table of: *1X400* MS1, MS2 *7X510* FS7, FS8, FS9	*2X210*	Table of: FS3, FS4 MS10, MS11		Table of: MS5, MS6 FS12, FS13

3X300 *8X240*   *4X140*   *5X20*   *9X160*   *6X30*

Table of: FS14, FS15 MS20, MS21	*10X150*	Table of: FS16, FS17 MS22, MS23,	Table of: FS18, FS19 MS24

11X30   *12X30*   *13X20*

Desk of: MS25	Desk of: FS26	Desk of: MS27	Desk of: empty	Desk of: empty

14X90   *15X210*   *16X120*

Reading area

Work Table

Resource Table

Teacher's Desk

Storage Cabinets, and Charts

Selma's first day of volunteering at the school caught her by surprise. The principal asked her to spend some time in classes at each grade level, starting with the pre-school. When she was in each room she was to observe the students and see if she could see examples of behavior on a list (Form C3B). Looking at the list, Selma realized that her own children had progressed through some of these behaviors as they had gotten older. Drawing on her introduction to child development course, Selma aligned the list of behaviors with Piaget's theory. Here is what she developed:

simple reflexive moves	reflexive schemes
imitations centered on own body	primary circular reactions
retrieves partially hidden objects	secondary circular reactions
retrieves hidden object from first place hidden	coordination of secondary circular reactions
searches in many places for hidden object	tertiary circular reactions
engages in deferred imitation	mental representations
unaware of other's viewpoints	egocentrism
inanimate objects have lifelike qualities	animistic thinking
judges based on current perceptions	perception-bound thought
centers on one aspect of a situation	centration
focuses on present, not past and future	momentary states
cannot go backward through a series of steps	irriversibility
wrong linking of events as cause and effect	transductive reasoning
cannot group objects into categories	lack of hierarchical classification
knows mass stays same as shape changes	conservation
understands relations of distance and time	spatial operations
coordinates several features of a task	decentration
arranges items in logical series	seriation
can work backwards through a problem	reversibility
can infer relationships among objects	transitive inference
can group objects into categories	hierarchical classification
tests hypothesis in an orderly manner	hypothetico-deductive reasoning
evaluates abstract verbal statements	propositional thought

Reflective Questions:
- Based on what you know about Piaget's theory, how would you expand or change Selma's form?
- Based on what you know about Piaget's theory, what other objective observations of the application of this theory might you develop?

COGNITIVE DEVELOPMENT: Information Processing Perspectives

There are many cognitive theorists who have different models about how we learn and deal with information. Although their various models differentiate themselves in various ways, as a group these theorists hold more or less to some basic tenets about how we process information. In the classroom, the concern is on the perception of the student, the attention given to the task, the ways the student plans to learn, the strategies the student uses to organize information, the amount of time it takes a student to learn, the way(s) that the student deals with processing/memorizing tasks, the ways the student shows comprehension, the ability of the student to retrieve information which was previously learned, the sequencing of the learning events, and the awareness of the student about how his/her memory works.

Form C3B: Some Indicators of Cognitive Development Applying Piaget's Theory

School:_____ Room:_____ Teacher:_____

Grade Level____ Subject Matter:_____ Number of Students:_____

Date:_____Start Time:_____ Finish Time:_____Total Observation Time:_____

Room Set-up/Special Information:_____

Definition of Observation:_____

___simple reflexive moves
___imitations centered on own body
___retrieves partially hidden objects
___retrieves hidden object from first place hidden
___searches in many places for hidden object
___engages in deferred imitation
___unaware of other's viewpoints
___inanimate objects have lifelike qualities
___judges based on current perceptions
___centers on one aspect of a situation
___focuses on present, not past and future
___cannot go backward through a series of steps
___wrong linking of events as cause and effect
___cannot group objects into categories
___knows mass stays same as shape changes
___understands relations of distance and time
___coordinates several features of a task
___arranges items in logical series
___can work backwards through a problem
___can infer relationships among objects
___can group objects into categories
___tests hypothesis in an orderly manner
___evaluates abstract verbal statements

Fran and Alton compared notes from their class. Both of them were assigned to observe for evidence of information processing in two students. Fran's classmates had discussed this in their small group work, and had decided that there were limited defined behaviors that they could observe in a normal classroom setting that dealt with such an internal process as how one learns. Rather, they could observe if the student evidenced learning through his/her responses, the amount of time a student spends working on a task, the questions the student asks, and the number or kind of interactions a student has with the teacher or others. Fran decided to make a verbatim observation of one student. When she told Alton what she was doing, and showed him how easy it was to set-up the form for this observation, Alton said that he would do the same thing, but on a different student. Then, they could compare their notes. Alton decided to record the verbatim statements of the frequently-out-of-seat student. Fran decided to record the verbatim statements of another student who sits at the same table. Form C3C-example 1 shows a small part of what Alton recorded. Form C3C-example 2 shows the total of what Fran recorded.

Form C3C-example 1: Alton's Record of One Student's Verbalizations

School:_____Lincoln Middle_____ Room:_Pod 2___ Teacher:____RB_____

Grade Level_8__ Subject Matter:____social sciences_____ Number of Students:_21__

Date:____10/5____Start Time:_1:10 pm_ Finish Time:_1:50 pm_ Total Observation Time:_40 min

Room Set-up/Special Information:____nothing special noted_____

Definition of Observation:____Student verbalizations: MS1_____

Event___Student verbalization_____

1   What do you think we are supposed to do so we can get our work done? Do you think that anyone else knows what they are supposed to do? I'll check with another group and see if they know. I'll go now so I won't interrupt them later, and so we will have plenty of time to get our work done.

2   I'm sorry to interrupt you. Do you know what we are supposed to do to get our work done? We are having a problem figuring it out. Did you figure it out? You all seem to be working very hard.

3   Thank you. That was helpful. When is this due? How much time did it take you to do it? Did you find it difficult? Are there special assignments for each of us?

4   How are you today? Did you get your work done? We aren't sure what to do, do you know?

5   No, we didn't ask the teacher. We should do that. I'll tell them to do that. Thanks so much. We should have thought of that. Good thinking!

6   We are supposed to ask the teacher. We all have different assignments. Each group is working on something different. We have to ask the teacher to tell us what we are supposed to do to get our work done. I can't believe that we didn't ask yesterday. Who has the role of being the contact with the teacher today?

7   What did the teacher say?

8   We have much to do. I know some of this already, but, we need to know the answers for all of these. Does everyone know the answer to the first item? Can we go on to the second item?

9   Excellent job, Martha. You seem to know this much better than last week. I hope that you can explain item #4 to the rest of us. I really am having problems with this. I just don't get the big rule. What do you think the big rule is for doing these problems?

10   Wow, I get it now! I understand it. This is much easier than I thought, once you get the hang of it. Why didn't I understand this earlier? Thanks everyone. You were all a big help. What do you think we should do next? We will have time left over after we check our work. Should we try to work ahead? Should I check how everyone else is doing?
....

Form C3C-example 2: Fran's Record of One Student's Verbalizations.

School:___Lincoln Middle_____ Room:_Pod 2___ Teacher:___RB_____

Grade Level_8___ Subject Matter:____social sciences_____ Number of Students:_21__

Date:____10/5____ Start Time:_1:10 pm_ Finish Time:_1:50 pm_ Total Observation Time:_40 min_

Room Set-up/Special Information:___nothing special noted_____

Definition of Observation:_____Student Verbalizations: MS2_____

Event___Student verbalization_____

1   What did you say?

2   That's okay with me.

3   I don't know. You decide.

4   I don't know. I was sick yesterday. I'll do mine at home tonight.

> **Reflective Questions:**
> • Based on what you know about information processing, how would you expand or change Fran's form?
> • Based on what you know about information processing, what other objective observations of the application of this model might you develop?

COGNITIVE DEVELOPMENT: *Vygotsky's Socialcultural Theory*

Vygotsky (1928) was interested in how a culture transmits its values, beliefs, customs and skills to the next generation. He proposed that each individual develops and masters the cultural system based on the activities that he/she engages in. It is through social interactions of working on a learning task with a more mature person who has mastered the task that the student learns to master the task and to think about the task in meaningful ways. Vygotsky explained that this learning happened when the student was in his/her zone of proximal development, that is, cognitively ready to learn with the help of someone else. Unlike some other theories, there are not clear categories or student behaviors that can be easily described or observed. Rather, there are a variety of teaching behaviors that are believed to enhance the learning through this theory. Therefore, although the theory is mentioned here, observational techniques will be discussed in the next chapter.

INTELLECTUAL/ABILITY DIFFERENCES & SITUATED COGNITION

There are many theories of intelligence and it's relationship to thinking. Theories differ in their perspectives as to what constitutes intelligence, what phenomena contribute to the development of intelligence, and how intelligence may be assessed. In many schools intelligence is generally defined as the ability to complete tasks which require analytical thinking and/or verbal proficiency. Although

Form C3D: Some Possible Intelligence Considerations Based on Typical School Definitions of Intelligence

School:_____ Room:_____ Teacher:_____

Grade Level____ Subject Matter:_____ Number of Students:_____

Date:_____ Start Time:_____ Finish Time:_____ Total Observation Time:_____

Room Set-up/Special Information:_____

Definition of Observation:_____

Student is able to:

___decode and recognize written words
___correctly spell words orally
___correctly spell words in writing
___listen to spoken prose
___write prose
___speak prose
___listen to a passage and supply deleted words
___read a passage and supply deleted words
___use vocabulary correctly when responding orally
___use vocabulary correctly when responding in writing
___listen to material and immediately recall it verbally
___listen to material and immediately recall it in writing
___use symbols as abbreviations for words
___after studying, recall material that is not required
___after studying, recall material that is required
___listen to a foreign language and repeat the words
___listen to a passage and respond verbally to provide information
___read a passage and respond verbally to provide information
___listen to a passage and respond in writing to provide information
___read a passage and respond in writing to provide information
___listen to a passage and respond verbally to comprehension questions
___read a passage and respond verbally to comprehension questions
___listen to a passage and respond in writing to comprehension questions
___read a passage and respond in writing to comprehension questions
___listen to a passage and discuss how concepts are similar and different
___read a passage and discuss how concepts are similar and different
___listen to a passage and respond in writing how concepts are similar and different
___read a passage and respond in writing how concepts are similar and different
___listen to a problem and do the mathematical calculations without paper
___read a problem and do the mathematical calculations without paper
___do mathematical calculations with the help of a calculator
___listen to and then repeat sequences of words or numbers forward
___listen to and then repeat sequences backwards
___construct a pattern from something that is presented visually
___construct a pattern from something that is presented auditorily
___look at an incomplete picture and identify what is missing
___listen to an incomplete passage and identify what is missing
___look at a set of pictures and place them in sequence
___listen to a set of sentences and place them in sequence
___look at a set of pieces and put them together to form an object
___compare different groups of items presented visually and indicate what they have in common
___work from the beginning to the end of a task, staying with the sequence needed
___work through a task, not necessarily using the generally recognized sequence

___interact appropropriately with other
___physically reproduce movements of others
___sustain conversation
___determine what to study
___complete required tasks
___attend to details
___think about things in a new way
___ask for help when needed
___organize a learning task
___make supplementary material useful
___correctly paraphrase
___choose among learning tasks

this is a limited definition, it is a useful start point to think about individual differences in abilities. Teachers make decisions about students' abilities regularly, and use these decisions to place students into groups, give assignments, determine how best to teach a task and assess that the task was learned, etc. Surviving and learning in the school setting may require different abilities than surviving and learning at home or at a job. In recent years, research by various theorists has supported the concept the different abilities are needed in different situations, and some people have more of the ability to remember and use one skill to another situation. While this idea may seem obvious, it has lead to a line of inquiry into what people think in different situations, and when provided with specific tasks. Research into this thinking, called situated cognition (Lave, 1988), is helping clarify the nature of intelligence, and the ways that thinking develops within and across individuals. Today, rather than trying to define and identify "intelligence" in their students, teachers may find their students learning more when the teacher has identified the ways that students engage in tasks, and what they think about as they try to learn.

Danielle knew how important it was to set-up the right situation for learning. The stimuli should be related to the learning task, and different tasks required different behaviors on the part of the teacher and the students. Danielle thought that if the task was situated correctly, it should improve the chances of it being correctly learned. While this idea may work, it is missing the point that the nature of the task, and the idea of what "learning" means and how "learning" is measured is also situational. Therefore, when Danielle thought about how to objectively observe situated cognition in her students, she initially missed defining some important components of the process. Danielle started out by asking the students to do a series of math problems as part of the science lesson. When students looked confused, she asked them to share what they were thinking. Among the comments were that "math is math," and "that doesn't apply here." While the verbal information was helpful, Danielle knew that there was more information that she ought to be considering.

Danielle reconsidered what she knew about abilities and performance, and could objectively observe. Pulling together a list based on various definitions of intelligence and learning, Danielle developed a form that helped her think about the ways that a student may best learn (Form C3D). Applying that form to each individual student, she was then able to group students, and set up learning tasks that she felt might best meet their needs.

Reflective Questions:
- Based on what you know about intelligence, how would you expand or change Danielle's form?
- Based on what you know about intelligence, what other objective observations of the application of this concept might you develop?

PERSONAL/LEARNING STYLES: Field Dependent/Independent Model

There are a variety of models for explaining how people learn and how they prefer to learn. In the field, there are differences in labels for the various models. The general category for the conceptual issues related to styles of learning is usually labeled as personal style. The specific area of study for this model is either called a cognitive style or a learning style. For the sake of allowing you to draw comparisons among the styles, the same terminology will be used throughout. The field dependent/independent model (Witkin, et.al., 1977) has been researched, and tends to hold up as a model to explain general learning preferences across much of the globe. Although various cultures may tend to put more emphasis on one style over another, generally, both styles are found in any culture. Therefore, regardless of the cultures in your classroom, you will find both styles presented.

The field dependent learning style is exhibited by the person who looks at things globally, adhering to the structure which is given, and making broad general distinctions among concepts, seeing relationships through a social context. The student who is field dependent attends to material which is relevant to his/her own experience, but is organizationally structured with goals and reinforcements. This student likes to learn concepts through watching others. He/she is motivated through verbal praise, external rewards, helping the teacher, and showing the value of the task to others.

The field independent learning style is exhibited by the person who looks at things analytically, imposing his/her own structure or restrictions on the experiences, making specific concept distinctions, and learning new concepts for their own sake. The student who is field independent takes an impersonal orientation and learns social material only as an intentional task, preferring self-defined goals and reinforcements while using hypothesis testing to attain concept information. He/she is motivated through competition and personal attainment charts, knowing how a task is useful, and being allowed to self-structure the task.

Reflective Questions:
- Based on what you know about this model, what objective observations of the application of this theory might you develop?

PERSONAL/LEARNING STYLES: Kolb's Model

Kolb (1971) believes that there are four major learning style preferences. Each student has one main style, which tends to be fairly stable over time. However, the style may be modified with experiences, or in a classroom where the preferred style is not encouraged, and one has to change to try to learn.

The Converger is the style name given for someone whose greatest strength is the practical application of ideas, the ability to solve problems. This person seems to learn best through hypothetical-deductive reasoning in situations such as conventional learning where there is one correct answer or solution to a problem. Research has found that convergers are relatively unemotional, prefer to deal with things instead of people, and tend to have narrow technical interests, often specializing in the physical sciences.

The Diverger is the style name given for someone whose greatest strength is the ability to assimilate disparate observations. This person seems to learn best through brainstorming which allows viewing concrete situations from many perspectives, and the use of imagination. Research has found that divergers tend to be emotional, have broad cultural interests, and often specialize in the arts.

The Assimilator is the style name given for someone whose greatest strength is the ability to create theoretical models. This person seems to learn best through inductive reasoning, organizing information, and assimilating disparate observations into an integrated explanation, often disregarding the facts if they do not fit with the theory. Research has found that assimilators like to do research and planning, and are often working in basic sciences and mathematics.

The Accommodator is the style name given for someone whose greatest strength is doing things, carrying out plans and involving self in new experiences. This person seems to learn best through intuitive trial-and-error experimenting or adapting to immediate circumstances. Research has found that accommodators are at ease with people, but sometimes seen as impatient as they rely heavily on others for information instead of asserting their own analytic ability. The accommodator tends to be found in technical or practical "action-oriented" jobs such as marketing and sales.

Steve had attended an inservice on learning styles years ago. Since then, he had experimented with the concept in his classroom. Using Kolb's model, he tried to make sure that he differentiated the types of tasks he required, and the ways that he provided instruction. Recently he had begun applying the concept in conjunction with cooperative learning. When he had cooperative learning groups for general conceptual learning, he would place students together based on their learning styles. He liked the idea that students with similar styles could learn a task in the ways that best met their needs, and could produce different things to show their learning. Steve placed identified

Form C3E: Learning Styles Adapted from Kolb's Model:

School:_____ Room:_____ Teacher:_____

Grade Level____ Subject Matter:_____ Number of Students:_____

Date:_____Start Time:_____ Finish Time:_____Total Observation Time:_____

Room Set-up/Special Information:_____

Definition of Observation:_____

> Directions: For the student you are observing, place a check next to the item which describes what you see happen in the classroom. At the bottom, make any notes that help explain or provide examples of the decisions you made.

Converger
___likes active experimentation
___uses hypothetical-deductive reasoning
___likes learning where there is one correct answer
___does not challenge ideas
___likes to work alone with things
___does not show emotion
___likes to problem solve
___likes technical tasks

Diverger
___likes to think about things instead of experiment with them
___likes brainstorming
___likes to consider multiples perspectives
___is imaginative
___is interested in various cultural dimensions, especially the humanities
___shows emotion
___is oriented toward feelings
___is open-minded

Assimilator
___uses inductive reasoning
___likes to create models and designs
___questions the facts if they don't seem to fit
___likes to follow a plan for learning
___is interested in math and quantitative tasks
___likes to work alone when thinking
___is good at designing experiments
___does not like to make decisions

Accommodator
___likes active experimenting in a trial-and-error manner
___is usually busy
___takes risks, tries new experiences
___likes to interact with others
___often relies on others for analysis
___is able to push his/her ideas on others
___adapts to new situations well
___uses trial and error to solve problems

Notes:

students' learning styles based on what he observed in the classroom. He knew that he could obtain a form for each student to answer and then score that to determine learning styles. However, he was suspicious that his students would answer as they thought they should, or in a way that made them look good to their peers. He decided to look again at the literature, and develop an actual form for his use when he observed his videos. He also decided to ask Danielle to try-out the form and see if they had agreement when using the form on the same students. Form C3E shows Steve's form.

Reflective Questions:
- Based on what you know about Kolb's model, how would you expand or change Steve's form?
- Based on what you know about Kolb's model, what other objective observations of the application of this model might you develop?

PERSONAL/LEARNING STYLES: Dunn and Dunn's 12 Variables Model

Dunn and Dunn's classroom observations lead them to conclude that no two learners have the exact same learning style. They have identified 12 distinct environmental variables (1978) that differ in the amount of concern that the individual learner prefers as part of his/her learning style. For each learner, each variable may be placed on a continuum ranging from "not a concern at all" to "a major concern." The variables include time, schedule, amount of sound, type of sound, type of group work, amount of pressure, type of pressure, place, physical environment and condition, type of assignments, perceptual strengths and styles, and type of structure and evaluation.

Danielle had learned about a variety of different learning styles. She was concerned because she felt that Kolb's style choice was too narrow. She liked the Dunn and Dunn model, but found it very difficult to think about in the classroom. much less observe in her students. She knew that she could purchase a learning style inventory for her students to answer. She could then have this computer scored and get a print-out for each student. However, her team wasn't sold on the Dunn and Dunn idea, so, if she applied it, She agreed to use Steve's quick-check to see if she could establish reliability with Steve on their students. In turn, Steve agreed to try to help Danielle develop a form to observe students based on the Dunn and Dunn model. Starting with the twelve variables, they decided to use a standard four-point continuum to try to categorize the behaviors and characteristics that they observed. They recognized that within each variable there were various characteristics, so each needed to be rated as a separate item using the continuum. Form C3F shows the form that they developed.

Reflective Questions:
- Based on what you know about Dunn and Dunn's model, how would you expand or change Danielle's form?
- Based on what you know about Dunn and Dunn's model, what other objective observations of the application of this model might you develop?

PERSONAL/LEARNING STYLES: COGNITIVE TEMPO

Cognitive tempo, or conceptual tempo is typically associated with information-processing tendencies, and labeled along a continuum from impulsivity to reflectivity. Learners who are impulsive tend to respond faster and commit more performance errors. Learners who are reflective tend to have longer response times and commit fewer performance errors (Kagan, 1965). Reflective learners also tend to gather information more systematically and evaluate it more thoroughly when they are problem-solving.

Form C3F: Learning Style Descriptors Adapted from Dunn and Dunn

School:_____ Room:_____ Teacher:_____

Grade Level____ Subject Matter:_____ Number of Students:_____

Date:_____Start Time:_____ Finish Time:_____Total Observation Time:_____

Room Set-up/Special Information:_____

Definition of Observation:_____

Directions: For each behavior or characteristic, place the number that best describes the placement on the continuum scale:
- 1= not observed as a concern
- 2= observed as a minor concern, happens once in awhile
- 3= observed as a concern, happens a few times in class
- 4 =observed as a major concern, happens frequently in class

TIME:
___Student asks what time it is/is seen looking at the clock/is seen looking at his/her watch
___Student asks how much time is allotted for a task
___Student does more work when challenged to "beat the clock"

SCHEDULE:
___Student works on a task over a short interval of time, gets it all done at once
___Student works on a task over a long interval of time, does part now and part later
___Student works on a variety of tasks at once

AMOUNT OF SOUND:
___Student works when there is total quiet
___Student creates noise when there is total quiet
___Student works when there is conversation
___Student works when there are many noisy disruptions
___Student wears ear plugs when working

TYPE OF SOUND:
___Student hums when he/she works
___Student listens to music when he/she works
___Student sings when he/she works
___Student taps out beats when he/she works

TYPE OF GROUP WORK:
___When given choice, student chooses to work alone
___When given choice, student chooses to work in small groups
___When given choice, student chooses to work when whole class is involved

AMOUNT OF PRESSURE AND MOTIVATION:
___Student works when others tell him/her to
___Student works when has own set goals and deadlines
___Student works when others set goals and deadlines
___Student works when given public recognition
___Student works when given external rewards

PLACE:
___Student works in the normal classroom
___Student works at the computer
___Student works in the library
___Student does homework
___Student homework completed, seatwork not completed
___Student seatwork completed, homework not completed

PHYSICAL ENVIRONMENT AND CONDITIONS:
___When given choice, student sits at desk
___When given choice, student sits at table
___When given choice, student sits on the floor
___When given choice, student stands
___When given choice, student sits near window or light
___When given choice, student sits away from window or light
___When given choice, student wears sunglasses
___Student wears heavy clothes even in warm weather
___Student wears light clothes, even in cold weather

TYPE OF ASSIGNMENTS:
___When given choice, student chooses self-directed tasks
___When given choice, student chooses teacher-assigned tasks
___Student works when has work contract
___When given choice, student chooses peer-directed tasks

PERCEPTUAL STRENGTHS AND STYLES:
___Student chooses visual materials to learn
___Student chooses aural materials to learn
___Student chooses printed materials to learn
___Student chooses hands-on/tactile materials to learn
___Student chooses a variety of different kinds of materials to learn

STRUCTURE AND EVALUATION:
___Student chooses a strict structure for the class work
___Student chooses a flexible structure for the class work
___Student self-starts on tasks
___Student inquires as to how well he/she is learning
___Student develops a time-line to complete an ongoing task
___Student does all he/she can on a task at one time

Form C3G: Cognitive Tempo in the Classroom

School:_____ Room:_____ Teacher:_____

Grade Level_____ Subject Matter:_____ Number of Students:_____

Date:_____Start Time:_____ Finish Time:_____Total Observation Time:_____

Room Set-up/Special Information:_____

Definition of Observation:_____

Response #	Student							
	#1 Time	#1 Error	#2 Time	#2 Error	#3 Time	#3 Error	#4 Time	#4 Error
1								
2								
3								
4								
5								
6								
7								
8								
9								
10								

Fran knew that it was difficult to measure reflectivity and impulsivity in the classroom. She couldn't give tests to determine cognitive tempo. However, she had a stop watch, and she could observe students to see how long it took them to respond, and how many errors they made. She knew that she could not watch an entire classroom of students and try to clock everyone's response times. Rather, she could focus on a few students who sat close to one other and try to clock their times. She developed a form (Form C3G) for keeping track of response times and errors. She found that using the form was easy, and she was able to differentiate response times and the number of errors among students.

Reflective Questions:
- Based on what you know about the cognitive tempo model, how would you expand or change Fran's form?
- Based on what you know about the cognitive tempo model, what other objective observations of the application of this model might you develop?

PERSONAL/LEARNING STYLES: THE SOCIAL, AFFECTIVE PERSPECTIVE

Grasha and Reichmann (1974) believe that learning styles involve the social and affective aspects of how the individual interacts with his/her environment. Their model postulates that learners interact along three continuums. The first continuum is participant/avoidant, how much a student wishes to become involved in the classroom environment. The second continuum is collaborative/competitive, how much the student views peers as competition or peers to work with. The third continuum is independent/dependent, how much freedom and control the students wants in his/her environment.

When Steve read about this learning style, he realized that he often used this intuitively in his class. Without having had the label, he tended to put students into categories and design their learning tasks around these three main ideas. The students who were dependent were placed together in a part of the room where he could easily access them, and could tell them what to do. The students who were competitive were always finding ways to compete, even in collaborative groups, so he tended to group the competitors together. The avoidant students tended to be "doing their time," and skipped doing work or coming to class when they could. He made sure he did not put avoidant individuals together, because then that group would stand out.

Steve thought about this construct, and what he intuitively had observed in students. He developed a form (Form C3H) to use to try to quickly place a student along each of the three continuums. He found that with practice of watching a student for some time, he could categorize each student so that he could make decisions about how to best group the student in the classroom.

Reflective Questions:
- Based on what you know about the social, affective model, how would you expand or change Steve's form?
- Based on what you know about the social, affective model, what other objective observations of the application of this model might you develop?

PSYCHOSOCIAL DEVELOPMENT: Erikson's Theory

Erikson's (1950) theory of psychosocial development proposes that the individual student faces a certain developmental "crisis" as he/she gets older. How that conflict is resolved is the basis for the development of the person's psychosocial characteristics. The age-related crisis are:

Trust versus Mistrust	Birth - 1 year old
Autonomy versus Shame and Doubt	1 - 3 years
Initiative versus Guilt	3 - 6 years
Industry versus Inferiority	6 - 11 years
Identity versus Identity Confusion	Adolescence
Intimacy versus Isolation	Young adulthood

Fran and Alton were both observing at Lincoln Middle School. Applying Erikson's theory, they ought to be able to see students who had resolved the crisis of industry vs. inferiority, and may now be facing the crisis of identity versus identity confusion. Fran was interested in trying to observe the students to determine how they had resolved earlier crisis. Did they trust? Did they have autonomy? Were they showing initiative? Did they exhibit industry? Fran considered the behaviors that went with each of these psychosocial concerns. She determined that there were a few key behaviors she could identify and objectively observe in the students in the classroom. if she developed these in a hierarchical manner, she could develop a sort of checklist form. After reviewing the theory and reading some of Erikson's work, Fran developed a list of indicators. She then expanded the potential

Form C3H: Social, Affective Learning Style Differences

School:_____ Room:_____ Teacher:_____

Grade Level____ Subject Matter:_____ Number of Students:_____

Date:_____Start Time:_____ Finish Time:_____Total Observation Time:_____

Room Set-up/Special Information:_____

Definition of Observation:_____

Student Characteristics

Participant _____ **Avoidant** _____

___engages in learning course content
___attends class regularly
___assumes responsibility for learning
___participates in class
___completes required work

___does not engage in learning course content
___misses class
___assumes no responsibility
___does not participate
___does not complete required work

Collaborative _____ **Competitive** _____

___shares with others
___is cooperative
___enjoys working with others
___interacts with others in class
___is not concerned about winning

___competes, does not share
___tries to do better than others
___enjoys competing
___"shows off" to others
___tries to win

Independent _____ **Dependent** _____

___creates own structure
___works on own without supervision
___will work to learn what is needed
___listens to others
___confident
___curious

___relies on teacher for structure
___needs supervisor to tell what to do
___learns minimum that is required
___listens to teacher only
___lacks confidence
___lacks intellectual curiosity

observation form by adding some time-related and event-related components. She determined that the best way for her to use the form (Form C3I) was to focus on one individual student at a time, and to try to determine where that student was in the psychosocial development process, given that form. She then decided that if the form worked she would use it on a few different students and compare her results. She shared her form and the development process with Alton. He added a few suggestions, and agreed to try to use it himself.

Fran used the form with the two different students each on three different days. Fran learned that the same student exhibited different behaviors on different days. She concluded that observations for such complex concepts as psychosocial indicators need to be done over a longer period of time, and may require additional information beyond that which one gets by being an uninformed observer in the classroom.

Alton was not as familiar with Erikson's theory, and didn't do the reading that Fran had done. He found it difficult to use the form when he lacked the theory-base. He didn't know how to categorize the behaviors as indicators. He also had trouble sometimes decided what constituted a task in the classroom. He decided that he needed better definitions of behaviors which were identified on the checklist before he would draw any conclusions in isolation.

Alton hesitantly shared his concerns with Fran. He didn't want to make her feel bad, nor did he want to make it look like he didn't know the theory, so he carefully explained that sometimes he just wasn't sure what all to check. He and Fran agreed to observe the same student from different places in the room at the same time. When they did this, and compared notes, they found that they had a reliability correlation of .92, which was fine. They decided that such checklists may be helpful for some other observations.

Reflective Questions:
- Based on what you know about Erikson's theory, how would you expand or change Fran's form?
- Based on what you know about Erickson's theory, what other objective observations of the application of this theory might you develop?

PERSONALITY TYPES: THE "BIG 5" FACTORS

Over the years personality theorists have constructed various models to describe the personality traits and characteristics of individuals. Over the past several years, the majority of the theorists have come to accept McCrae's (1989) that there are a consistent set of five factors that make up personality type and describe dimensions of personality. These factors are:

surgency:	talkative-silent, social-reclusive, adventurous-cautious
agreeableness:	good natured-irritable, mild-headstrong, cooperative-negativistic
conscientiousness:	responsible-undependable, perservering-quitting, tidy-carelessness
emotional stability:	calm-anxious, composed-excitable, poised-nervous
intellect:	intellectual-nonreflective, imaginative-simple, artistic-insensitive

While individuals exhibit many different traits, for the most part, with observation, the individuals' variations in each of the dimensions ought to be able to be charted on a continuum. Steve set-out to do just that. It was well into the school year, and although he had been placing his students into work groups based on learning styles and their achievement levels, he was concerned that he was missing something. As he made plans for the second half of the year, and the ways that students would complete performance assessments to show learning over the year, the personality dimensions kept coming forefront to his thoughts. He could put S1 and S2 together, but not with S3 because S3 made everyone edgy and nervous. He decided that if he tried to use the theory to chart each student's personality dimensions, maybe he could put students into groups in a more equitable

FORM C3I: A Modified Checklist of Indicators of a Student's Psychosocial Development Applying Erikson's Theory

School:_____ Room:_____ Teacher:_____

Grade Level_____ Subject Matter:_____ Number of Students:_____

Date:_____Start Time:_____ Finish Time:_____Total Observation Time:_____

Room Set-up/Special Information:_____

Definition of Observation:_____

Student behavior
- [ ] Allows contact with others
- [ ] Initiates contact with others
- [ ] Allows others near his/her desk
- [ ] Allows others near his/her body
- [ ] Says "No" to some task choices
- [ ] Moves away from others
- [ ] Tries to learn show skills through counting, recitation, etc.
- [ ] Scolds self aloud
- [ ] Shakes head as engages in tasks
- [ ] Refuses to choose a task when given a choice
- [ ] Asks adults for confirmation it is okay to try a task
- [ ] Asks adults if tasks are accomplished appropriately or correctly
- [ ] Initiates play by self with the toy _____ for _____ seconds/minutes
- [ ] Chooses the task of _____, and is seen engaging in this task
- [ ] Tries a task and stays with it for _____ seconds/minutes
- [ ] Imitates a modeled behavior of _____ for _____seconds
- [ ] Initiates play with others for _____ seconds/minutes
- [ ] Plays with others for _____seconds/minutes
- [ ] Works with others on a task for _____seconds/minutes
- [ ] Work with students in a small group for _____seconds/minutes
- [ ] Cooperates/works with the teacher
- [ ] Refuses to engage in tasks
- [ ] Says aloud is not smart enough to do the task
- [ ] Asks other students for help when engaged in a task
- [ ] Asks teacher for help when engaged in a task
- [ ] Complies with teacher request of _____ for _____seconds/minutes
- [ ] Complies with student request of _____ for _____seconds/minutes
- [ ] Works on a task by self for _____seconds/minutes
- [ ] Comes back to a task when given free time in the class
- [ ] Cleans up after self when completes a task or task time is over
- [ ] Cleans up after self and others when done with small group activity
- [ ] Tells others why task is important
- [ ] Tells others own vocational goals
- [ ] Tells others why learning is important
- [ ] Tells others who they are, what they feel, what they believe
- [ ] Expresses opinions as own in front of peers in classroom
- [ ] Expresses own opinions in front of teacher in classroom
- [ ] Labels friends as such in front of others in classroom
- [ ] Labels close friends/special relationships as such in front of others in classroom
- [ ] Says aloud does not know what will do in the future

Form C3J: Personality Differences as Observed in the Classroom

School:_____ Room:_____ Teacher:_____

Grade Level____ Subject Matter:_____ Number of Students:_____

Date:_____Start Time:_____ Finish Time:_____Total Observation Time:_____

Room Set-up/Special Information:_____

Definition of Observation:_____

The Individual Student:

Surgency

Talkative	Silent
___engages in discussion in class	___engages in discussion only when called upon
___is seen initiating conversation with peers	___is not seen initiating conservation with peers
___talks out during classtime	___is silent during classtime
___talks to teacher during class	___does not talk to teacher during class

Social	Reclusive
___is seen initiating contact with others	___is not seen initiating contact with others
___engages others in work/play	___works/plays alone
___shares with others	___does not share with others
___enjoys working with others	___enjoys working alone
___interacts with others during class	___interacts with others only when forced to do so
___energetic	___easily fatigued

Adventurous	Cautious
___tries new learning tasks	___stays with known tasks
___looks to outside world	___looks inward
___takes chances	___does not take chances
___moves around the classroom	___stays in seat or assigned area
___tries out new ideas in class	___only does assigned work
___speaks mind/ideas	___keeps ideas to self

Agreeableness

Good natured	Irritable
___interacts with others in class	___complains about others
___jokes with others	___finds nothing funny
___does not complain, goes with the flow	___complains about things in the room

Mild	Headstrong
___listens to others	___listens to teacher only
___accepts more than one way of thinking	___believes own way of thinking is correct
___accepts differences with others	___believes differences are wrong

Cooperative	Negativistic
___shares with others	___does not share
___presents things positively	___presents things in negative manner
___finds ways to deal with problems	___believes problems can't be solved

Conscientiousness

Responsible	Undependable
___engages in learning course content	___does not engage in learning course content
___assumes responsibility for learning	___assumes no responsibility
___participates in class	___does not participate
___completes required work	___does not complete required work
___can be relied upon for leadership	___cannot be relied upon for leadership

Persevering	Quitting
___attends class regularly	___misses class
___works on own without supervision	___needs supervisor to tell what to do
___will work to learn what is needed	___learns minimum that is required
___continues to work on a task until done	___works on task only during assigned time
___refuses to give up on a complicated task	___gives up on a complicated task

Tidy	Carelessness
___cleans up after self	___leaves work area messy
___offers to help clean up room	___does not offer to help clean up room
___carefully erases mistakes	___papers contain smudges and dirty erasures
___papers are handed-in that are clearn	___papers are handed-in that are dirty

Emotional Stability

Calm	Anxious
___calm, relaxed	___restless, tense
___normal rate of speech	___increased rate of speech
___focused attention	___easily distracted
___does not seem threatened	___threatened easily

Composed	Excitable
___confident	___lacks confidence
___emotions are appropriate to situation	___shows emotions inappropriately
___thinks before acts	___immediately reacts in situations

Poised	Nervous
___secure	___insecure
___performs well on tasks	___performs based on others approval
___self-assured, self-confident	___questions self, lacks confidence
___mature	___immature, childish

Intellect

Intellectual	Nonreflective
___curious	___lacks intellectual curiosity
___engages in thinking tasks	___does not think about how to do tasks
___presents alternative ways to do tasks	___does tasks with direction
___accepts new ideas	___rejects new ideas
___tolerates ranges of answers	___looks for right and wrong answers only

Imaginative	Simple
___creates own structure	___relies on teacher for structure
___elaborates	___does not elaborate
___flexible	___inflexible

Artistic	Insensitive
___expands on learning	___does only what is required
___creates designs on worksheets	___not seen doodling, designing
___likes to show work to others	___does not show work to others

Form C3K: Categorizing Student Personality on Introversion/Extroversion

School:_____ Room:_____ Teacher:_____

Grade Level____ Subject Matter:_____ Number of Students:_____

Date:_____Start Time:_____ Finish Time:_____Total Observation Time:_____

Room Set-up/Special Information:_____

Definition of Observation:_____

Directions: Check all those that are observed as applying to the individual student:

Student name:_____

Extroverts tend to: **Introverts tend to:**

___perform complex motor sequences   ___read instead of doing motor activities
___be conditioned by positive experiences   ___be conditioned by negative experiences
___use short-term retention skills   ___use long-term retention skills
___seek affiliation   ___seek academic achievement
___tolerate frustration   ___be intolerant of frustration
___be impulsive   ___be reflective
___be friendly, sociable   ___avoid friendship/social situations
___take risks   ___avoid risks
___be energetic   ___tire easily
___enjoy numerous tasks at once   ___work on one thing at a time
___focus on stimuli   ___ignore interruptions
___be influenced by others   ___use personal values as guides
___be aggressive   ___shrug from confrontation
___enjoy change   ___enjoy stability
___like disorder   ___like order
___go with the moment   ___plan ahead

manner, and the performance choices that they made may make for less problems than he had the year before. Steve developed Form C3J to determine each student's personality. He knew that it was not as accurate as giving a personality test, but, for his purposes, he believed that this would work. Additionally, he wanted to have Danielle complete this form on some of the same students when they were in her room. That way he could compare his results with Danielle's to see if the students were different in different classrooms.

Reflective Questions:
- Based on what you know about the "Big 5" theory of personality, how would you expand or change Steve's form?
- Based on what you know about the "Big 5" theory of personality, what other objective observations of the application of this theory might you develop?

PERSONALITY DIFFERENCES: INTROVERSION/EXTROVERSION

H.J. Eysenck (1960) says that he did not coin the terms introversion and extroversion, as they have been in the European vernacular for hundreds of years. However, he is usually credited with developing the terms in their psychological sense, and for developing the model and researching the characteristics of this personality difference. In Eysenck's classification, introversion and extroversion do not fit on opposite ends of a continuum. Rather, an individual can be classified as to the extent to which he/she is introverted and the extend to which he/she is extroverted in a situation. If you look across behaviors in different situations, you get a general sense of the characteristic expression within the individual.

Danielle was working with her pod to develop learning tasks for the students. She had just tried Steve's personality dimensions form, and found it interesting, but cumbersome. As she was still developing her repertoire of instructional skills and creating tasks for students, she wanted something that was easier for her to determine the types of tasks that might best work with students. As she read about introversion and extroversion, she learned that there was a strong research base on which to give different tasks to different students based on these dimensions. She learned that she could give a test to the students to categorize them, or she could observe for the characteristics in the classroom. She developed Form C3K to observe each student. Based on the strength of the characteristic, she could then provide extroverts with different tasks than introverts.

Reflective Questions:
- Based on what you know about Eysenck's theory, how would you expand or change Danielle's form?
- Based on what you know about Eysenck's theory, what other objective observations of the application of this theory might you develop?

LANGUAGE DEVELOPMENT: *Interactionist Theories*

In recent years the interactionist theories of language development have arisen, and received much attention in accounting for the individual differences in language development across individuals. The theories stress that biology, cognition, and social interaction all play a role in the development of language. Different theorists give varied import to the different aspects, and provide different focuses to different parts of language. The development of phonology, semantics, grammar, pragmatics, and metalinguistic awareness have all been points of focus to differentiate and determine developmental progress. As with the other theories and models, various cultures will promote various developmental trends, and there will be wide variations in the development both within and across cultures. Therefore, the general trends by age should not be taken as absolute.

Age:	Birth-1 year
	Phonology: speech sounds become organized phonemic categories; begins babbling Semantics: babble sounds appear in contexts Grammar: sensitivity to natural phrase units begins Pragmatics: starts to engage in vocal exchanges with caregiver Metalinguistics: not known to be present
Age:	1 - 2 years
	Phonology: systematic strategies to simplify word pronunciation begin Semantics: first words, usually objects, are pronounced; vocabulary built to several hundred words Grammar: two word utterances, first grammatical morphemes Pragmatics: takes turns in conversations Metalinguistics: not known to be present
Age:	3 - 5 years
	Phonology: pronunciation improves Semantics: word coinage expands and metaphors appear Grammar: sentences mimic adult grammar with complex structures Pragmatics: adjusts speech with social expectations Metalinguistics: awareness starts to emerge
Age:	6 - 10 years
	Phonology: subtle differences in meaning are mastered in the pronunciation Semantics: vocabulary is 14,000+ words with appreciation of multiple meanings for same word Grammar: passive voice and other complex grammatical structures further developed Pragmatics: able to engage in advanced conversational strategy use in unfamiliar situations Metalinguistics: rapid development of awareness
Age:	11 years and older
	Phonology: difficult word endings and syllabic changes are mastered Semantics: vocabulary builds to 30,000 words, abstract and nonliteral meanings developed Grammar: continues refinement of complex grammatical structures Pragmatics: referential communication continues to expand Metalinguistics: refinement of awareness

In Selma's class on introduction to languages, she learned that most humans develop language along a standard pattern, regardless of culture. She was fascinated by the idea that if language did progress along a systematic course, second language should do the same thing. She read about the need to have good language models and the need to have practice. She told the principal that she would like to volunteer in the primary grades where students were rapidly developing their language, and she would have the opportunity to interact and continue her language development while helping them.

The principal assigned her to a split first and second grade classroom where she could tutor students to help them develop their reading skills. After a few hours of tutoring students, Selma decided that it was going to be difficult to keep track of where each of the students were and who needed what help without some kind of record keeping. Selma discussed this with the classroom teacher who suggested that Selma have each student develop a word log. They could write down every word that they knew how to pronounce, and if they knew what it meant, they could underline the word. Students could put new words in at anytime, but, if they couldn't explain one when someone asked, they had to circle the word and then it nolonger counted on the log. Students could compare logs and try to help each other discover new words to build their logs. Selma could then chart the number of words in each student's log and then know how much growth students had on a weekly basis. Selma decided to start her own English word log and also chart her vocabulary growth each week.

SOCIAL DEVELOPMENT: Selman's Model

Social development involves developing an awareness of self, the development of perspective taking, and the development of the skills to socialize appropriately with others. Selman (1981) proposed a five stage model of perspective taking that fits with the play behaviors normally found in youngsters. As one's perspective taking advances, one's ability to socialize with others should be expanded . Putting what we know about socialization with Selman's theory, we have these major stages:

Selman's stage	age	behavior	socialization behaviors
undifferentiated	3-6 years	confuse thoughts and feelings	parallel play, peer modeling
social-informational	4-9 years	different perspectives self and others	sociodramatic play, rough-and-tumble play, peer groups emerge
self-reflective	7-12 years	view own thoughts from another's perspectives	interpreting and responding to others prosocial behaviors grow
third party	10-15 years	can imagine how third party would view the situation	dominance hierarchies become stable conformity to peer groups
societal	14 + years	third party can be influenced by society	individualization in friendships

Alton was interested in the friendships that students had in the school. He knew that in preadolescent students there was a development of being able to take a third person's perspective, and students engaged in forming various cliques and groups which take on emerging importance. Alton wanted to interview students to find out what cliques they were in and how they viewed situations. However, this was not possible given that he was not a teacher. After much thought, Alton decided that he could observe who students were with when they had free time in the classroom. Alton decided to use a kind of sociogram schematic to chart who was with whom in the room. Instead of drawing the room, he kept track of which students approached other students, and if the approach was acknowledged or not. Form C3L is an example of what Alton found.

MORAL DEVELOPMENT: Kohlberg's Model

Kohlberg (1976) proposed a six stage model of moral development that he believed was universal and invariant. He believed that people everywhere moved through the stages in a fixed order, with each stage requiring successively more reasoning, and a more developed concept of justice. Kohlberg believed that moral development is promoted by grappling with moral issues. Kohlberg's theory has been criticized as too rigid, not applying to females, dependent upon cognitive

Form C3L-Example: Tracking Classroom Socialization

School:____Lincoln Middle_____ Room:_Pod 3___ Teacher:_____TS_____

Grade Level_6_ Subject Matter:___social sciences and language arts_ Number of Students:___18_

Date:_10/21___Start Time:_12:15pm__Finish Time:_12:35pm_Total Observation Time:_20 minutes_

Room Set-up/Special Information:___desks, nothing unusual_____

Definition of Observation:___student interactions when given free time, who they choose to be with

Student	Gender	Who socializes with
1	Male	3, 2, 4, 5
2	Female	1, 6
3	Male	1, 4, 5
4	Male	1, 3, 5
5	Male	1, 12, 3, 4
6	Female	2
7	Female	8, 9, 10
8	Female	7, 9, 10
9	Female	7, 8, 10
10	Female	7, 8, 9, 12, 13, 14, 15
11	Female	
12	Female	10, 5
13	Male	10, 15, 18
14	Male	10
15	Male	10, 13
16	Female	17
17	Female	16
18	Male	13

development, too focused on rights and justice, and not applicable to other cultures. Kohlberg's stages are:

Preconventional Level	Stage 1: Punishment and disobedience orientation
	Stage 2: Instrumental purpose orientation
Conventional Level	Stage 3: "Good boy-Good girl" orientation
	Stage 4: Social-order-maintaining orientation
Postconventional level	Stage 5: Social-contract orientation
	Stage 6: Univsersal ethical principle orientation

Selma was surprised when she found that some students were entering words in their word logs that they didn't know. She asked them why, and they said that they were helping each other. She then told them that they should help each other learn, but this was cheating. She then asked them what they thought of cheating. They immediately asked if they would be punished, and said that they were taught it wasn't wrong to help each other. Selma believed that the students were giving responses that fit in Kohlberg's stage 1. Selma explained that there were times, places, and ways to help each other, and that they should make sure that the teacher wanted them to help each other on a project before they did help each other. She then talked to the teacher to find out if the teacher wanted the students to help each other on this project. The teacher told Selma that the students often work cooperatively, and that instead of labeling the behavior as cheating, she would tell the students that each log should be kept only by the individual student.

Reflective Question:
- Based on what you know about Kohlberg's theory, what objective observations of the application of this theory might you develop?

MORAL DEVELOPMENT: Eisenberg's Model

Eisenberg (1982) believes that children's moral development is dependent upon their reasoning, which is situational and variable. She suggests that Kohlberg's model of moral development is too rigid as it does not allow for children to reason at several different levels. She believes that a child can use any of the levels of reasoning for which he/she is capable, however just because a child has the capability doesn't mean that he/she will choose to use it. Also, higher levels of reasoning will tend to be found in older children who have more experience with thinking and reasoning. Eisenberg puts cognitive and affective components of morality together.

Additionally, Eisenberg's model was developed keeping both genders in mind. Research with Eisenberg's model has held that it not only works for both males and females, but it also works in different cultures. Eisenberg's model is:

Self-centered reasoning: concern with consequences to oneself
Needs-oriented reasoning: concern for the expressed needs
Stereotyped and/or approval-oriented reasoning: concern is on good/bad, winning approval
Empathetic reasoning: concern with emotional consequences
Partly internalized principles: justifications for actions involve internalized values
Strongly internalized principles: justifications for actions involve strongly internalized values and self-respect

Form C3M: Example of Danielle's Application of Eisenberg's Model

Directions: Read the following story carefully. Then, answer each of the questions.

Torry is a good student. He does his work, and generally earns passing grades. Torry's parents are going through a divorce, and right now he spends half of his week with one parent and the other half with the other parent. Torry left his project homework, which is worth one-quarter of his grade for this grading period, at his mother's house, and won't see her for another four days. If he calls either parent and asks for help, Torry thinks that it is likely that the other parent will be angry at him, and he doesn't know if either parent would leave work to help him. His mother lives across town, and it takes about 40 minutes to get to her house. Torry does have a key for her house, as well as his father's house. The work is due in a couple of hours. Torry goes to his friends and asks them to help him figure out what to do. His friends make lots of different suggestions. Which ones to do think Torry should consider? Would you add any other suggestions? Which one do you think that Torry should do?

___borrow and copy someone else's work
___call mother and ask her to leave work, get it, and bring it to school
___call father and tell him that he needs to take you to mothers to get the work
___skip school for the rest of the day
___tell the teacher you are sick and will have it later
___tell the teacher that the work is at his mother's and he will not be able to get it until he is back there
___tell the teacher that the work was ruined and he needs time to redo it tonight
___tell the teacher that because of the divorce he couldn't get the work done and start crying
___take someone else's work and claim it as his
___go to father's house and do what can of the work, bring it in when it is due

My other suggestions are:

I would tell Torry to:

Danielle wanted to know what the moral thinking of her students. She looked at Kohlberg's and Eisenberg's theories, and decided that the best way to determine her students' reasoning was to ask each of them to tell their thinking about a moral situation. She knew that she could use any of the standard dilemmas, but she instead chose to use an example of something that had occurred in the school. Form C3M shows an example of what she developed.

Reflective Questions:
- Based on what you know about Eisenberg's model, how would you expand or change Danielle's form?
- Based on what you know about Eisenberg's model, what other objective observations of the application of this model might you develop?

ECOLOGICAL SYSTEMS: Bronfenbrenner's Theory

Bronfenbrenner (1989) views the student as developing within a complex system of relationships affected by multiple levels of the environment. The environment surrounds the student in a series of structures which react and interact with the student, impacting his/her development. Bronfenbrenner postulated that there are four layers of the environment. The first layer, the microsystem is the activities and interaction patterns in the student's immediate surroundings. The mesosystem, the second layer, is the connections among the student's immediate settings. The exosystem, the third layer, is the settings that impact on the student, but do not affect the student's immediate settings. The macrosystem is the final layer. It consists of the values, laws, and customs of a culture that influences the experiences and interactions at the lower levels of the environment.

Objectively observing the environment, and how it impacts on the student is difficult. Making any decisions about impact necessarily means that you are making judgments. Observing the environment means that you have to clarify your definition of the environmental layer you are observing. After trying various ways to observe the various layers, I have found that focused anecdotal reports are a good source for generating information which can be used to try to "objectify" the situation. using this method, the layer and the portion of it that one is reporting on needs to be defined. For instance, for the student who is at school, the school is in the microsystem. The interactions of the school with the immediate family of the student is part of the mesosystem. While an observer could objectively make a list of the items which are sent between school and family, an anecdotal report which lists and explains the interactions could also be considered objective, and provide more information for decision-making.

Danielle choose to keep a focused anecdotal report concerning the interactions she knew about between school and Terrance's (a student in her homeroom) family. Terrance's permanent file indicated that his parents were divorced, and only his mother had access to school records and reports. Yet, Terrance reported that he now was staying with his father. Terrance did not share any details about this arrangement, and Danielle was not sure how to handle things when she was new to the school and just trying to get to know everyone. Danielle clarified the focus of the anecdotal report as being "any contact with any primary or secondary caretaker of Terrance." See Form C3N-example to see a portion of what her anecdotal report contained.

Reflective Questions:
- Based on what you know about Bronfenbrenner's theory, how would you expand or change the observation form?
- Based on what you know about Bronfenbrenner's theory, what other objective observations of the application of this theory might you develop?

Form C3N: Example of an Anecdotal Report That Applies Bronfenbrenner's Model:

School:___Lincoln Middle_____ Room:_____ Teacher:___Danielle (self)___

Grade Level____ Subject Matter:__DNA_____ Number of Students:DNA___

Date:___DNA___Start Time:__DNA___ Finish Time:__DNA___Total Observation Time: _DNA_____

Room Set-up/Special Information: Does not apply_____

Definition of Observation: Report on: any contact with any primary or secondary caretaker of Terrance.

Date	Time	Contact with	Explanation of contact
9/8	3pm	step-father	inquired on phone if Terrance was at school. I requested that mother provide written release to talk with step-father, explained school legalities and confidentiality. Step-father agreed.
9/8	3:15pm	mother	inquired on phone why would not give information to step-father. I explained confidentiality. She agreed to send a letter so the school could talk to the step-father. She asked that I call her if Terrance was not in school. I explained the school attendance clerk would do that automatically. She told me she is concerned that Terrance is at school when he should be.
9/9	9am	Terrance	handed me a letter from his mother. Copy of letter put into his school file and the team file.
9/13	8am	father	phoned, Terrance would not be in school because he was ill
9/13	8:05am	mother	I phoned, and told her that the father had called and said Terrance would not be in school. I told her that school records indicated that she was the contact and father was not to have information. I was unsure how to handle his call. I asked her to clarify if I should be speaking with the father. She said Terrance is at his father's during the week, and I would take messages from him, but I should not give him information. I requested that she put that in writing so we have it in the records to share with the team.
9/26	4pm	mother	first parent-team conference. Terrance's progress and learning contracts provided. Mother explained that Terrance is a very emotional child who needs a great deal of support and care. Mother agreed to conference again in early November.
10/3	11am	mother	I phoned, Terrance is not in school and there was no call that he would be out. She said he is at the dentist and would be in this afternoon.....he came I at 12:15pm
10/14	3pm	mother	Terrance has not had homework done for the past week. I called and notified her that this was a concern. She said that Terrance was having some problems with her husband, and she would try to make sure it was done.
10/21	8am	father	Came to school and gave me a copy of a temporary court order for Terrance to live with him, he to have school contact. He asked to speak to Terrance. I referred him to the Principal. I gave a copy of the order to the Principal and asked if this meant that no one could talk to the mother. The Principal said she would talk to the school lawyer for clarification.

HUMANISTIC DEVELOPMENT: Maslow's Hierarchy of Needs

Discussion continues among theoreticians and practitioners as to what constitutes self-concept and self-esteem, how one assesses them, and how important they are to a student for the learning process. When one ties this to the discussion as to what needs an individual has and how to meet those needs in the classroom, the discussion gets much more complicated. One of the older standard models in the field that approaches human development from the humanistic perspective is that of Maslow. Maslow (1962) postulated that everyone had needs that fit into categories. When the base categories were mostly fulfilled, one went on to develop self-esteem, and then, as that need was met, move on to still higher categories. In the later years of Maslow's life, he revised his earlier model of the theory. The revision takes different forms with different interpretations of his work. However, there seems to be little disagreement about the first model of five categories or levels, which would be the ones primarily observed in school-age students.

Self-Actualization
Self-Esteem
Love and Belongingness
Safety and Security
Basic Physiological Needs

When Fran's instructor engaged the pre-service teachers in a discussion of the relevance of this theory for teacher's today, there seemed to be agreement that it would be important to know the needs of each student, and to try to figure out ways to meet those needs in the classroom. Fran agreed, but then asked how, given these rather general categories, one could objectively observe needs of students. Fran's instructor noted that whenever one was trying to observe characteristics or behaviors to put them into categories, then one was making judgments. However, some objectivity could be preserved if one carefully read for the defined behaviors within the categories, and tried to maintain as much as possible the behaviors and categories as defined by the theory.

After doing further reading on the theory, the class broke into small groups to try to isolate specific needs in each category. After they reached some agreement as to needs which fit in each category, they discussed what type of observation form and process would best allow them to observe the individual needs of a student, or to compare students. They decided that ultimately a two-step observation would be most beneficial. First, they would observe the student in the classroom in an uninformed, unobtrusive manner. That is, they would not have any information about the student, nor have the student know that he/she was being observed. Second, they would conduct a limited, structured interview with the student. That is, in an individual situation they would ask the student to verbally respond to a set of questions. The instructor reminded the pre-service teachers that if they asked questions they should be very careful not to violate confidentiality, and to adhere to ethics. They should have the permission of the student, the student's parent/guardian, the teacher, the principal. They should also have the questions screened by someone else to insure that they were not asking questions which violated privacy laws of the state, etc. As the instructor provided these cautions and considerations, the list of questions for an interview was revised, and the questions that were included were done so with the understanding that the second part of each question may have to be reworded or removed if the teacher thought that any judgments might be made based on the responses of the student. The final form that the pre-service teachers agreed they would use consisted of two parts (see Form C3O). They decided that if they could not obtain an interview, then, they would have less accurate information on which to base their decisions, but they still might be able to make some tentative decisions about areas in which they should further explore the needs of a student.

Form C3O: Observing the Humanistic Needs of Students Adapted from Maslow's Theory

School:_____ Room:_____ Teacher:_____

Grade Level____ Subject Matter:_____ Number of Students:_____

Date:_____Start Time:_____ Finish Time:_____Total Observation Time:_____

Room Set-up/Special Information:_____

Definition of Observation: Physiological, safety and security, love and belongingness, self-esteem, self-actualization observed in students.

Checklist part:

☐ Student is dressed in weather-appropriate attire
☐ Student's clothes are clean
☐ Student is bathed, groomed
☐ Student has food for meals and snacks
☐ Student has no visible bruises, injuries
☐ Student has own desk or workspace in classroom
☐ Student moves around classroom appropriate to activities
☐ Student expresses work-related emotions in the classroom
☐ Student cooperates with other students and with the teacher
☐ Student raises hand to ask or respond to questions
☐ Student praises others for good work
☐ Student shows own work to others

Interview part:

1. What things need to be in a classroom so that you feel safe? Are those things in this classroom?

2. What things need to be in a classroom so that you feel that you are part of the classroom? Are those things present in this classroom?

3. Tell me what you know about how you learn. Are the things you need to help your learning provided in this classroom?

4. Tell me what you need to feel good about your self, to feel important. Are the things you need to help you feel good about yourself provided in this classroom?

Reflective Questions:
- Based on what you know about Maslow's theory, how would you expand or change the observation form?
- Based on what you know about Maslow's theory, what other objective observations of the application of this theory might you develop?

REVIEW QUESTIONS:

1. What are the major differences in cognitive development theories? How would you observe cognitive development of students in the classroom?
2. What are the major differences in models of learning styles? How would you observe student learning styles in the classroom?
3. What are the major differences in personality development theories? How would you observe student personality characteristics in the classroom?
4. What are the major differences in models of moral development? How would you observe student moral development in the classroom?
5. Compare and contrast the various theories of development. How are each observed in the classroom?

DISCUSSION QUESTIONS:

1. Within each developmental theory there are wide ranges of individual differences in how students develop and how they exhibit the behavior or characteristics associated with the theory. Which theories lend themselves to a wide range of individual differences? Which theories lend themselves to a narrow range of individual differences? How does the range of individual differences impact the observation process?
2. If you were observing in a brand new situation and could only observe for two hours, which individual difference would be most important for you to observe in students in a classroom? Support your decision.
3. What types of observation lend themselves to use with looking at individual differences? What are the advantages of using objective observation of students? What are the disadvantages?

CHAPTER 4:
OBSERVING TEACHERS AND THEIR
INSTRUCTIONAL PROCESSES IN THE CLASSROOM

LEARNING OBJECTIVES:

After you read this chapter you should know:
1. How to observe teacher application of motor development in the classroom.
2. How to observe teacher application of student cognitive development in the classroom.
3. How to observe teacher application of student personal/learning styles in the classroom.
4. How to observe teacher application of student personality characteristics in the classroom.
5. How to observe teacher application of student language development in the classroom.
6. How to observe teacher application of student social development in the classroom.
7. How to observe teacher application of student moral development in the classroom.
8. How to observe teacher application of student environmental considerations in the classroom.
9. How to observe teacher application of student humanistic needs in the classroom.
10. How to observe teacher application of student social learning in the classroom.
11. How to observe teacher application of student motivation in the classroom.

After you read this chapter, you should be able to:
1. Identify and describe various teacher applications of theories and models of student individual differences and development in the classroom.
2. Use the forms provided to observe for a variety of teacher applications of theories and models of student individual differences and development in the classroom.
3. Develop your own forms to observe for a variety of teacher applications of theories and models of student individual differences and development in the classroom.
4. Explain to others how to observe students in the classroom.

INTRODUCTION

The previous chapter's focus was on how to observe various theories and models related to student individual differences as they might be applied in the classroom. Objective observation of students allows us to know what characteristics they have, and where they are developmentally. We can then make decisions about if and how to deal with what is observed. In this chapter, we will also learn that observation can be applied to teachers, and as a result of the observations, we can make decisions about what is occurring in the teaching-learning process, and if changes in the process might help the student, and the teacher.

Many of the thousands of studies about educational process have used various types of observation processes as part of their methodology. The results of these studies have been used to compare and make recommendations for changes in teaching processes. For instance, Nielsen (1988) asserted that through observation, a teacher's questioning technique can be described. By noting the types of questions asked, the distribution of questions, and the ways that students and teachers interact during questioning, the teacher can then make changes in the technique.

After making a series of observations in high school science classes, Jones (1989) found that teachers at all levels of experience tended to interact more with male than with female students. Others have found that levels of experiences are an important factor when looking at teacher behavior. For instance, Mitchell and Williams (1993) found that there were differences in how novice and expert teachers deal with teaching and learning tasks. Experts were more than twice as likely as novices to focus on content and process, to determine the task difficulty, to restructure the task as necessary, to redirect student thinking, and to check individual student work. They also praised student behavior more and corrected student performance twice as much.

Clarification of what constitutes an expert teacher is important. Lisia (1982) found that teachers who possessed a master's degree had less student time-on-task than teachers who did not possess the degree but had the same years of teaching experience. Comparing results of studies such as Lisia, and Mitchell and Williams is important because it leads us to further understanding, and to further questions. It should serve to remind us that we need to be careful about defining the behaviors we are observing, to be objective, and to remember that what we observe at one point of time may not be representative of what we would observe at another point in time, or would see with another subject.

In this chapter we will look at how to observe instructional processes in the classroom, focusing on observing the teacher, and sometimes the teacher-student interaction. After meeting some new case examples, the theories that were used in the previous chapter will be used as a basis to discuss teacher behavior and instructional processes. Then, additional theories will be reviewed and their application to the observation of teacher behavior will be explored. As with other chapters, there will be opportunities to reflect upon your learning, and to modify the forms presented for your own use.

The forms presented in this chapter indicate a wide variety of teacher behaviors. Sometimes, those behaviors are at opposite ends of continuums, based within a particular theory or model. The behaviors listed are not meant to be condoned as appropriate or good practice. At times, they may even be poor practice. However, they provide for reference within the models, and therefore are important for the observation process.

THE CASES:

A Pre-School and Kindergarten Teacher Uses Observation to Enhance Student Learning: The Case of Geri

Geri has a master's degree in early childhood education. She owns, manages, and teaches part-time at her own pre-school and kindergarten center. There were four pre-school rooms and two kindergarten rooms, one for full-days and one for two half-days. Geri recently obtained special government moneys to teach students who were identified as at-risk for problems at school. One of the stipulations of the funds was that Geri observe the teachers and provide inservices to help the teachers enhance student learning. Geri decided that before she could provide inservices she needed to see what behaviors her teachers were engaging in, how they were interacting with their students, and what concerns they identified.

A Primary School Teacher Agrees to Help Her Colleagues Learn New Instructional Techniques: The Case of Nell

Nell has been teaching second grade for the past eight years. She recently enrolled in a master's degree program to become a teacher leader. This semester, one of her classes requires that she spend 25 hours observing other teachers, and providing them with feedback. When her principal agreed to have her observe in the school, she did so with the stipulation that Nell focus her observations on the instructional techniques that the teachers use and try to provide them with feedback focused on them learning about what they were doing and what new instructional techniques they could replace old behaviors with. Nell knows that most of the teachers at her school had been teaching longer than she had, and many of the teachers had advanced degrees in various educational fields. She looked forward to the observations, but was unsure how she would gather information that would allow her to give appropriate feedback to her peers.

A High School Teacher Finds Himself Part of a Peer Observation Group: The Case of Juan

Juan never really considered himself as an expert or master teacher. He knew he was good at what he did, but, he was always learning about and trying out new ways to teach. He was blessed to be teaching. These days there were tons of social studies teachers who didn't have jobs. He kept thinking that the school would replace him with a younger, less experienced, and thus less expensive teacher. However, in the meantime, he kept doing his job. His school superintendent announced that the school district teachers will be using peer observation groups to build their own practice, and as the first line of supervision. The superintendent explained that a teacher team would determine its own goals, and work on those. Teachers could choose team members, but teams had to be accountable to file all paperwork and evidence of doing their jobs with both the principal and the superintendent on a routine basis. The teacher's union had agreed to this, and had agreed to help provide training to the teachers for this new process of development and supervision. The superintendent said that peer observation would alleviate concerns that principals did not know the subject matter area, and that there were too many other roles for principals in busy high schools. Juan looked forward to this change, but wondered how it would add to his already busy life.

Juan was assigned to a group of four teachers. Each of them was to observe the others at least four times over two months. Initially, they were given observation forms based on the extent to which teachers met individual differences in the classroom. Then, they were to meet to discuss their observations, and to make selections for later observations.

Reflective Questions:
- What are the issues that Geri, Nell, and Juan have in common? What are some of their differences?
- Do you think that Geri, Nell, and Juan will be observing for the same kinds of teacher behaviors? Do you think that they will be able to use the same forms?
- What do you think will be some of the ways that they will observe?

OBSERVING CLASSROOM TEACHERS AND THEIR INSTRUCTIONAL PROCESSES BASED ON MAJOR THEORIES

Although some of the theories covered in Chapter 3 will be revisited here again, the focus of the observation will be on the teacher. Therefore, the defined behaviors for observation, and the forms we use will be different.

PHYSICAL DEVELOPMENT: Body and Motor Skills

When we look at instructional processes that promote physical development, there are both general and specific concepts that need to be considered. In general, we would look to see that the students are provided with opportunities to engage in physical activity, to have proper nutrition, to rest, etc. Specifically, we may be concerned that the teacher is teaching needed motor skills, such as holding a pencil, writing, keyboarding, sitting in a desk, etc. Then, there are concerns that the teacher is using all of the senses in the instructional process, building vision, hearing, smell, etc.

Another focus involving motor skills is how the teacher is using his/her own motor skills. Is the teacher using physical, nonverbal cues? Is the teacher moving around the room? Is the teacher physically modeling skills that are desired in the students?

Geri had two concerns about how her teachers were using their own motor skills. First, were they modeling the behaviors that they were trying to instill in their students? Were they resting during rest time? Were they sitting at their desks when they were working on papers? Were they running, chasing, or doing other things that were not encouraged in the students? To answer her questions, Geri decided to observe teachers' physical activities. She knew that she couldn't begin to adequately keep a running list of the physical behaviors of any teacher. Instead, she decided that every five minutes she would look at the teacher, and use specific categories to describe what the teacher did. She developed form C4A to use with each teacher.

Reflective Questions:
- Based on what you know about physical development and motor skills, how would you expand or change Geri's form?
- Based on what you know about physical development, what other objective observations of teachers might you develop?

Form C4A: Physical Behaviors of a Teacher

School:_____ Room:_____ Teacher:_____

Grade Level____ Subject Matter:_____ Number of Students:_____

Date:_____Start Time:_____ Finish Time:_____Total Observation Time:_____

Room Set-up/Special Information:_____

Definition of Observation:_____

Five-minute Interval	Position of Teacher	# of Students Interacting With	Description of Teacher Physical activity
1			
2			
3			
4			
5			
6			
7			
8			
9			
10			

COGNITIVE DEVELOPMENT: Piaget's Theory

Although Piaget's Theory is not adhered to as strongly as it used to be, there are still parts of the theory that are important for the classroom teacher. One of the easy ways to observe this theory and teacher behavior is to look at the specific behaviors that Piaget predicted for each stage of his theory of development. Then, look to see if the teacher is providing opportunities for the learner to engage in those behaviors. Using the previously developed list of student behaviors as a building point, it is fairly easy to turn the student behaviors around into teacher behaviors.

Geri knew that Piaget vastly underestimated the skills and cognitive development of the child, including the baby. However, using the theory as a way to start to observe and describe behaviors, especially until Geri became more comfortable identifying and describing teacher behaviors, seemed feasible. Geri used Form C4B to do this, and found that with the addition of writing some notes about the behaviors that she observed, she was able to clarify some of the behaviors she was observing in her teachers.

T allows baby simple reflexive moves	reflexive schemes
T provides chances for imitations	primary circular reactions
T partially hides objects as baby watches	secondary circular reactions
T allows child to retrieve hidden object	coordination of secondary circular reactions
T allows child to search in many places for hidden object	tertiary circular reactions
T provides for child to engage in deferred imitation	mental representations
T allows for child to have own views, even when wrong	egocentrism
T provides interactions with inanimate objects	animistic thinking
T has child practice making judgments	perception-bound thought
T provides various situations for child to learn	centration
T focuses on present, but also tries to build past and future	momentary states
T provides chances to practice a series of steps	irreversibility
T provides chances to learn cause and effect	transductive reasoning
T provides various objects of different groups	lack of hierarchical classification
T provides hands on opportunities to work with mass and shapes	conservation
T provides problems with distance and time	spatial operations
T gives tasks with multiple features	decentration
T gives problems requiring sequencing	seriation
T gives multiple step problems	reversibility
T provides objects that have relationships	transitive inference
T provides objects that can be grouped	hierarchical classification
T provides chances to test hypothesis	hypothetico-deductive reasoning
T provides opportunities for discussion/reflection	propositional thought

Of course, the above behaviors are broad generalizations of the theory. There are many specific behaviors which could be added to the list if you wanted to go into detail with any of the particular stages of the theory.

Reflective Questions:
- Based on what you know about Piaget's theory, how would you expand or change Geri's form?
- Based on what you know about Piaget's theory, what other objective observations of the application of this theory to teachers might you develop?

Form C4B: Observation for Broad Piagetian Theory Applications in the Classroom

School:_____ Room:_____ Teacher:_____

Grade Level____ Subject Matter:_____ Number of Students:_____

Date:_____Start Time:_____ Finish Time:_____Total Observation Time:_____

Room Set-up/Special Information:_____

Definition of Observation:_____

Directions: Check those teacher (T) behaviors that are observed:

___T allows baby simple reflexive moves
___T provides chances for imitations
___T partially hides objects as baby watches
___T allows child to retrieve hidden object
___T allows child to search in many places for hidden object
___T provides for child to engage in deferred imitation
___T allows for child to have own views, even when wrong
___T provides interactions with inanimate objects
___T has child practice making judgments
___T provides various situations for child to learn
___T focuses on present, but also tries to build past and future
___T provides chances to practice a series of steps
___T provides chances to learn cause and effect
___T provides various objects of different groups
___T provides hands on opportunities to work with mass and shapes
___T provides problems with distance and time
___T gives tasks with multiple features
___T gives problems requiring sequencing
___T gives multiple step problems
___T provides objects that have relationships
___T provides objects that can be grouped
___T provides chances to test hypothesis
___T provides opportunities for discussion/reflection

Note: Describe any behaviors of the teacher that further provide evidence of meeting this theory.

COGNITIVE DEVELOPMENT: *Information Processing Perspectives*

The basic tenets of most information processing models hold that the perception, attention, organization, comprehension, and retrieval processes are all important. The ways that the teacher provides opportunities for, and supports these processes is fundamental for classroom learning. While the teacher cannot get inside each student's brain and find out how it is working, the teacher can use a variety of strategies that allow the teacher to make decisions about how the student best processes information. The teacher can also use a variety of strategies to then help the student process information.

Nell was interested in learning if the teachers were using strategies to promote information processing in the classroom. As Nell read more on the subject, she learned that there were a vast number of behaviors that the teacher might be engaging in that fit within the model. She decided that she would limit her list of behaviors to those that most teachers would be likely to use, and not include behaviors that were designed to specifically meet a special learning need in this area. Nell developed Form C4C as a checklist for behavioral occurrences.

Reflective Questions:
- Based on what you know about information processing, how would you expand or change Nell's form?
- Based on what you know about information processing, what other objective observations of the application of this model to teachers might you develop?

COGNITIVE DEVELOPMENT: *Vygotsky's Socialcultural Theory*

Vygotsky (1928) believed that when one was below one's zone of proximal development, one could learn the task without help. When one was in one's zone of proximal development, one could learn the skill with the help of others. When one was above one's zone, one could not learn the skill, even with the help of others. The teacher's role in using zone theory is to determine readiness for learning, make sure that the student has the prior knowledge needed to learn the task, and determine what social construction teaching should occur that will help the student move through the zone and learn the task. Typically, the social construction teaching involves the use of scaffolding (providing task assistance or simplification strategies), the use of intersubjectivity (negotiating a mutual understanding of the task and how to proceed with its solution), the use of cooperative learning, and the use of reciprocal teaching (members of a collaborative group take turns leading dialogues on the content). Of course, all of this teaching should occur taking the cultural context of the learner into consideration.

Nell had been trying to institute Vygotsky's theory in her own teaching. She had set-up learning centers with specific tasks. Her students worked in small groups at the particular learning centers where they had to learn. Each group contained at least one student who could learn the task without assistance, and sometimes knew the task. However, she didn't know if any other teachers were using any Vygotskian strategies. She developed Form C4D to observe for Vygotskian strategies at use in the classroom.

Reflective Questions:
- Based on what you know about Vygotsky's theory, how would you expand or change Nell's form?
- Based on what you know about Vygotsky's theory, what other objective observations of the application of this model to teachers might you develop?

Form C4C: Checklist for Teacher Behaviors that Support Student Information Processing

School:_____ Room:_____ Teacher:_____

Grade Level_____ Subject Matter:_____ Number of Students:_____

Date:_____ Start Time:_____ Finish Time:_____Total Observation Time:_____

Room Set-up/Special Information:_____

Definition of Observation:_____

____T has students prepare for a new task
____T tells students what kind of learning they will be engaging in
____T tells students what the objectives of the learning are
__.__T cues students to the task, tells them to pay attention
____T tells students what prior knowledge they will need to use for this task
____T tells students why this learning/task is important
____T tells students how the information is organized
____T tells students how they will be tested to show they have acquired/can use the information
____T provides learning task which involves more than one sense/modality
____T provides information at a pace that students have time to work with the information
____T groups individual bits of data into a chunk
____T provides that no more than five chunks have to be worked with at a time
____T provides information chunks within a conceptual framework
____T shows students more than one way to put the information together
____T allows time for the students to process the information
____T refers to prior learning as it connects to new learning
____T uses familiar terms when explaining the information
____T focuses students on salient information/task cues
____T tells students to ignore extraneous stimuli
____T has students practice the new information
____T provides specific links of the new information to previous learned information
____T asks students questions about their learning
____T tells students to think about what they are learning
____T tells students how to use this information in practice
____T tells students how to use this information in future work
____T provides visual information in accompaniment with aural information
____T labels pictures, graphs, and other visual stimuli
____T associates specific new items with specific familiar items as part of the place method mnemonic device
____T provides an image for linking new items together as part of the link method mnemonic device
____T associates specific new items with familiar pegs as part of the peg method mnemonic device
____T uses a keyword to link items that are to be associated as part of the keyword method mnemonic device
____T uses imagery to associate new items
____T points out the main idea
____T tells students if part of their learning is more important than other parts
____T points out common misconceptions and shows how and why they are incorrect
____T asks adjunct questions about the learning
____T cues students to take notes, underline, draw pictures, etc.
____T provides review of material
____T provides for further learning practice
____T works individually with students on their learning
____T has students work in small groups or individually
____T questions student learning
____T allows three to five seconds after asking a question before seeking a response
____T monitors student practice/work

Form C4D: Vygotskian Strategies in the Classroom

School:_____ Room:_____ Teacher:_____

Grade Level____ Subject Matter:_____ Number of Students:_____

Date:_____ Start Time:_____ Finish Time:_____Total Observation Time:_____

Room Set-up/Special Information:_____

Definition of Observation:_____

Scaffolding:

___T uses direct instruction for students who indicate that they do not know how to proceed
___T demonstrates task performance while verbalizing aloud the thinking that guides it
___T simplifies the task by reducing the task to steps
___T provides prompt or dues that help student move on with the task
___T provides questions that focus on the reasons for errors
___T encourages alternative strategy use
___T provides feedback to let students know how well they are learning
___T withdraws support as students show they can work on the task alone

Intersubjectivity:

___T and student discuss how to proceed with task
___T and student negotiate how the learning will occur
___T and student negotiate how to proceed with finishing the task
___T helps students discuss how to proceed with task
___T helps students negotiate how the learning will occur
___T helps students negotiate how to proceed with finishing the task

Cooperative learning:

___T assigns students to mixed ability groups
___T assigns groups to work on tasks
___T holds individuals and the group accountable for the learning
___T has different groups working on different learning
___T monitors group interactions

Reciprocal Teaching:

___T forms collaborative learning groups
___T monitors groups members as they read a passage
___T, or a student monitored by the T, asks questions about the content of the passage
___T, or the student monitored by the T, manages the group as they pose answers, raise additional questions
___T, or the student monitored by the T, summarizes the passage
___T, or the student monitored by the T, leads discussion to achieve consensus on the summary
___T, or the student monitored by the T, helps the group clarify ideas that are ambiguous
___T, or the student monitored by the T, encourages the group to predict upcoming content

INTELLECTUAL/ABILITY DIFFERENCES & SITUATED COGNITION

As in Chapter 3, we will not begin to cover all of the theories of intelligence. Rather, focusing on the verbal proficiency and analytical thinking tasks generally required in schools as a way to show intelligence, the concern is what opportunities the teacher provides the student to show intelligence and build skills. While the list of such opportunities could be endless, the focus is on some general principles and ideas that are typically seen in classrooms. Form C4E is designed to note what behaviors the teacher engages in that are related to building student intelligence/skills and cognition.

Reflective Questions:
- Based on what you know about intelligence, how would you expand or change the form?
- Based on what you know about intelligence, what other objective observations of the application of this concept to teachers might you develop?

LEARNING STYLES: Field Dependent/Independent Model

The field dependent/independent model can be applied two ways when considering the teacher. First, there is the consideration as to what is the teacher's style. Second, there is the consideration as to what the teacher does in the room to meet each of the different styles. This was the focus of Juan's first observation. He went into the classroom of another history teacher and used FormC4F. As he completed the observation, he noticed that primarily one learning style was met by the teacher. He noted his question as to if this was the teacher's learning style.

Reflective Questions:
- Based on what you know about this model, how would you expand or change the form?
- Based on what you know about this model, what other objective observations of the application of this theory to teachers might you develop?

LEARNING STYLES: Kolb's Model

The same way that the student will primarily exhibit one of the four major learning style preferences in the Kolb model, the teacher is also likely to exhibit one of these. The form used for observing students and determining their styles can also be used to determine a teacher's style. Also of concern is the ways that the instructional opportunities provide for all four styles. As Juan became familiar with the various learning style models and forms for observing them in the classroom, he used Form C4G with two teachers from different subject matter areas. Juan found the form easy to use, but wondered if the lessons he saw were specially designed to meet the various needs because he was observing, or if the teachers really tried to meet the different styles in every lesson.

Reflective Questions:
- Based on what you know about Kolb's model, how would you expand or change the form?
- Based on what you know about Kolb's model, what other objective observations of the application of this model to teachers might you develop?

Form C4E: Teacher Behaviors Related to Student Classroom Intellectual Skills

School:_____ Room:_____ Teacher:_____

Grade Level_____ Subject Matter:_____ Number of Students:_____

Date:_____Start Time:_____ Finish Time:_____Total Observation Time:_____

Room Set-up/Special Information:_____

Definition of Observation:_____

Teacher provides classroom opportunities for the student to:

___decode and recognize written words
___correctly spell words orally
___correctly spell words in writing
___listen to spoken prose
___write prose
___speak prose
___listen to a passage and supply deleted words
___read a passage and supply deleted words
___use vocabulary correctly when responding orally
___use vocabulary correctly when responding in writing
___listen to material and immediately recall it verbally
___listen to material and immediately recall it in writing
___use symbols as abbreviations for words
___after studying, recall material that is not required
___after studying, recall material that is required
___listen to a foreign language and repeat the words
___listen to a passage and respond verbally to provide information
___read a passage and respond verbally to provide information
___listen to a passage and respond in writing to provide information
___read a passage and respond in writing to provide information
___listen to a passage and respond verbally to comprehension questions
___read a passage and respond verbally to comprehension questions
___listen to a passage and respond in writing to comprehension questions
___read a passage and respond in writing to comprehension questions
___listen to a passage and discuss how concepts are similar and different
___read a passage and discuss how concepts are similar and different
___listen to a passage and respond in writing how concepts are similar and different
___read a passage and respond in writing how concepts are similar and different
___listen to a problem and do the mathematical calculations without paper
___read a problem and do the mathematical calculations without paper
___do mathematical calculations with the help of a calculator
___listen to and then repeat sequences of words or numbers forward
___listen to and then repeat sequences backwards
___construct a pattern from something that is presented visually
___construct a pattern from something that is presented auditorily
___look at an incomplete picture and identify what is missing
___listen to an incomplete passage and identify what is missing
___look at a set of pictures and place them in sequence
___listen to a set of sentences and place them in sequence
___look at a set of pieces and put them together to form an object
___compare different groups of items presented visually and indicate what they have in common
___work from the beginning to the end of a task, staying with the sequence needed
___work through a task, not necessarily using the generally recognized sequence

___interact appropriately with others
___physically reproduce movements of others
___sustain conversation
___determine what to study
___complete required tasks
___attend to details
___think about things in a new way
___ask for help when needed
___organize a learning task
___make supplementary material useful
___correctly paraphrase
___choose among learning tasks

Form C4F: Teacher's Use of Learning Styles: Field Dependence and Field Independence

School:_____ Room:_____ Teacher:_____

Grade Level_____ Subject Matter:_____ Number of Students:_____

Date:_____Start Time:_____ Finish Time:_____Total Observation Time:_____

Room Set-up/Special Information:_____

Definition of Observation:_____

Teacher provides opportunity for students to:

Field Dependent
___engage in global thinking
___follow a given structure
___be externally directed
___attend to social information
___resolve conflict
___be social
___affiliate with others
___have friends
___work with a provided hypothesis
___work with facts
___be influenced by the format
___use others decisions
___be sensitive to others
___use stress for learning

Field Independent
___engage in analytic thinking
___generate own structure
___be internally directed
___be inattentive to social information
___think things through philosophically
___be distant in social relations
___work alone
___have acquaintances
___generate own hypothesis
___work with concepts
___generate own format
___use own decisions
___be insensitive to others
___ignore external stress for learning

Form C4G: Teacher's Use of Learning Styles Adapted from Kolb's Model

School:_____ Room:_____ Teacher:_____

Grade Level_____ Subject Matter:_____ Number of Students:_____

Date:_____Start Time:_____ Finish Time:_____Total Observation Time:_____

Room Set-up/Special Information:_____

Definition of Observation:_____

Teacher provides opportunities for students to:
___engage in active experimentation
___use hypothetical-deductive reasoning
___engage in learning where there is one correct answer
___challenge ideas
___work alone with things
___show emotion
___think about things instead of experiment with them
___brainstorm
___consider multiples perspectives
___be imaginative
___explore various cultural dimensions, especially the humanities
___show emotion
___use inductive reasoning
___create models and designs
___question the facts if they don't seem to fit
___follow a plan for learning
___work alone when thinking
___actively experiment in a trial-and-error manner
___take risks, try new experiences
___interact with others
___share analysis with others
___share ideas on others

Notes:

LEARNING STYLES: Dunn and Dunn's 12 Variables Model

Designing a classroom so that each learner's learning style can be met is a difficult task. In most schools, it is too cumbersome for teachers to do this. Many times, the students' major style issues are considered and met when possible. Juan wondered how much the teachers in his assigned group were trying to meet learning styles which fit with the Dunn and Dunn model. He used Form C4H to observe his colleagues. When he was done, he noted that it was difficult to determine if the teachers had engaged in some of the behaviors, but he didn't know it because when teachers individualized, it may not be seen by the observer.

Reflective Questions:
- Based on what you know about Dunn and Dunn's model, how would you expand or change the form?
- Based on what you know about Dunn and Dunn's model, what other objective observations of the application of this model to teachers might you develop?

PERSONAL/LEARNING STYLES: COGNITIVE TEMPO

Teachers, just like their students, will fall somewhere along the continuum from impulsive to reflective. The concern becomes how much they promote students to be one or the other in the classroom. By now, Juan felt fairly assured of himself as he observed his colleagues. He had used checklists and looked for particular behaviors or incidents in the classroom. For this observation, the process was going to change. He watched a question and answer session that was lead by the teacher. Each time the teacher asked a question, he counted the number of seconds before the teacher called on a respondent. He knew that in the educational field, this lag of time was called wait time. Then, if the teacher went on to ask the question again, he counted this as a continuation of the question, and again looked at the wait time. Theoretically, the longer the wait time, the more the teacher was encouraging students to be reflective. As he counted the time, he also noted if the respondent who the teacher called upon had raised his/her hand. He did this using Form C4I.

Reflective Questions:
- Based on what you know about the cognitive tempo model, how would you expand or change the form?
- Based on what you know about the cognitive tempo model, what other objective observations of the application of this model to teachers might you develop?

PERSONAL/LEARNING STYLES: THE SOCIAL, AFFECTIVE PERSPECTIVE

Applying the Grasha and Reichmann (1974) continuums to the teaching process was easy for Steve. He had been using this in his classroom to place students into groups. Now, he wanted to modify the form so he could apply it to his own teaching through observing videotapes. He found it easy to modify the form, keeping in the continuums as a reminder for him. He then watched a couple of tapes of his classes and tried to complete the form (Form C4J). He found that he primarily made modifications for one side of each continuum, but hardly any for the other sides. He decided he had to think about how much he really was willing to make modifications for students who were avoiders in his class.

PSYCHOSOCIAL DEVELOPMENT: Erikson's Theory

Applying Erikson's theory of psychosocial development to the teacher was a challenge for Geri. She knew that given the range of ages in her students, there were potentially three "crisis" for students. A few would be dealing with trust and mistrust. More would be dealing with autonomy versus shame and doubt. Even more would be dealing with initiative versus guilt. Geri knew that how the teachers reacted in the classroom was a very important part of how each student resolved the crisis. Geri decided to observe for this in the classroom, and used Form C4K on two teachers, one in the pre-kindergarten, and one in the kindergarten. Geri found differences in the ways the two teachers interacted with their students.

PERSONALITY TYPES: THE "BIG 5" FACTORS

Every teacher brings his/her own personality to the classroom. Anyone observing a student, or a teacher, could use the form from Chapter 3 to try to discern the personality characteristics that are present in someone in a classroom situation. However, knowing the teacher's personality, while important, is probably not as important as knowing what instructional processes are presented that meet the needs of students' different personality factors.

Steve had previously developed a form for observing student personality factors. He found it easy to modify that form (Form C4L) and use it in his own observations of videotapes of his room. He also asked Danielle to use the form when observing him, to see if they had agreement as to how he tried to meet student needs.

Form C4H: Teacher's Use of Learning Style Descriptors Adapted from Dunn and Dunn

School:_____ Room:_____ Teacher:_____

Grade Level____ Subject Matter:_____ Number of Students:_____

Date:_____Start Time:_____ Finish Time:_____Total Observation Time:_____

Room Set-up/Special Information:_____

Definition of Observation:_____

TIME:
___Teacher allows for the task to be completed with different time frames
___Teacher tells students how much time is allotted for a task
___Teacher allows students to challenge themselves to "beat the clock"

SCHEDULE:
___Teacher allows students to work on a task over a short interval of time, get it all done at once
___Teacher allows student to work on a task over a long interval of time, do part now and part later
___Teacher allows students to work on a variety of tasks at once

AMOUNT OF SOUND:
___Teacher provides a place for students to work in quiet
___Teacher provides a place for students to work where there is noise.
___Teacher allows students to work and converse.
___Teacher allows students to wear ear plugs when working

TYPE OF SOUND:
___Teacher allows students to hum when working
___Teacher allows students to listen to music when working
___Teacher allows students to sing to selves when working
___Teacher allows students to tap out beats when working

TYPE OF GROUP WORK:
___Teacher gives students choice to work alone
___Teacher gives students choice to work in small groups
___Teacher gives students choice to work in large groups

AMOUNT OF PRESSURE AND MOTIVATION:
___Teacher tells students when to work
___Teacher tells students to set their own goals and deadlines
___Teacher tells students to help each other set goals and deadlines
___Teacher gives students public recognition
___Teacher gives students external rewards

PLACE:
___Teacher has students work in normal classroom
___Teacher has students work at the computer
___Teacher has students work in the library
___Teacher assigns students homework
___Teacher assigns students seatwork
___Teacher has some students do seatwork but not homework
___Teacher has some students do homework but not seatwork

PHYSICAL ENVIRONMENT AND CONDITIONS:

___Teacher gives students choice to sit at desk
___Teacher gives students choice to sit at table
___Teacher gives students choice to sit on the floor
___Teacher gives students choice to stand
___Teacher gives students choice to sit near window or light
___Teacher gives students choice to sit away from window or light
___Teacher gives students choice of clothing to wear

TYPE OF ASSIGNMENTS:

___Teacher gives students choices of tasks
___Teacher gives students choices of self-directed tasks
___Teacher gives students work contract
___Teacher gives students choices of peer-directed tasks

PERCEPTUAL STRENGTHS AND STYLES:

___Teacher gives students choice of visual materials for learning
___Teacher gives students choice of aural materials for learning
___Teacher gives students choice of printed materials for learning
___Teacher gives students choice of hands-on/tactile materials for learning
___Teacher gives students choice of different kinds of materials for learning

STRUCTURE AND EVALUATION:

___Teacher gives student choice of structure for the class work
___Teacher allows students to self-start on tasks
___Teacher allows students to inquire as to how well they are learning
___Teacher allows students to develop a time-line to complete an ongoing task
___Teacher allows students to do all they can on a task at one time

Form C4I: Teacher's Use of Cognitive Tempo in the Classroom

School:_____ Room:_____ Teacher:_____

Grade Level_____ Subject Matter:_____ Number of Students:_____

Date:_____Start Time:_____ Finish Time:_____Total Observation Time:_____

Room Set-up/Special Information:_____

Definition of Observation:_____

Teacher Question #	Amount of Seconds Before Seeks Respondent	Hand Was Raised? Yes/No	Amount of Seconds Before Seeks Respondent Again	Hand Was Raised? Yes/No
1				
2				
3				
4				
5				
6				
7				
8				
9				
10				

Form C3J: Teacher Dealing with Student Social, Affective Learning Style Differences

School:_____ Room:_____ Teacher:_____

Grade Level_____ Subject Matter:_____ Number of Students:_____

Date:_____Start Time:_____ Finish Time:_____Total Observation Time:_____

Room Set-up/Special Information:_____

Definition of Observation:_____

Teacher provides opportunities for students to:

Participant _____ **Avoidant** _____

___engage in learning course content   ___avoid engaging in learning course content
___attend class regularly   ___miss class
___assume responsibility for learning   ___not take responsibility
___participate in class   ___not participate
___complete required work   ___not complete required work

Collaborative _____ **Competitive** _____

___share with others   ___compete
___be cooperative   ___try to do better than others
___work with others   ___work alone
___interact with others in class   ___"show off" to others
___focus on participating, not winning   ___try to win

Independent _____ **Dependent** _____

___create own structure   ___rely on teacher for structure
___work on own without supervision   ___have a supervisor tell them what to do
___work to learn what is needed   ___learn the minimum that is required
___listen to others   ___listen to the teacher only
___be confident   ___be unsure of self
___be curious   ___lack intellectual curiosity

<u>**Form C4K: Teacher Application of a Modified Checklist of Indicators of a Student's Psychosocial Development Using Erikson's Theory**</u>

School:_____ Room:_____ Teacher:_____

Grade Level_____ Subject Matter:_____ Number of Students:_____

Date:_____Start Time:_____ Finish Time:_____Total Observation Time:_____

Room Set-up/Special Information:_____

Definition of Observation:_____

Teacher provides opportunities for students to:

☐ Have contact with others
☐ Initiate contact with others
☐ Have others near his/her desk
☐ Have others near his/her body
☐ Say "No" to some task choices
☐ Move away from others
☐ Try to learn show skills through counting, recitation, etc.
☐ Scold self aloud
☐ Shake head as engages in tasks
☐ Refuse to choose a task when given a choice
☐ Ask adults for confirmation it is okay to try a task
☐ Ask adults if tasks are accomplished appropriately or correctly
☐ Initiate play by self with the toy _____ for _____ seconds/minutes
☐ Choose the task of _____
☐ Try a task and stay with it for _____ seconds/minutes
☐ Imitate a modeled behavior of _____ for _____seconds
☐ Initiate play with others for _____ seconds/minutes
☐ Play with others for _____seconds/minutes
☐ Work with others on a task for _____seconds/minutes
☐ Work in a small group for _____seconds/minutes
☐ Cooperate/work with the teacher
☐ Refuse to engage in tasks
☐ Say aloud is not smart enough to do the task
☐ Ask other students for help when engaged in a task
☐ Ask teacher for help when engaged in a task
☐ Comply with teacher request of _____ for _____seconds/minutes
☐ Comply with student request of _____ for _____seconds/minutes
☐ Work on a task by self for _____seconds/minutes
☐ Come back to a task when given free time in the class
☐ Clean up after self when completes a task or task time is over
☐ Clean up after self and others when done with small group activity
☐ Tell others why task is important
☐ Tell others own vocational goals
☐ Tell others why learning is important
☐ Tell others who they are, what they feel, what they believe
☐ Express opinions as own in front of peers in classroom
☐ Express own opinions in front of teacher in classroom
☐ Label friends as such in front of others in classroom
☐ Label close friends/special relationships as such in front of others in classroom
☐ Say aloud does not know what will do in the future

Form C4L: Teacher Application of Personality Differences as seen in the Classroom

School:_____ Room:_____ Teacher:_____

Grade Level____ Subject Matter:_____ Number of Students:_____

Date:_____ Start Time:_____ Finish Time:_____ Total Observation Time:_____

Room Set-up/Special Information:_____

Definition of Observation:_____

Teacher provides opportunities for the individual student to:

Surgency

Talkative	**Silent**
___engage in discussion in class	___engage in discussion only when called upon
___initiate conversation with peers	___initiate conservation with peers
___talk out during classtime	___be silent during classtime
___talk to teacher during class	___not talk to teacher during class

Social	**Reclusive**
___initiate contact with others	___not initiate contact with others
___engage others in work/play	___not engage others in work/play
___share with others	___not share with others
___work with others	___work alone
___interact with others during class	___interact with others only when forced to do so
___be energetic	___be fatigued

Adventurous	**Cautious**
___try new learning tasks	___stay with known tasks
___look to outside world	___look inward
___take chances	___not take chances
___move around the classroom	___stay in seat or assigned area
___try out new ideas in class	___only do assigned work
___speak mind/ideas	___keep ideas to self

Agreeableness

Good natured	**Irritable**
___interact with others in class	___complain about others
___joke with others	___find nothing funny
___not complain, goes with the flow	___complain about things in the room

Mild	**Headstrong**
___listen to others	___listen to teacher only
___accept more than one way of thinking	___believe own way of thinking is correct
___accept differences with others	___believe differences are wrong

Cooperative	**Negativistic**
___share with others	___not share
___present things positively	___present things in negative manner
___finds ways to deal with problems	___believe problems can't be solved

Conscientiousness

Responsible | **Undependable**

___engage in learning course content | ___not engage in learning course content
___assume responsibility for learning | ___assume no responsibility
___participate in class | ___not participate
___complete required work | ___not complete required work
___be relied upon for leadership | ___not be relied upon for leadership

Persevering | **Quitting**

___attend class regularly | ___miss class
___work on own without supervision | ___need supervisor to tell what to do
___work to learn what is needed | ___learn minimum that is required
___continue to work on a task until done | ___work on task only during assigned time
___refuse to give up on a complicated task | ___give up on a complicated task

Tidy | **Carelessness**

___clean up after self | ___leave work area messy
___offer to help clean up room | ___not offer to help clean up room
___carefully erase mistakes | ___have papers contain smudges and dirty erasures
___hand-in papers that are clean | ___hand-in papers that are dirty

Emotional Stability

Calm | **Anxious**

___be calm, relaxed | ___be restless, tense
___talk at a normal rate of speech | ___talk at an increased rate of speech
___focus attention | ___be easily distracted
___not seem threatened | ___be easily threatened

Composed | **Excitable**

___be confident | ___lack confidence
___show emotions appropriate to situation | ___show emotions inappropriately
___think before acts | ___immediately react in situations

Poised | **Nervous**

___be secure | ___be insecure
___perform well on tasks | ___perform based on others approval
___be self-assured, self-confident | ___question self, lack confidence
___be mature | ___be immature, childish

Intellect

Intellectual | **Nonreflective**

___be curious | ___lack intellectual curiosity
___engage in thinking tasks | ___not think about how to do tasks
___present alternative ways to do tasks | ___do tasks with direction
___accept new ideas | ___reject new ideas
___tolerate ranges of answers | ___look for right and wrong answers only

Imaginative | **Simple**

___create own structure | ___rely on teacher for structure
___elaborate | ___not elaborate
___be flexible | ___be inflexible

Artistic | **Insensitive**

___expand on learnings | ___do only what is required
___create designs on worksheets | ___not engage in doodling, designing
___show work to others | ___not show work to others

PERSONALITY DIFFERENCES: INTROVERSION/EXTROVERSION

Observing a teacher's introversion and extroversion could be accomplished using the form from Chapter 3 that was developed for use with students. Knowing the teacher's personality on this dimension is helpful, but it is also helpful to know if the teacher is meeting the needs of both extroverts and introverts in the classroom.

Danielle had found it easy to observe introversion and extroversion in students. She modified the form she developed for that, and now used it (Form C4M) to observe Steve and the rest of her team in the classroom. First, she observed to determine if the teacher was introverted or extroverted, and then she observed the extent to which the needs were met in the classroom. She was surprised to find that the teachers met the needs of both dimensions in most classrooms.

Reflective Questions:
- Based on what you know about Eysenck's theory, how would you expand or change Danielle's form?
- Based on what you know about Eysenck's theory, what other objective observations of the application of this theory to teachers might you develop?

Form C4M: Teacher Application of Introversion/Extroversion in the Classroom

School:_____ Room:_____ Teacher:_____

Grade Level_____ Subject Matter:_____ Number of Students:_____

Date:_____Start Time:_____ Finish Time:_____Total Observation Time:_____

Room Set-up/Special Information:_____

Definition of Observation:_____

Teacher provides student opportunities to:

Be Extroverts:	**Be Introverts:**
___perform complex motor sequences	___read instead of doing motor activities
___be conditioned by positive experiences	___be conditioned by negative experiences
___use short-term retention skills	___use long-term retention skills
___seek affiliation	___seek academic achievement
___tolerate frustration	___be intolerant of frustration
___be impulsive	___be reflective
___be friendly, sociable	___avoid friendship/social situations
___take risks	___avoid risks
___be energetic	___tire easily
___enjoy numerous tasks at once	___work on one thing at a time
___focus on stimuli	___ignore interruptions
___be influenced by others	___use personal values as guides
___be aggressive	___shrug from confrontation
___enjoy change	___enjoy stability
___like disorder	___like order
___go with the moment	___plan ahead

LANGUAGE DEVELOPMENT: Interactionist Theories

Most teachers use language on a daily basis in their classrooms. Most have their students use language in a variety of ways each day. Despite the use of language, the concern remains if teachers are actually trying to develop language in their students. Nell knew that many of the students at her school came to school speaking another language, or lagging in their use of English. Nell was interested in knowing what the teachers at her school did to promote language development in the classroom. After reading about various theories of language development, Nell developed Form C4N to observe teachers at her school. One of Nell's frustrations was that she found it difficult to define and clarify for observation many of the specific skills that are involved in language development. So, she ended-up developing the form with generalities that she could observe across grade levels and across different teachers.

Reflective Questions:
- Based on what you know about language development, how would you expand or change Nell's form?
- Based on what you know about language development, what other objective observations of teachers might you develop?

<u>Form <u>C4N</u>: <u>Teacher</u> <u>Language</u> <u>Development</u> in the <u>Classroom</u></u>

School:_____ Room:_____ Teacher:_____

Grade Level____ Subject Matter:_____ Number of Students:_____

Date:_____Start Time:_____ Finish Time:_____Total Observation Time:_____

Room Set-up/Special Information:_____

Definition of Observation:_____

Teacher does the following:
___uses adult language, not baby talk
___engages in vocal exchanges with students
___encourages proper pronunciation of works
___gives students new words to learn
___takes turns in conversations with students
___uses proper grammar
___adjusts speech with social expectations
___gives students words to learn that have multiple meanings
___uses multi-syllabic words
___uses passive voice and other complex grammatical structures
___uses words which have abstract meanings
___uses referential language
___has students make up stories and conversations
___uses visual aids to supplement printed materials
___allows students to use dialect
___allows students to use vernacular
___allows students to use native language
___gives feedback to students about their language development
___praises students for attempting to use language
___explains grammar
___explains irregularities in language

SOCIAL DEVELOPMENT: Selman's Model

While cognitive and personality, and language development are all important in the classroom, teachers also need to engage in behaviors that promote social development and self-awareness. Teachers need to know if students have differentiated themselves from others and developed their cognitive processes to the point that they can take different perspectives and understand a third party's perspective. They also need to know if students have friends and know how to appropriately play and interact with their friends. Teachers need to know which students are viewed as "popular" and which ones are those that everyone ignores. Teachers need to know how to build social skills, and how to promote the use of these in the classroom. Some teachers mistakenly believe that if they assign students to work in cooperative groups, the students will automatically socialize and make friends. Other teachers mistakenly believe that if you leave kids alone to play they will get along and learn to play together.

Nell's school had recently instituted a new policy. The students had a fifteen minute in-class recess in the mornings and in the afternoons. They also had a thirty minute lunch, and after they ate they could go outside to play, as long as there was an aide or teacher supervising them. Nell was surprised by the policy. Students had always had recess outside. Moving it to the classrooms didn't give students much opportunity to meet with other students, or to engage in play. Nell made a note to try to get into each classroom to observe the recess time and see how the teachers handled the time. Did they interact and play with the kids? Did they teach social skills? Did they allow kids to engage in rough-and-tumble play? Nell developed Form C4O to observe teacher behavior related to developing social skills.

Reflective Questions:
- Based on what you know about Selman's model, how would you expand or change Nell's form?
- Based on what you know about Selman's model, what other objective observations of the application of this model to teachers might you develop?

MORAL DEVELOPMENT: Kohlberg's Model and Eisenberg's Model

Classroom teachers need to be careful when they engage in dealing with issues related to moral development in the classroom. While they can teach students about rights and justice under the laws of the country, school districts and laws vary widely in terms of what teachers can teach that is considered "moral." The concerns becomes one of whose morals, whose values, and if religion is involved. Teachers certainly can teach that people are punished when they are caught violating laws. They can also teach what the social order is, and what societal behaviors are considered normal.

One of the ways that the teacher teaches moral development in the classroom is by the way that the classroom is managed. The rules that are set, the consequences for rule violations, the responsibilities that the students are given, the justifications for actions that are used, and the other disciplinary actions that are evident are all parts of developing a moral system in the classroom. Of course, the rules, consequences, justifications, etc., that the teacher uses are all indicators of the teacher's moral thinking. While this may be a concern for some, what the teachers are doing to develop moral thinking in their students is usually more of a concern for the observer.

Alton was curious about the ways that teachers presented basic moral values in the classroom. He knew about the use of dilemmas for measuring moral development, but he didn't think that teachers presented dilemmas regularly in the classroom. He thought about the various ways that he could observe in the classroom, tired to develop a few different forms, and finally decided on a limited structured interview to observe the moral development of students in the classroom. He developed Form C4P and used it with two different teachers.

Reflective Questions:
• Based on what you know about Kohlberg's model and Eisenberg's model, how would you expand or change Alton's form?
• Based on what you know about Kohlberg's model and Eisenberg's model, what other objective observations of the application of this model to teachers might you develop?

Form C4O: Teacher Social Development in the Classroom

School:_____ Room:_____ Teacher:_____

Grade Level_____ Subject Matter:_____ Number of Students:_____

Date:_____Start Time:_____ Finish Time:_____Total Observation Time:_____

Room Set-up/Special Information:_____

Definition of Observation:_____

Teacher provides students the opportunity to:
___engage in play activities with other students
___give help to each other
___receive help from each other
___practice taking turns
___seek help from other students
___tease others appropriately
___practice kindness to other students
___practice fairness to other students
___practice giving consideration to other students' needs
___practice giving consideration to other students' opinions
___provide encouragement to other students
___provide praise to each other
___play games that have rules
___learn how to play games with rules
___explain how to play games to others
___practice self-control with others
___engage in play activities
___interact with various groups of students
___develop friendships with age mates
___develop friendships with both genders
___practice using emotions
___practice imitating appropriate behaviors
___accept strengths and weaknesses of peers
___choose to conform or not conform to peer demands
___respond negatively to direct peer pressures
___practice modeling peer behaviors
___engage in rough-and-tumble play
___interpret other people's thoughts and feelings
___respond to other people's thoughts and feelings
___practice taking other people's perspectives
___practice third party thinking and feeling

Form C4P: Interview for Teacher Development of Morals in the Classroom

School:_____ Room:_____ Teacher:_____

Grade Level____ Subject Matter:_____ Number of Students:_____

Date:_____Start Time:_____ Finish Time:_____Total Observation Time:_____

Room Set-up/Special Information:_____

Definition of Observation:_____

Directions: This is a structured interview. Use the questions below. Write down the responses for each question. Try not to show emotion as you ask the questions or listen to the answers.

1. Tell me what you know about the state laws regarding your teaching about morals in the classroom.

2. Tell me about how you run your classroom. What are the classroom rules? What are the rewards for following the rules? What are the consequences for not following the rules?

3. What vocabulary do you use with the students to explain the rules and procedures in the classroom?

4. What responsibilities do your students typically have on a day-to-day basis?

5. What, if any, responsibilities do your students get to earn?

6. What do you tell a student that you are giving consequences or punishments? Please give me an example.

7. What are your procedures for special disciplinary issues?

8. Tell me what you teach about the social order, and what societal behaviors are considered normal. Please give me an example.

9. Tell me how you handle the concept of teaching moral development in the classroom.

10. Tell me what you teach your students about justice and ethics.

11. Please tell me anything else I should know about moral development in your classroom.

ECOLOGICAL SYSTEMS: Bronfenbrenner's Theory

When a teacher tries to consider the complex system of relationships found in Bronfenbrenner's (1989) theory of development, the observation is typically complicated by the fact that the teacher is part of the environment. The same problem occurs when trying to look at the teacher and use ecological systems theory, the observer is part of the environment. How do you look at the reactions and interactions when you are part of the system?

Geri knew that the interactions between students and teachers was part of the systems theory. She could record the statements each made to the other, or those students made to other students. However, as she focused on the teachers, she became more interested in the interactions of teachers with other teachers. Who initiated interactions? What were the interactions? Did the interactions focus on students? What other things were the interactions about? Geri developed Form C4Q to record the interactions of one teacher with other teachers.

Reflective Questions:
- Based on what you know about Bronfenbrenner's theory, how would you expand or change the observation form?
- Based on what you know about Bronfenbrenner's theory, what other objective observations of the application of this theory to teachers might you develop?

HUMANISTIC DEVELOPMENT: Maslow's Hierarchy of Needs

Any two students have different needs. When teachers have a class of any number of students, they have a lot of different needs in the room. When we apply the humanistic development theory to teaching, the focus becomes on how the teacher determines the needs, and what the teacher does once the determination has been made. A simple form (Form C4R) which can be used for a structured interview, or to have the teacher self-report, is commonly used when applying Maslow's hierarchy. If the teacher presents enough detailed information, the observer can determine the level of the needs the teacher focuses on, and the level of needs the teacher is trying to move the students to.

Reflective Questions:
- Based on what you know about Maslow's theory, how would you expand or change the observation form?
- Based on what you know about Maslow's theory, what other objective observations of the application of this theory to teachers might you develop?

SOCIAL LEARNING/SOCIAL COGNITIVE LEARNING: Bandura's Theory

Bandura (1986) believes the learning involves operant conditioning and cognitive processes. Learning occurs through the process of observation, with the learner watching (attending to) a model, retaining the information learned from the observation, producing the learning, and receiving reinforcement. The roles of the teacher in applying the theory are to call attention to the behavior that is being modeled, provide models, help the student practice producing the behavior, and then provide reinforcement for the learning. The classroom observer can objectively observe the application of social learning theory in the classroom by watching the behaviors of the teacher, or recording the verbalizations of the teacher as they relate to the learning process.

Geri knew that one of the ways that her young students learned was by watching someone else do something and then trying it out themselves. Sometimes they imitated a behavior at home that they learned from another student at school, and Geri would receive a call from a parent asking

Form C4Q: Applying Bronfenbrenner's model to teachers

School:_____ Room:_____ Teacher:_____

Grade Level_____ Subject Matter:_____ Number of Students:_____

Date:_____Start Time:_____ Finish Time:_____Total Observation Time:_____

Room Set-up/Special Information:_____

Definition of Observation:_____

Directions: Record the interactions of one teacher with other teachers. While this is an anecdotal record, make sure you are as objective as possible.

Date	Time	Interacted with whom?	Description of the nature of the interaction	Length of interaction

Form C4R: Teacher Report of Meeting the Humanistic Needs of Students as Adapted from Maslow's Theory

School:_____ Room:_____ Teacher:_____

Grade Level_____ Subject Matter:_____ Number of Students:_____

Date:_____Start Time:_____ Finish Time:_____Total Observation Time:_____

Room Set-up/Special Information:_____

1. Please describe how you determine the humanistic needs of your students.

2. Please describe how you determine what student needs are important to meet in your classroom.

3. Please describe how you try to meet the important student needs in your classroom.

4. Please describe how you deal with students having different needs.

how a child had learned to use a particular word or do a particular activity. Sometimes Geri would see a student engage in a behavior that seemed to have been learned at home and brought into school. Geri was curious about the behaviors that her teachers consciously modeled for the students. She decided to develop Form C4S to observe the modeling behaviors in the classroom, focusing on the behaviors of the teacher.

Reflective Questions:
- Based on what you know about Bandura's theory, how would you expand or change the observation form?
- Based on what you know about Bandura's theory, what other objective observations of the application of this theory to teachers might you develop?

Form C4S: Teacher Modeling Behaviors in the Classroom per Social Learning Theory

School:_____ Room:_____ Teacher:_____

Grade Level____ Subject Matter:_____ Number of Students:_____

Date:_____Start Time:_____ Finish Time:_____Total Observation Time:_____

Room Set-up/Special Information:_____

Behavior Modeled:_____
___Teacher tells students to pay attention/watch
___Teacher performs/models the behavior of _____
___Teacher has a student perform/model the behavior
___Teacher has the class students perform/practice the behavior
___Teacher provides the reinforcement of _____for students who successfully model the behavior.

Behavior Modeled:_____
___Teacher tells students to pay attention/watch
___Teacher performs/models the behavior of _____
___Teacher has a student perform/model the behavior
___Teacher has the class students perform/practice the behavior
___Teacher provides the reinforcement of _____for students who successfully model the behavior.

Behavior Modeled:_____
___Teacher tells students to pay attention/watch
___Teacher performs/models the behavior of _____
___Teacher has a student perform/model the behavior
___Teacher has the class students perform/practice the behavior
___Teacher provides the reinforcement of _____for students who successfully model the behavior.

Behavior Modeled:_____
___Teacher tells students to pay attention/watch
___Teacher performs/models the behavior of _____
___Teacher has a student perform/model the behavior
___Teacher has the class students perform/practice the behavior
___Teacher provides the reinforcement of _____for students who successfully model the behavior.

MOTIVATING THE STUDENT: LOCUS OF CONTROL AND SELF-REGULATION THEORIES

Over the course of childhood, students learn a sense of control over their environment. Those who learn that they are not in control, do not have choices, and are at the whim of others are labelled as "externals" in regard to their locus of control. They typically blame others for their successes and failures, refer to others to make choices for them. Those who learn that they do have control, have choices, and if they try can successfully complete their task choices are labelled as "internals" in regard to their locus of control. They typically blame themselves for their successes and failures, and take responsibility for the choices they make and their learning (Rotter, 1966).

The theory of self-regulation says that students have their own internal standards of acceptable performance. When they engage in a task, they apply this standard to self-evaluate. This self-evaluation leads to their making changes in their behaviors to better their performance, should they decide that they are not performing to their own internal standards. The theory holds that those who have learned to self-regulate will probably be internal in their locus of control orientations, and probably will be likely to maintain their work on a task longer, and do more to complete a task than those who are not self-regulated.

In the classroom, the observer can listen to the students' verbalizations related to their successes and failures and determine if they are internal or external in nature. The observer can also keep track of how long a student persists at a task. When it comes to the role of the teacher, the observer can do the same thing, focusing on the teacher's verbalizations about the students' successes and failures, how long the teacher persists at a task, and how long the teacher allows students to persist at a task. Form C4T was developed to use for such a focus.

Reflective Questions:
- Based on what you know about locus of control and self-regulation theories, how would you expand or change the observation form?
- Based on what you know about locus of control and self-regulation theories, what other objective observations of the application of this theory to teachers might you develop?

REVIEW QUESTIONS:

1. What are the major differences in observing teacher application of cognitive development theories in the classroom?
2. What are the major differences in observing teacher application of learning style models in the classroom?
3. What are the major differences in observing teacher application of personality theories and models in the classroom?
4. What are the major differences in observing teacher application of moral development theories in the classroom?
5. How do you observe a teacher motivating students in the classroom?

DISCUSSION QUESTIONS:

1. How do the various theories and models covered in this chapter lend themselves to the various observation processes? Why would observing the application of these theories and models be important for the teacher?

2. Provide one strength and one weakness for each theory in this chapter. Based on your analysis, what are the three most important theories for the teacher to apply? Which are the least important? Support your decisions.

3. What are the advantages of using objective observation of teachers? What are the disadvantages?

4. If you observe a teacher engaging in a behavior which may be dangerous to the students, how should you handle the situation?

Form C4T: Teacher Use of Locus of Control and Self-Regulation Theories in the Classroom

School:_____ Room:_____ Teacher:_____

Grade Level____ Subject Matter:_____ Number of Students:_____

Date:_____Start Time:_____ Finish Time:_____Total Observation Time:_____

Room Set-up/Special Information:_____

Definition of Observation:_____

Incident #	# minutes teacher does task	# minutes teacher has students do task	Teacher verbalization about responsibility for student successes and failures (who is to blame?)

CHAPTER 5

OBSERVING TEACHER-STUDENT INTERACTION AND CLASSROOM INSTRUCTIONAL EFFECTIVENESS

LEARNING OBJECTIVES:

After you read this chapter you should know:
1. How to observe different types of cooperative learning are used in the classroom.
2. How to observe different types of peer tutoring are used in the classroom.
3. How to observe teachers interact with students who are labeled as at-risk, having special needs, or gifted.
4. How to observe teachers as they develop creativity in their students.
5. Ways to observe teachers promoting gender equity in the classroom.
6. How to observe teachers interact with students of different ethnicities.
7. How to observe teachers building multicultural awareness in the classroom.
8. Ways to observe teachers using technology in the classroom.
9. Ways to observe teachers applying motivational techniques to students.
10. Some of the types of assessments teachers may use in the classroom.
11. How conflict resolution may be used in the classroom.
12. Ways to observe teachers managing the classroom.
13. Ways that schools and teachers promote interaction with parents.
14. What the learner-centered principles are.
15. What the model of clinical supervision entails when observing in the classroom.

After you read this chapter, you should be able to:
1. Describe typical teacher-student interactions during cooperative learning and peer tutoring.
2. Describe typical teacher-student interactions that promote multicultural awareness, and enhance student ethnic and gender equity.
3. Describe how teachers and students may engage in using various assessments in the classroom.
4. Describe typical teacher-student interactions related to using technology, motivating, and managing the classroom.
5. Identify teacher behaviors that maintain conflict and those that seek to resolve conflict in the classroom.
6. Identify ways that schools can promote interactions with parents.
7. Describe how to use the clinical supervision model when working with a teacher.
8. Use the forms to observe for a variety of teacher-student interactions in the classroom, and determine which of those interactions are learner-centered.

INTRODUCTION

In the previous two chapters, as the various theories and models of individual differences were applied to observing students and teachers, there were occasions in which the teacher-student interactions became a point of focus. There were also references made to specific teacher behaviors which could promote learning and development. This chapter will cover other theories and models found in the educational psychology literature as they apply to instructional effectiveness. Some of these theories could fit within the previous chapters. However, they are presented here because they lend themselves to observation of teacher-student interactions, which will expand our observational processes.

One of the frustrations that supervisors and colleagues who are assigned to observe others commonly report is that they don't know the subject matter. They assume that subject matter knowledge is needed for a good observation. They ask, "How can I observe if I don't know anything about the subject matter?" My reply would be, "what is the defined behavior you are observing?" Usually that leads to a discussion about what constitutes effective teaching, for which subject matter knowledge is part, but knowing about and effectively applying the instructional processes that work with the subject matter are also important. One can easily engage in observing the teacher using teaching techniques and strategies, and come away with a great deal of valuable information, without ever knowing the subject matter. Many of the observations in the last chapter, and in this chapter, are examples of that. The trick is to have a defined observable focus when you observe.

There are hundreds of observations of teacher-student interactions reported in the educational literature. One of the common features of these observations is that as they have defined the behavior that they are observing, they have either taken a primary focus on what the teacher does or what the students do. Observing a teacher and one or more students at one time becomes more difficult. It typically requires that symbols and codes are developed to keep track of behaviors. Additionally, it is usually recommended that the observer already has experience with the observation process, and is skilled at managing multiple tasks at one time. As the observations of the concepts covered in this chapter are developed further, the levels of skill requirements should become clearer.

Even though most of the observations in this chapter do require more practice and some developed observational skills, the novice observer should still read this chapter. One of the benefits of doing so should be to advance your own thinking about the observational process. As you expand your thinking, you should be able to draw upon your earlier learning and think about how you could apply these new ideas to the prior concepts. Additionally, you should be more cognizant of the possibilities for your own development.

THE CASE:

A School Principal Engages in Classroom Observations: The Case of Miguel

Juan's principal, Miguel Moreales, is in the third year of his principalship. In addition to trying to implement the initiates undertaken by the superintendent, he was trying to develop his own action plan for the school. Miguel knew that most of his teachers were well-trained, having one or more masters degrees in various areas of specialization in education. Some of these degrees were in educational administration, with teachers hoping to become principals themselves. Other teachers were new to teaching, and brought current field knowledge with them to the classroom. Other teachers were neither new, nor continuing their education. These teachers posed the biggest challenge to Miguel. He wondered how they were doing in teaching their classes. Were they using latest known effective teaching methods? Were they respected by their students and their colleagues? Were their students achieving at the same rates as other teachers' students? As Miguel pondered these questions, he wondered how he could obtain this information. He thought about using objective observations to address these, and other concerns he had. He knew that he had to follow the policies of his district, as they were worked out with the teachers' union, and follow a special observation process if he engaged in any observations which were evaluative of the individual teacher. He decided to notify his supervisor whenever he was going to observe, and to keep a log of his observations.

OBSERVING SOME INSTRUCTIONAL PROCESSES IN ACTION IN CLASSROOMS

ORGANIZING AND USING COOPERATIVE LEARNING

There are a variety of specific methods for developing learning tasks and grouping students together to complete those tasks which are collectively called cooperative learning. Cooperative learning, while not a new instructional technique, is currently being widely used by teachers, although the extent to which they understand the basic concepts and have appropriately developed the learning tasks varies greatly. Johnson and Johnson (1987, 1994) have identified a number of important elements that should occur if cooperative learning is used successfully. Among these are face-to-face interaction, group processing, positive interdependence, collaborative skills, and individual responsibility.

Face-to-face interaction means that students are placed in a situation where they can talk with each other and discuss the learning, learn from each other, and make sure that each other has learned. Group processing refers to the idea that the members of the group are able to function as a group, not as individuals who are sitting together but working entirely alone. Positive interdependence is developed when the task is developed in such a way that each student must rely on other students to provide some information or resources for the entire learning to be accomplished. Students thusly know that their learning is dependent upon information sharing. Collaborative skills are developed through practice and having role models engage in leadership, working as a team, developing consensus, resolving conflicts, etc. Individual responsibility means that ultimately the individual student must be able to show that he/she has accomplished the learning task and is held to be accountable for his/her own learning. An observer should be able to look to see if the task is set-up to allow for these elements to occur.

Kagan (1985) is known for his descriptions of six varieties of cooperative learning, including student teams-achievement divisions (STAD) (Slavin, 1980), teams-games-tournaments (TGT), Jigsaw I (Aronson et al. 1978), Jigsaw II (Slavin, 1980), Group investigation (Sharan & Herta-Laxarowitz, 1980), and Co-op Co-op (Kagan, 1985). In student teams-achievement divisions, there are five instructional steps. First, the material is presented to the whole class. Second, the students work in teams using a peer tutoring format to try to insure that all team members master the material. Third, the students individually complete a quiz to assess their learning. Fourth, the teacher keeps track of each individual student's record of achievement. Fifth, there is team recognition for high individual performance.

The teams-games tournaments model is the same as the STAD model except that the third step of taking a quiz is replaced by academic games. Students demonstrate their knowledge of the material by sitting in homogenous ability groups of three and playing the game. The lowest scorer of the game is given two points and moves to another group of students who also scored two points. The middle scorer of the game is given four points and moves to another group of students who also scored four points. The highest scorer of the game is given six points and moves to another group of students who also scored six points. A new game is played, and the process of scoring and moving is repeated. The entire process is repeated a number of times while the scores of students are collected and then recorded as a team total.

In Jigsaw I, the interdependence of students is stressed. The students are given different parts of the information so that each has to learn his/her unique information and then teach it to their team. Jigsaw II extends this by having different teams assigned to different topics. Once each team learns their individual topics, the teams are changed so that a member from each original team is on the second team. The second team then has each team member teach his/her topic to the new team. The learning is followed by an individual quiz. The quiz scores are compiled to form team scores. Both the individual and the team receive recognition for learning.

Group investigation involves a six stage process. First, students choose among identified topics and form research groups based on a topic. Second, each research group has the individual members choose subtopics to determine how these will be investigated. Third, the students engage in investigation. Fourth, the group shares the information, selects and organizes it, and prepares a final report. Fifth, the final report is presented to the rest of the class through a means that is appropriate for sharing the information. Sixth, there is evaluation of the cognitive and affective learning.

Co-op Co-op uses a compilation of the other cooperative methods. First, a class discussion about a topic or issue is held. Second, students work in teams. Each team has a different topic. These teams are heterogeneous, and are supposed to include students of different abilities, gender, and ethnicities. Third, the team members each determine a subtopic to work on, learn, and teach the rest of the team. Fourth, the team prepares a presentation of the topic to the entire class. Fifth, the presentations are made. Sixth, evaluation processes occur in which teammates evaluate the work of their own members, classmates evaluate the presentations, and teachers perform an evaluation on each individual student.

An observer who is aware of the different types of cooperative learning will be able to accurately observe the processes as they are applied in the classroom, and differentiate the types of work the students are engaged in, and the types of instructional support offered by the teacher. Additionally, a knowledgeable observer will also know that the teacher-student interactions will be different depending upon the model which is being used. The observer may want to observe some individual differences among students, including how one student engages in the cooperative activity. The observer may want to focus on the teacher and how the teacher supports the individual differences in the classroom. Either of these could be done through processes explained in the earlier chapters. An alternative focus is on the teacher-student interactions during the cooperative learning process.

Juan knew that students typically came to his high school with a good working knowledge of various cooperative methods. What he wasn't sure of is if and how the teachers continued to use cooperative methods. Juan decided to observe the teacher-student interactions during a cooperative learning task. He started by meeting with the teacher he was going to observe to review key process components. In some cooperative methods, students are given different roles. He needed to know if for each team one student each was assigned the task of managing the group and time related to the task, getting work from and communicating with the teacher, encouraging the other learners, writing the group decision, etc. He also needed to know what the teacher perceived as his/her role. Did the teacher work as a sort of tutor individually moving to work with each group? Did the teacher serve as a resource facilitator and students came to the teacher's work area? Did the teacher walk around monitoring progress and focusing learning on critical parts? Did the teacher focus on the learning or on the cooperating, or on both? How did the teacher handle student complaints, or students not learning the task? Did the teacher respond to students individually, only to the team, or sometimes interrupt and respond to the whole class? Did the teacher respond verbally, or only in writing?

Janet Gerg was eager to have Juan observe the cooperative learning in her class. As a relatively new teacher she had learned the processes of cooperative groupings during her preservice training. She did make sure that each student had an assigned role in the group, and she tried only to meet with the contact student unless she felt that the issue raised needed to be addressed to the entire group. She tried to resource around the room, but also spent time at her work area, so students could also come to her. She reported that she rarely interrupted the entire class, but she did try to respond to issues as they arose and found that given the short time she had the students, it was easier to tell the team her response than to tell a team member who then had to tell the team. Janet had learned that within a few weeks of the start of school her freshmen were settled in and sometimes used cooperative tasks as an excuse to be silly. She found that instead of trying to reprimand when an entire group was off-task, it was easier to tell that particular group that from that time on she would only respond to them in writing. Typically that sobered them up, and they would try to get back to task so that she would again deal with them verbally.

Juan worked with Janet to develop the observation and coding that Juan would use. Juan decided to put a key system to identify several aspects of the situation. He then decided to focus his observation on the actual teacher-student interactions. He decided to put an arrow moving from the student when the student initiated contact with the teacher. He then would put an arrow moving toward the student when the teacher initiated the contact with the teacher. Each new contact instance would require a new arrow. However, sustained interaction within one contact would be noted by placing arrow tips on top of each other, with the appropriate direction noted. To begin, Juan decided to only focus on the one team that Janet said she typically had a moderate level of contact with. Form C5A-example presents an example of what Juan observed over a 40 minute cooperative learning session. As soon as Juan had completed the notations, he wrote the summary information. This provided him the opportunity to make sure that he was in agreement with what he had noted.

Form C5A: **Student-Teacher** **Interaction** **During** **Cooperative** **Learning** **Session**

School:___Juan's high school_____ Room:_____ Teacher:___Gerg_____

Grade Level_9__ Subject Matter:____biology_____ Number of Students:__28_

Date:__Jan 18_Start Time:_10am___ Finish Time:_10:40amTotal Observation Time:_40 min___

Room Set-up/Special Information:__cooperative groups_____

Definition of Observation:_teacher-student interaction for one group_____

Key: @ = student who has assigned role to interact with teacher as contact
      # = student who has assigned role as manager
      % = student who has assigned role as writer
      * = student who has assigned role as encourager
      < = student interaction with teacher
      > = teacher interaction with student
      ] = teacher interacts with whole team
      } = teacher interacts with whole class
      1, 2, 3... = order of interaction

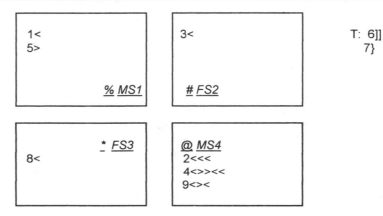

Summary: There were nine different interactional exchanges between the teacher and the cooperative group of students. The writer initiated one interaction and was the recipient of one interaction. The manager initiated one interaction. The encourager initiated one interaction. The contact initiated three interactions. in the first of these, he addressed the teacher three times. In the second of these, he addressed the teacher. The teacher then addressed him twice, and he then addressed the teacher twice. In the third interaction, he addressed the teacher, the teacher addressed him, and then he addressed the teacher. The teacher initiated contact with the whole team once, during which time she addressed them twice. The teacher also addressed the entire class once.

Reflective Questions:
- Based on what you know about cooperative learning, how would you expand or change the observation form?
- Based on what you know about cooperative learning, what other objective observations of the application of this idea might you develop?

ORGANIZING AND USING PEER TUTORING

Peer tutoring has been used in a variety of educational settings for many years. Many times it is a method that teachers use to help develop basic skills in students. While some teachers reserve the use of peer tutors for those students who are identified as having special needs, other teachers use peer tutors regularly regardless of needs. Peer tutoring can involve same-age tutors, in which pairs of students are developed among the students who are all in the same classroom. Peer tutoring can also involve cross-age tutors, in which older students are paired with younger students. In both of these situations, there is an implication that one member of the pair knows more, and has more ability, than the other member. However, the situation and task can be developed so that the pairs can learn together without implying a teaching responsibility in the relationship. In this case, if the peers are from different backgrounds, ethnicities, languages, etc., the tutoring may be a means to build culturally relevant socialization and communication, as well as improve task performance (Webb & Palinscar, 1996). Studies conducted on peer tutoring indicate that the situation and task do need to be constructed so that the learners feel they need to work in the task, and so that the minimal acceptable level of performance does not become the upward limit of what the students do (Stacey, 1992).

Nell's school had a cross-age peer tutoring program in place that followed Vygotskian principles of learning. The teachers identified those students who were having problems learning a basic skill on their own, but seemed to be ready to learn with some help. They also identified the students that already knew each basic skill. Then, those students who seemed ready to learn were paired up with students who knew the information. The student tutors and tutees changed for each task, with a student being tutor for one skill, but a tutee for another. This concept was applied on a voluntary basis across the school each Wednesday, with students moving in and out of various rooms and various learning centers of the teachers who were part of the program. Teachers reported much success as students carried around their skills lists and proudly showed their various teachers the tasks they had accomplished, or how many other students they had helped with learning a skill. However, other teachers who were not involved in the project argued that the teachers still ended-up doing the teaching, and this was just more work for them. They said that the tutees would ask for teacher help anyway, and the teacher ended up repeating items many times that could be given to a larger group once. They believed that this technique also lead to less skill development as the students would talk about other things. They argued that more skills could be developed using traditional direct teaching than with peer tutoring.

Nell thought about this, and decided that there was potential objective observation of teacher-student interaction. As the pairs engaged in the peer tutoring, who interacted with the teacher? How frequently? Did the students or the teacher initiate the contact? If the students started the contact, was it one or both of them, the tutor or the tutee? If the teacher started the contact, was it to both students or to one of them? If to one of them, was the student the tutor or the tutee? How much got accomplished, that is how many tasks or skills were learned over a set time of peer tutoring? How did these things all compare to a non-peer-tutoring situation? She decided to set-up observations to try to answer these questions. The results of one of these observations is shown as Form C5B-example. She also observed in a regular classroom during the same time, using the same form but changing the key to one found in C5A. She then could compare the contact of the students and the teachers in the two situations.

Form C5B-example: Who Initiates Student-Teacher Contacts

School:___Nell's_____ Room:_2B_____ Teacher:_____

Grade Level:Multi_Subject Matter:_Multi_____ Number of Students:_8 of 32_

Date:__Feb 2__Start Time:_1pm_____ Finish Time:_1:50pmTotal Observation Time:_50 min__

Room Set-up/Special Information:_Wed. peer tutoring set-up, leaing centers, students moving classroom to classroom and center to center as needed_____

Definition of Observation:__who initiates contact during peer tutoring session_____

key:	R< = student who is tutor initiates contact with teacher
	E< = student who is tutee initiates contact with teacher
	#< = both students initiate contact with teacher
	>R = teacher initiates contact with student who is tutor
	>E = teacher initiates contact with student who is tutee
	># = teacher initiates contact with both students
	1, 2, 3...= actual number of tasks completed for each group

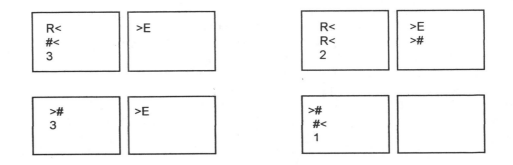

Summary: There were eleven different interactions between the teacher and the students. Two student tutors initiated contact with the teacher, one of them twice. There were two groups where both students in a pair initiated contact with the teacher, each once. The teacher initiated contact with three different tutees, each once. The teacher initiated contact with both students in a pair for three groups, each once. A total of 9 separate learning tasks were checked off as completed at the end of the session.

Reflective Questions:
- Based on what you know about peer tutoring, how would you expand or change the observation form?
- Based on what you know about peer tutoring, what other objective observations of the application of this idea might you develop?

INSTRUCTING STUDENTS AT-RISK FOR FAILURE

Students who are at-risk to fail are those more likely to experience problems in the school or community (Good & Brophy, 1995). Most schools employ programs to help these students that are based on the assumption that the student needs to learn how to deal with the school's academic culture. In the early grades the students may have felt rejection because of school failure. They may have come to school lacking the preparation of other students. They not have the same early learning experiences or support. They may come from various types of situations such as extremely low-income families, disorganized families, homeless families, drug-abusing families, or families where there are serious mental health problems. They may come to school and behave as they do at home, trying to protect themselves, to survive. They may come to school and act out behaviors they see at home. They may come to school and not have any friends, nor trust anyone enough to try to make friends. They may never have had a friendship, and may not know how to interact with others to even build a friendship.

Instructing an at-risk student typically involves the teacher developing the socialization of the student with other students and with the teacher. The teacher may assign the student a peer tutor or buddy to work with the student. The teacher may also use cooperative learning to try to assimilate the student. The teacher also needs to get to know the student, voice empathy to the student, assign responsibilities that make the student feel part of the class, and provide learning opportunities that also provide information for the student. Such learning opportunities include: 1) using books which the child can relate to and use to help generate coping and learning skills (bibliotherapy), 2) developing learning tasks in which students can succeed and also express emotions, 3) using tasks that allow for mistakes, 4) providing learning that is focused on effort and that develops higher-level thinking skills, and 5) having tasks that demand seatwork and homework. These students need to be a part of the class, seated where they feel they are part, and where they have opportunities to interact. Teachers need to be careful to not reprimand inappropriate interactions, but instead focus on appropriate models and encourage the student to try the appropriate behavior instead.

Miguel knew that there were many students in his school that were at-risk to fail. There were many students that dropped-out as soon as they were legally of age to do so. There were also many students that rarely came to school, even though they were too young to drop-out. These students were rarely found by the truant officers, and many times their parents moved in and out of the school attendance area so many times that the district had a hard time keeping track of which school they were supposed to be in. Additionally, some of these students were homeless, and finding where they spent time was very difficult. Miguel decided that if he knew how teachers were interacting with at-risk students in the classroom, he might be able to help them develop skills which would help the students stay in school. Miguel developed Form C5C to keep track of teacher verbal and non-verbal behaviors directed at one at-risk student, and also keep track of that student's behaviors. Miguel then used the form to observe a few different teachers interacting with a few different students.

Reflective Questions:
- Based on what you know about at-risk students, how would you expand or change the observation form?
- Based on what you know about at-risk students, what other objective observations of the application of this idea might you develop?

Form C5C: Teacher and At-Risk Student Interactions

School:_____ Room:_____ Teacher:_____

Grade Level_____ Subject Matter:_____ Number of Students:_____

Date:_____Start Time:_____ Finish Time:_____Total Observation Time:_____

Room Set-up/Special Information:_____

Definition of Observation:_____

Time	Student Verbalization	Student Behavior	Teacher Verbalization	Teacher Behavior

INSTRUCTING SPECIAL NEEDS STUDENTS

There are a variety of students who have special needs in the classroom. Typically, special needs students are those who are legally identified as having some disabling condition which qualifies them for help under Public Law 94-142 and its amendments, which is now called the Individuals With Disabilities Education Act (IDEA). The law allows for a wide range of conditions to qualify as disabilities. It also specifies that whenever possible, the student should stay in the regular classroom (mainstreamed or included) and receive services there. Most teachers have students who are mainstreamed, and who have an Individualized Education Plan (IEP) which specifies key learning objectives and instructional processes. While the IEP provides some specific things for teachers to do, it generally does not specify the typical teacher-student interactions that might be helpful for the student.

In addition to providing cooperative learning activities and peer tutoring, teachers also usually have to make modifications for the student learning. These modifications may include allowing students to respond differently to show learning, allowing for poor mechanics in reports, providing study-skill and learning strategy-building sessions, using technology, presenting material using different modalities, providing various reminders, providing the task in small steps, establishing routines, and focusing on each student's abilities.

Steve had always made accommodations for his students who had an IEP. He also made sure that in trying to mentor Danielle, he explained the ways that he made changes, and provided examples of success when modifications were made. Danielle said that she was trying to meet the IEPs of the students, but she was not sure if she was making modifications which promoted her interactions with these students. Together they identified four students that Danielle wanted to explore her interactions with. Then, they developed Form C5D for Steve to observe in Danielle's classroom, using one sheet for each identified student.

Reflective Questions:
- Based on what you know about special needs students, how would you expand or change the observation form?
- Based on what you know about special needs students, what other objective observations of the application of this idea might you develop?

Form C5D: Teacher and Special Needs Student Interactions

School:_____ Room:_____ Teacher:_____

Grade Level____ Subject Matter:_____ Number of Students:_____

Date:_____Start Time:_____ Finish Time:_____Total Observation Time:_____

Room Set-up/Special Information:_____

Definition of Observation:_____

Student Name:	Special Need:
Teacher:	Student responds by:
says to student:	
indicates that the learning task for the student is modified by:	
indicates that the learning assessment for the student is modified by:	
references study skills and learning strategies for the student:	
provides routine for the student of:	
focuses on student's abilities by:	

INSTRUCTING GIFTED STUDENTS

The definition of what constitutes a gifted student varies from school to school. In many schools it is the students who are academically achieving (scoring in the top five or ten percent) in some subject area. In other schools it is the students who have artistic, musical, spatial, bodily-kinesthetic, or other special abilities. The same way that there are variations in definitions, there are also variations in how schools deal with gifted students. Some provide acceleration activities, what is they grade skip, make recommendations for early college admission, etc. Some provide grade compacting in which the student can work at his/her own pace through the materials based on his/her strengths. Some schools provide enrichment programs in which the student may leave the classroom or attend after school activities which are an enrichment to the normal curriculum. Some schools provide technology training, special thinking groups, and other specialized programs for their gifted students. Other schools may develop their own IEPs for gifted students and individualize the programs for each student.

While teachers often try to remember that every single student is a unique individual, and deserves modifications in the curriculum to meet the student's learning needs, they sometimes feel especially challenged by the gifted student. This is because the gifted student may ask questions for which the teacher is not prepared to answer, or the student may challenge the teacher's authority. As teachers make modifications to meet the needs of gifted students in the classroom, they usually try to provide a chance for students to pre-test the material and test-out of the learning, provide special explorations and activities for gifted students based on their giftedness, provide opportunities for students to expand upon their abilities through special projects, and provide student learning experiences that allow students to move ahead with their learning.

Steve and Danielle found the form on observing teacher-student interactions for students with special needs easy to use. They decided to also use the form, with modifications for looking at the accommodations made for gifted students in the classroom. They developed Form C5E for this purpose.

Reflective Questions:
- Based on what you know about gifted students, how would you expand or change the observation form?
- Based on what you know about gifted students, what other objective observations of the application of this idea might you develop?

Form C5E: Teacher and Gifted Student Interactions

School:_____ Room:_____ Teacher:_____

Grade Level____ Subject Matter:_____ Number of Students:_____

Date:_____Start Time:_____ Finish Time:_____Total Observation Time:_____

Room Set-up/Special Information:_____

Definition of Observation:_____

In this school, gifted is defined as:_____

Student Name: _____ Special gift:	
Teacher:	Student responds by:
says to student:	
indicates that the learning task for the student is modified by:	
indicates that the learning assessment for the student is modified by:	
references the student's giftedness by:	
provides special opportunities for the student by:	
focuses on student's abilities by:	

INSTRUCTING TO BUILD STUDENT CREATIVITY

The same way that it is difficult to define and measure giftedness in students, it is also difficult to define and measure creativity. Guilford (1959) defined creativity as involving divergent thinking as represented by the fluency, flexibility, and originality of thought processes. Fluency involves the production of many ideas in a short period of time. Flexibility involves the changing to different approaches as needed. Originality involves developing new, unique, different suggestions or solutions to problems. While many teachers would argue that every student has some creative potential, some teachers work hard to develop that potential in the classroom, and others work hard to develop that potential only within the particular domain that they are teaching, such as math, literature, etc.

Teachers develop creativity by giving students choices of tasks, focusing on internal (rather than external) evaluation, providing opportunities for groups of students to collaborate among themselves and compete with other groups, removing time constraints, encouraging brainstorming, encouraging varied student task-related productions, encouraging imaginative, original ways to engage in problem-solving, and by modeling creative thinking.

While Juan was observing the ways that teachers made accommodations for individual learning styles in their classrooms, he thought about the ways that teachers and students interacted. It was one thing for a teacher to report that he/she tried to develop divergent thinking in the classroom. It was quite another for the teacher to actually do this. Juan had picked-up on the divergent thinking of two of his students in his own classroom. He decided to observe these students and see if they also evidenced divergent thinking in their interactions with other teachers. He developed Form C5F to observe each student as he/she interacted with another teacher.

Reflective Questions:
- Based on what you know about creativity, how would you expand or change the observation form?
- Based on what you know about creativity, what other objective observations of the application of this idea might you develop?

Form C5F: Creative Student Interactions with the Teacher

School:_____ Room:_____ Teacher:_____

Grade Level____ Subject Matter:_____ Number of Students:_____

Date:_____Start Time:_____ Finish Time:_____Total Observation Time:_____

Room Set-up/Special Information:_____

Definition of Observation:_____

Student Name:	
Student:	Teacher responds by:
indicates his/her choice of learning tasks by:	
engages on working on a learning task by:	
changes to other approaches to learn by:	
focuses on evaluation by:	
develops new, unique solution of:	
otherwise evidences creativity by:	

INSTRUCTING WHILE BUILDING AND MAINTAINING GENDER EQUITY

Gender is a culturally and socially defined concept. In our educational settings, there is often a focus on gender differences, what a student can or can't do based on gender. One of the problems with such a focus is that it often is self-fulfilling, as observers and teachers bring their own gender stereotypes to the situation. Many meta-analytic reviews of gender differences have found that differences related to mathematical, verbal, and spatial abilities really do not exist, or are so tiny that they really are insignificant (Eisenberg, Martin, and Fabes, 1996). Yet, when we look at achievement, gender differences emerge. These differences may be related to the differential expectations and experiences that students have, and the ways that teachers interact with them in the classroom.

In recent years, there has been an increased focus on researching if students are being provided gender-fair or gender-equitable learning situations and interactions in the classroom. That is, does the teacher interact differently with boys than with girls? Does the teacher have different expectations for success, and define task learning differently for boys than for girls? Do the texts and materials contain sex-equitable materials, or are boys and girls treated and tested differently? Do the tests contain examples which are primarily written for boys and about boys? Does the word "she" appear as often as the word "he" on a test or in teaching materials? Are these words presented in an unbiased context? Does the teacher provide the same kind of praise at the same frequency to students, regardless of gender? There has also been an increased focus on if the teacher actively challenges gender misconceptions, models sex-equitable behavior, uses gender fair materials, encourages girls to engage in using equipment and doing things which are "traditionally male," organizes the classroom so that boys and girls are not segregated, and allows both males and females to have emotional reactions to events.

We are all sexual beings. All teachers have the opportunities to deal with students who are exploring their developing sexuality, including sexual orientations and sexual expressions. These explorations may be played out in the classroom by students flirting, having special friendships, and engaging in sexual play. Sometimes, teachers are the targets for the student trying out some of these behaviors. How the teacher handles this, as well as the student-to-student interaction is very important. The teacher needs to be kind and sensitive to the student's development, and also seek gender equity. The teacher needs to be careful not to put-down a student because of his/her behavior. The teacher also needs to be careful not to react in a way that is taken by the student as acceptance of sexual advances, or promoting inappropriate behaviors in the classroom. The teacher also needs to be aware of the messages that he/she, and the school policies, send about sexuality. Some school policies ignore equity issues around orientation, only allowing opposite-gender pairs of students to attend school-sponsored dances as "a couple." Other schools have policies that allow sexual harassment by students to other students to go unchecked. In many schools, female students report male students making lewd comments toward them, touching them in appropriate ways, and even engaging in attempted sexual behaviors that constitute various levels of rape. When schools and teachers ignore these behaviors, accept them as "normal," fail to provide support services to the victims, and fail to help the victim file charges, then they are promoting problems, and not engaging in promoting gender equity.

Geri was aware that from a young age children start to develop their perceptions of the role of males and females in our society. She also was aware that the ways that teachers interact with students was important in this developmental process. She decided to observe her teachers interact with students to see what, if any, gender stereotypical behaviors they were engaging in. She developed form C5G to observe these interactions in the various settings that her school provides.

Miguel was interested in an entirely different type of observation. The student council had recently conducted a survey among students. Many of the females, and some of the males reported being the recipients of unwanted touching in the classrooms. Unfortunately for Miguel, the question had been asked in such a way that it was unclear who the touchers were. While Miguel was concerned that any unwanted touching was occurring, he knew that the school, and he as principal, had to react entirely differently if the touchers were teachers, or if they were other students. Years ago the school had encouraged teachers to only touch a student with the permission of the student. He wondered if the teachers were still doing this. He also wondered if other students engaged in this behavior. He developed Form C5H to observe touching behaviors in the classroom.

Reflective Questions:
- Based on what you know about gender equity in the classroom, how would you expand or change the observation form?
- Based on what you know about touching behaviors in the classroom, how would you expand or change the observation form?
- Based on what you know about gender equity in the classroom, what other objective observations of the application of this idea might you develop?

INSTRUCTING STUDENTS OF VARIOUS ETHNICITIES

The same way that there have been increased concerns about gender equity in classrooms, there has been an increased focus on ethnic equity and meeting the needs of students of various ethnicities in the classroom. When some think of ethnic differences, they automatically assume that the student speaks a different language, or is from a family that has low-income. The truth is that while students from many ethnic groups will speak other languages, some will also speak English. Many students will be second or third generation in the United States, and while their parents may not speak English, they will. The income levels of the families of these students will also vary greatly. The concern for teachers is that these students' cultures often are not completely understood by their teachers or their peers. Students who are from minority cultures are unlikely to have full access to the benefits provided to those of the majority culture. They are unlikely to have the some resources to prepare them to succeed in school, and they may have lower expectations for success, or define success differently than the majority culture. Additionally, they may engage in behaviors which are appropriate in their cultures, but are not considered appropriate in the majority culture.

Cultural studies indicate wide differences in what behaviors are encouraged in the culture. For instance, some cultures value respect for elders, and consider it inappropriate to address an elder (teacher) unless spoken to. Even then, the younger (student) may be taught that it is incorrect to look directly at the elder, to challenge the elder, or to provide more than a basic answer to the elder. Some cultures value the opposite, and younger and older members of the group freely interact, openly challenge each other, talk at the same time, engage in eye contact, etc.

Form C5G: Teacher-Student Interactions Related to Gender Equity in the Classroom

School:_____ Room:_____ Teacher:_____

Grade Level____ Subject Matter:_____ Number of Students:_____

Date:_____Start Time:_____ Finish Time:_____Total Observation Time:_____

Room Set-up/Special Information:_____

Definition of Observation:_____

Directions: For the first part, keep track of the number of times that the teacher says something related to, or uses the phrases, by putting a slash on the line prior to the item. Immediately following the item, make any specific notes for clarification or examples. For the second part, look at the task materials and test, and count the number of instances, again noting them with slashes on the line prior to the item. Note examples after the item.

Part One: Teacher verbalizations: Number of times teacher says:
_____"boys and girls"
_____"girls and boys"
_____boys can..
_____girls can...
_____calls on goys
_____calls on girls
_____something related to luck
_____how the teacher likes
_____boys clothes/dress are...
_____girls clothes/dress are...
_____girls can do what boys do
_____girls and boys/boys and girls are to work together
_____girls and boys/boys and girls can cry, have other emotions
_____boys and girls/girls and boys have same tasks to do
_____boys should put forth effort
_____girls should put forth effort
_____boys have ability
_____girls have ability
_____the task is hard for boys
_____the task is hard for girls

Part Two: Analysis of Materials and Tests: Number of times:
_____"he" appears in text
_____"she" appears in text
_____male examples
_____female examples
_____females in traditional male roles
_____males in traditional female roles
_____males in traditional male roles
_____females in traditional female roles

Form C5H: Observing Touching Behaviors in the Classroom

School:_____ Room:_____ Teacher:_____

Grade Level_____ Subject Matter:_____ Number of Students:_____

Date:_____Start Time:_____ Finish Time:_____Total Observation Time:_____

Room Set-up/Special Information:_____

Definition of Observation:_____

Person who initiates touching	Person who receives touch	Reaction of receiver	Permission to touch requested?

Some cultures value the cognitive and affective dimensions of learning and interactions. Students are encouraged to not only think, but also express themselves and their feelings. They are encouraged to use their feelings, and to react to the affective dimension of the learning. Other cultures value the opposite and students are taught to ignore or disavow their feelings, and not share them or show them in the classroom.

Some cultures stress that the student is part of the bigger culture, and responsible to everyone. The student is taught to act as part of a group, to share information and resources, to cooperate, to help everyone achieve. In other cultures, the focus is on the individual, who should sit alone, work alone, and try to compete for individual awards.

Every culture has limits of acceptable behavior. In some cultures, these limits are narrow, and little variation in behavior is tolerated. In other cultures, these limits are wide, and there are vast differences in behaviors that are tolerated. The challenge to the teacher is to accept not only variations based on culture, but variations within each culture. To do this, the teacher needs to clearly know what the expectations and limits are within his/her own culture. The teacher needs to know how these then impact on his/her classroom, and expectations for student behavior. Then, the teacher can start the process of exploring how to modify these to accommodate cultural differences in the classroom, while still helping the students understand the expectations of the majority culture.

The cultural accommodations that a teacher makes are based on the cultures that are present in the classroom, the ages of the students, the extent to which students are enculturated to the dominant culture, the expectations of the parents for enculturation of their children, etc.

More and more students who attend Miguel's school come from varied cultures and ethnicities. The teachers were also from various cultures, but not nearly as many as the students. Miguel wondered how culturally aware this teachers were. He knew that they had information about learning styles, and other individual differences, and that many of these differences were more prevalent in various cultural groups. He looked at various cultural awareness checklists and decided that they did not provide him with information about teacher-student interaction that involved various ethnicities. He devised a structured questionnaire for the teachers to respond to either verbally or in writing (Form C5I).

Reflective Questions:
- Based on what you know about students of various ethnicities, how would you expand or change the observation form?
- Based on what you know about students of various ethnicities, what other objective observations of the application of this idea might you develop?

Form C5I: Structured Interview with a Teacher Related to Cultural Interactions

School:_____ Room:_____ Teacher:_____

Grade Level____ Subject Matter:_____ Number of Students:_____

Date:_____ Room Set-up/Special Information:_____

Please respond to the following questions. Please be honest in your answers.

1. What culture(s) do you participate in, practice the beliefs of, and feel you are a part of?
2. What are the predominant cultural practices that you engage in in the classroom?
3. What language(s) do you speak?
4. What language (s) do your students speak?
5. A student speaks his/her non-English native language in your classroom. What is your response?
6. What specific things do you do to help students learn English in your classroom?
7. How do your students define success? How do you define success for your students? What do you do in the classroom to compare the differences in definitions?
8. What do you do when students lack the resources they need for learning in your classroom?
9. What behaviors do your students engage in that you do not think are part of the dominate/majority culture? How do you react when they do these things?
10. How do your students show respect, and to whom do they show it? How do you show you respect them?
11. How do your students show their feelings, and to whom do they show them? How do you show your feelings?
12. How do your students show that they know the answer, and to whom do they show this? How do you acknowledge this in the classroom?
13. How do your students show that they are thinking, and to whom do they show this? How do you acknowledge this in the classroom?
14. How do your students socialize with others in the classroom? What socializing do you have in your classroom? How do you socialize with your students?
15. What work do you have students do individually? What work do you have students do in groups? What do you tell students about the differences between individual and group accountability?
16. What interactions do you have with parents of your students? Please describe some typical interactions.

INSTRUCTING TO BUILD MULTICULTURAL AWARENESS

There are various approaches to multicultural education, building multicultural awareness in the classroom. The most well-known of these are the assimilation, and the cultural pluralism models.

The assimilation model of multicultural education seeks to move non-English speaking students into an all-English-speaking environment as quickly as possible and encourage students to accept as completely as possible the norms and values of the dominant society (Secada & Lightfoot, 1993). Under this model, the school studies are related to the dominant culture. There may be a day, or activity set aside to highlight differences (e.g., an ethnic dress day). Many adherents to this model believe in cultural deficits. That is, students from another culture are seen as lacking cultural skills, rather than having other kinds of skills which should be valued and more fully understood.

The cultural pluralism model of multicultural education seeks to help students understand and appreciate the various cultures that are present in their school and in our society. Under this model, the school studies are typically evolving to become multicultural. They may have multiethnic studies courses, they may have multiethnic education in which the materials and teaching strategies are modified and changed to help students of minority cultures achieve comparable to the majority culture. Once this has been achieved, they may move toward multicultural education in which the needs of the broader cultural groups are also acknowledged, studied, and dealt with. These groups may include various disabilities, religious groups, regional groups, etc. When these studies and changes in how teachers and students interact with each other are institutionalized, full multicultural education may be achieved (Banks, 1994).

Miguel knew that the teachers at his school were not yet at the point that full multicultural education could be achieved. However, he did want to get a sense of where the school was in the development process, and which teachers needed more learning and support to move ahead in their developing the curriculum. He revised the Banks (1994) Multicultural Education Program Evaluation Checklist to make the list observable when he visited classrooms (Form C5J). Although he realized that in any particular lesson he may not get a true sense of the multicultural aspects that the teacher was dealing with, he gave each teacher that felt that the lesson he observed was not representative, the opportunity to invite him to observe a lesson which they felt was representative of their multicultural instruction. This also gave him an opportunity to explore some issues related to the validity of the items on his checklist.

Reflective Questions:
- Based on what you know about building multicultural awareness in the classroom, how would you expand or change the observation form?
- Based on what you know about building multicultural awareness in the classroom, what other objective observations of the application of this idea might you develop?

Form C5J: Multicultural Education Integrated into a Lesson

School:_____ Room:_____ Teacher:_____

Grade Level____ Subject Matter:_____ Number of Students:_____

Date:_____Start Time:_____ Finish Time:_____Total Observation Time:_____

Room Set-up/Special Information:_____

Definition of Observation:_____

___ethnic content and perspectives are incorporated into the lesson
___instructional materials treat racial and ethnic differences and groups realistically
___instructional materials treat racial and ethnic differences sensitively
___resources for learning are representative of various racial, ethnic, and cultural groups
___classroom decorations reflect various racial, ethnic, and cultural groups
___instructional processes accommodate ethnic and cultural differences in learning styles
___instructional processes accommodate ethnic and cultural differences in behaviors
___instructional materials respect the dignity and worth of students as individuals
___instructional materials respect the dignity and worth of students as members of various
groups
___instructional processes provide opportunities for students to develop a better sense of self
___instructional materials provide support for students to strengthen their self concepts
___instructional materials allow the student to examine the diversity across and within groups
___instructional materials provide the student the opportunity to explore the similarities and
differences of groups within U.S. society
___instructional processes provide students opportunities to develop decision-making abilities
___instructional processes provide students opportunities to develop social participation skills
___instructional processes provide students opportunities to distinguish facts from opinions in
various cultures
___instructional processes provide students opportunities to develop skills in obtaining and
using information from various cultures
___instructional processes allow those students for whom English is a second language a
chance to clarify and develop their vocabulary
___assessment processes take into account ethnic and cultural differences among students

INSTRUCTING USING TECHNOLOGY

Technology holds the potential to open ways that teachers and students interact, breaking down barriers as global communication occurs, and individual student needs can be met. Effective use of technology allows teachers to present lessons through various modalities, to make modifications in lessons, to design special lessons for various students, to provide various alternative assessments, to keep track of each student's progress, to individually interact with students, to leave electronic messages for parents, to send work to students who are home due to illness, etc. Effective use of technology also helps students as they can engage in various tasks through various modalities, work on basic skills all the way through higher order thinking, develop and track their own learning progress, interact with other students in their school, their city, their state, their nation, and globally.

When calculators, computers, and other technology have been introduced to classrooms, typically their full potential has not been realized. Rather, they were used for basic skills drill and practice, and playing games. Now, teachers are learning how to use the technology beyond the basics, and students have opportunities to engage in real-time discussions with others around the word, use simulations, use graphics and assembler programs for developing and maintaining their own web sites, etc. Additionally, schools have the opportunities to use distance education to deliver instruction to various sites, meeting the needs of rural, isolated, and site-based students.

It was once thought that as technology became more readily available, teachers would be replaced in the classrooms. While some teaching tasks may have been replaced, teachers have not. Instead, technology has allowed teachers to expand on what they do and how they do it in the classroom. However, in some classes, the use of technology has changed the nature of teacher-student interactions. Miguel witnessed this in a number of the classes he visited. He decided to keep track of the kinds of technology used by a teacher, the ways the teacher used technology, the ways the students used technology, and the interactions of teachers and students which were related to technology. He developed Form C5K, which he could use across various classrooms, subject matters, and levels of students.

Reflective Questions:
- Based on what you know about using technology in the classroom, how would you expand or change the observation form?
- Based on what you know about using technology in the classroom, what other objective observations of the application of this idea might you develop?

Form C5K: Teacher and Student Interactions with Technology in a Classroom

School:_____ Room:_____ Teacher:_____

Grade Level____ Subject Matter:_____ Number of Students:_____

Date:_____Start Time:_____ Finish Time:_____Total Observation Time:_____

Room Set-up/Special Information:_____

Definition of Observation:_____

1. The classroom technology that is visible is:

2. The teacher uses the technology by:

3. The number of minutes that the teacher uses technology is:

4. The student uses the technology by:

5. The number of minutes that the student uses technology is:

6. The teacher interacts with the student related to technology by:

7. The teacher and the student(s) use technology together by:

8. An example of what the teacher says about technology is:

9. Examples of what the students say about technology are:

MOTIVATING STUDENTS

In the previous chapter, the models of locus of control and self-regulation were presented as ways to motivate students. There are many theories and models as to how to motivate students. Stipek (1996) summarized the classroom practices, student beliefs and student outcomes that researchers believe are related to good motivational practices in the classroom. These can be listed as specific, observable behaviors, as found in Form C5L.

Reflective Questions:
- Based on what you know about motivating students, how would you expand or change the observation form?
- Based on what you know about motivating students, what other objective observations of the application of this idea might you develop?

ASSESSING STUDENT LEARNING

Teachers at all grade and age levels for all subject areas typically have to engage in some sort of assessment of student learning. The ways that teachers engage in gathering, analyzing, and interpreting information about their students' progress vary greatly. Some teachers use tests. Typically these are tests are of the paper-and-pencil variety. Some teachers use other assessments, sometimes called alternative assessments. These may be observations, performances, holistic, or authentic. Whatever the type of assessment, there are some standards that typically apply. For instance, the assessment should be based on the range of learning and content, in a format that fits with the desired outcome, appropriate to the students, developed based on a standard for acceptable performance, developed to provide students with information about their learning, and involve students with the process.

As part of Selma's volunteer work in the classroom, the teacher asked Selma to help a couple of students complete a questionnaire related to their learning. The teacher said that this questionnaire would help the teacher, the students, and the parents of the students all understand what and how the student thought about and dealt with assessment processes. The teacher explained that some of the questions were too high level for the students, but, the form (Form C5M) was used across the school. Additionally, the students spoke the same native language as Selma, and the teacher hoped that Selma would help the students make the translations they needed to for the form to be completed. Selma helped two students complete the form. She was surprised because when she was in school, no one had ever asked her these kinds of questions, or showed this level of concern for her learning. She was pleased that she had done this, as it showed her some of the things that teachers had to deal with in classrooms today as they prepared lessons.

Selma also learned that the teacher used a variety of assessments in the classroom. The students each had a small box in which they kept samples of their work, the assessments they completed, and sheets on which they wrote comments about their learning. These portfolios of work were also available for the student's parent/care-giver to view. The teacher said that the portfolios had two parts, the first contained work from this year. The second contained work from each year, so the student and the teacher and the parents could see how much growth and learning had occurred. The teacher

Form C5L: Teacher Motivational Techniques and The Associated Student Outcomes

School:_____ Room:_____ Teacher:_____

Grade Level____ Subject Matter:_____ Number of Students:_____

Date:_____Start Time:_____ Finish Time:_____Total Observation Time:_____

Room Set-up/Special Information:_____

Definition of Observation:_____

Teacher:
___designs learning task that is challenging
___designs learning task that can be completed with a reasonable amount of effort
___divides difficult tasks into subgoals that are achievable without requiring excessive effort
___provides diverse opportunities for students to demonstrate mastery
___differentiates tasks across students and over time
___adapts instruction to students' knowledge and experience
___designs tasks for exploration and experimentation
___defines success in terms of mastery and personal improvement
___designs tasks where students have an equal opportunity to be involved, and if the task is competitive, students have an equal chance to win
___provides clear and frequent feedback conveying developing competence.
___provides rewards contingent on effort, improvement, and good performance
___avoids unnecessary differential treatment of high and low achievers
___focuses on effort and strategy as primary causes of failure
___uses rewards only when necessary
___emphasizes the informational purpose of rewards
___provides substantive, informative evaluation that is based on mastery rather than on social norms
___treats errors and mistakes as a normal part of learning

Student:
___says/indicates expects to succeed
___says/indicates is academically competent
___says/indicates rewards on contingent on behavior
___says/indicates has ability to produce behavior upon which rewards are contingent
___says/indicates that poor outcomes are attributable to low effort or poor strategy
___approaches tasks without teacher reprimand to do so
___seeks help for task work
___persists when encounters difficulty
___takes pride in success
___says/indicates feelings of mastery
___says/indicates enjoys the task
___selects challenging tasks
___uses effective problem-solving strategies

told Selma that this was a great way for each student to feel personally responsible for the learning, and to interact with the teacher about the learning. The teacher showed Selma Form C5N which she used to interact individually with each student about any item that the student chose to put into his/her portfolio.

The teacher pointed out how easy it was the observer to note if the worksheet had been completed by both parties, and if it had been completed in a timely manner. The observer could also learn what the student felt he/she had learned, and compare that to the teacher's response. The teacher explained how completion of the form was one of the priorities that the administration had for the teachers, and if any supervisor found that portfolios had these forms without the teacher's response, the teacher was held accountable. The teacher said that she kept a listing of the forms turned in and when she gave each one back to the students, so that she knew the students received her feedback in a timely manner.

Reflective Questions:
- Based on what you know about assessing learning in the classroom, how would you expand or change the observation forms?
- Based on what you know about assessing learning in the classroom, what other objective observations of the application of this idea might you develop?

REDUCING VIOLENCE AND BUILDING CONFLICT RESOLUTION

Work by Olweus (1984) and others has shown that acts of aggression, whether they are direct or indirect, physical or mental, are typically committed by certain types of people, toward victims, who constitute other types of people. A wide variety of aggressive acts occur in schools, with estimates that 30% of students may either be aggressors or victims during their school years. Those who commit acts of aggression are typically impulsive, have positive self-concepts, have little anxiety, do not show empathy for others, and show a need for dominance. At the other end are the victims, who typically are anxious, insecure, socially isolated, cautious, and low in self-esteem.

Students who are engaging in bullying or other acts of aggression in the classroom may believe that the behaviors that they are engaging in are normal, appropriate ways to get attention or to deal with others. They may have learned these behaviors from observation of others who they admire. They may use these behaviors as they believe that they need to protect themselves from the world, from others who are more violent than they are. They typically believe that they are in conflict with others, and may purposefully create conflict because it is something they have come to expect in their lives.

Hocker and Williams (1991) define conflict as an expressed struggle between at least two people who perceive the situation differently and are experiencing interference from the other person in achieving their goals. Typically conflict involves one of six different types of issues: 1) control over resources, 2) preferences and nuisances, 3) values, 4) beliefs, 5) goals, and 6) the nature of the relationship between the people (Deutsch, 1973). While some conflict is inevitable, and may have positive effects, that which leads to violence, hostility, destruction, and pulls people away from each other is generally seen as negative.

Form C5M: Questionnaire for Students: Assessing Student Learning

School:_____ Room:_____ Teacher:_____

Grade Level_____ Your Name:_____

Today's Date_____ Person who helped with this form?_____

You are given a task to do, something to learn.
 What kind of task would you like it to be?
  What should the teacher give you do to?
 What kind of task do you do best?
  Did you ever tell the teacher that this is how you do best?
 Would you like to work on this task alone, or would you like help?
  If you want help, who would you like to help you?
 Should the teacher give you homework for this task?
  If you have homework, do you do it?
  If you have homework, what do you think about when you do it?
 Do you want to be graded for your work?
 Do you want to earn the grade alone or with others?
 What do you think a good grade is?
  What do you think when you earn a good grade?
  What do you think when you earn a grade that is not so good?

After you do the task, the teacher says that you have to show that you know how to do the task, that you learned the skill.
 If it was up to you, how would you show the teacher that you learned the task?
 If the teacher let you do this task, and you did well, why would you have done well?
  What would you say to yourself?
 If the teacher let you do this task, and instead of doing well you did poorly, why would you have done poorly?
  What would you say to yourself?
 Would you like to take a test?
  If so, what kind of test?
  If not, why not?
 Would you like to do something in front of others to show that you learned?
  If so, what would you like to do?
  If not, why not?

Pretend for a minute that the teacher says that you have to put away your books and take a hard test.
 What do you think about?
 If you start taking the test and you know the material, what do you think about?
 If you continue taking the test and it gets hard, and you don't know the material, what do you think about?

Pretend for a minute that your care-givers, your parents, relatives, or others who care about you, are coming to school to see your work.
 Who is most likely to come?
 What work are you going to show them? Why?
 What work are you not going to show them? Why?
 What will they say about the work that you show them?
 What will they tell the teacher about your work?

Form C5N: Student and Teacher Response Sheet for Portfolio Work

Student Completes This Part:

My Name Is:_____ Room #_____

Today's Date is:_____. My teacher is _____

This work is called:_____Grade_____

In completing this work I learned:

I want to put this in my portfolio because:

I did this work with the help of:

I would like to learn more about:

_____

Teacher response:

Date:_____ Room #_____Name_____

I have read the work. I think that the student learned:

The student should be proud of:

I would like the student to learn to:

Few teachers are taught how to deal with conflict in the classroom. As a result, they tend to engage in behaviors that may allow the conflict to continue, and may even encourage the conflict to grow. Teachers do this when they placate or conceal feelings they have, or others have; when they blame the other person; when they tend to be super-reasonable and deliver a lecture; or when they dismiss the issue as irrelevant, distracting students from the issue. They may try to "deflate" the self-esteem of the aggressor, or threaten punishments that are designed to raise anxiety. They need to learn to make appropriate "I" statements, and teach all students how to deal with conflict.

According to Gordon (1975) "I" statements are statements that someone makes that have four parts. They present an objective, non-judgmental description of the person's behavior in specific terms. They state how the individual (the "I") feels about this. They state the concrete effects on the individual. They state what the individual would prefer for the other person to do instead. "I" statements are particularly effective if the teacher makes sure this his/her nonverbal behavior is congruent with the verbal behavior. When delivering the "I" statement, the teacher should maintain direct eye contact, maintain an erect body posture, speak clearly, use appropriate gestures, and not whine or apologize (Alberti, 1991).

Whether the conflict is teacher and student, student to student, or the like, the steps for dealing constructively with the conflict are the same. First, the conflict needs to be defined in terms of needs, not solutions. The person needs to define his/her feelings and emotions. "I" statements should clearly define what is needed. Second, the problem and the unmet needs should to be stated appropriately. This means that the right time, place, and "I" statements should to be used to tell the other person what the defined problem is and what the unmet needs are. Third, the sender of the "I" statement needs to listen to the other person's needs. This will allow both parties to arrive at an agreed upon definition of the problem. Fourth, both parties should brainstorm possible solutions. Listing solutions without ownership is important for the parties involved to feel they are part of the solution. Fifth, the possible solutions should be evaluated, and the best one chosen. As each solution is evaluated, the possible consequences of the interaction should be considered. Sixth, the chosen solution should be implemented. There should be mutual agreement on who does what and the deadlines for doing this. Seventh, the solution should be evaluated at a later date to determine how it worked, and if further changes are needed (Walker & Brokaw, 1995). Form C5O is an example of a worksheet a teacher can give to two students who are experiencing conflict. The worksheet is designed to help them follow the process for conflict resolution with a minimum of interference by the teacher.

Reflective Questions:
- Based on what you know about dealing with conflict in the classroom, how would you expand or change the observation form?
- Based on what you know about dealing with conflict in the classroom, what other objective observations of the application of this idea might you develop?

Form C5O: Student Conflict Resolution Worksheet

My name is:_____My conflict is with _____

1. My problem is: OR: I need: (Use an "I" message)

2. Tell your problem to the person you have a conflict with. Make sure you use "I" messages.

3. Now, listen to the other person, what does the other person need? Write down what you think you heard the other person needs.

4. Once you have agreement that each of you has a clear understanding of the other person's needs, brainstorm possible solutions. Write down the possible solutions here.

5. For each solution you wrote in #4, write down a possible consequence after it. Then, discuss these, and choose the best solution. The solution we choose is:

6. Now, describe how you are going to implement the solution. Determine who is going to do what and by when.

MANAGING AND MAINTAINING THE CLASSROOM LEARNING ENVIRONMENT

When it comes to building and maintaining the classroom learning environment, most teachers rely on standard discipline and management processes. They may use behavioral theories, or cognitive theories to try to make sure that their students behave in an appropriate manner and that they can continue to provide instructional processes related to the curriculum.

Operant conditioning is a process for learning appropriate behavior which was developed by Skinner (1938, 1969). Skinner proposed that if a teacher has identified a problem behavior of a particular student, the teacher needs to then determine the behavior which the teacher would like to have occur in place of the problem behavior. Skinner was careful to note that this should be an observable behavior. He then said that the teacher should identify at least one satisfying consequence, something the student likes and will work to earn; and one aversive consequence, something the student does not like and will try to avoid. Then, applying this information, the teacher can set up four possible behavioral contingencies. For positive reinforcement, when the student would engage in the desired behavior, instead of the problem behavior, the student would be given the satisfying consequence. For negative reinforcement, when the student would engage in the desired behavior, instead of the problem behavior, the student would have the aversive consequence removed. For positive punishment, when the student would engage in the problem behavior, instead of the desired behavior, the student would receive the aversive consequence. For negative punishment, when the student would engage in the problem behavior, instead of the desired behavior, the student would lose the satisfying consequence. Once the four possible behavioral contingencies had been identified, it was up to the teacher to determine which one was best to use in the classroom when working with this particular student. Skinner (1968) argued that if teachers used operant conditioning correctly, they could teach a wide range of behaviors to their students. However, often they misused the process because they would reward or punish without clearly identifying the behaviors involved, or the behavioral contingencies that were possible, and without clearly specifying these to the student.

Cognitive theories of learning hold that the learner is actively involved in the learning process. When this is applied to classroom management, the same thing holds true. In applying cognitive management principles, the teacher needs to try to find out what the student who is engaging in inappropriate behavior is thinking. Then, the teacher needs to try to find out why the student is doing this. Often times, this leads to the teacher pointing out other ways to think about the situation and the behaviors. The teacher may also talk about the classroom climate, privileges afforded those who choose to be part of the classroom, and ways for the student and the teacher to work together to help the student make changes I his/her problematic behavior. Applying this idea, the learner is ultimately held responsible for his/her learning, and the thinking that accompanies that learning. The teacher is held responsible for trying to arrange the classroom, develop rules and procedures, and model ways to think about behavior, as well as modeling desired behaviors.

Nell knew that her young students had some cognitive abilities, but often times could not tell the teachers why they misbehaved. For some of the students, Nell suspected that fetal alcohol syndrome, or cocaine abuse by the mother when she was pregnant was the problem, and the students would have a long battle to learn to control their impulses. Nell knew that operant conditioning was a necessary part of the socialization and learning processes at her school. Young children who were having problems learning how to behave had to be provided clear, direct statements about what they were doing, what they should do instead, and what they would earn or lose. Nell knew that using external rewards for good behavior over a period of time was not a good idea. However, for the few students who needed help controlling behavior, she hoped that this system would impact positively upon the interactions of the teacher with the students. She also hoped that by the time students had matured a bit, the use of this sort of system could be lessened and cognitive systems relied upon more for management.

Nell set up Form C5P to observe the use of operant conditioning. She learned that it was important to interview the teacher before the observation so that the observer had enough information to complete the entire observation. Nell also found that when she sat down and interviewed a teacher, the teacher had entirely different ideas about what constituted inappropriate behavior and how to deal with this in the classroom.

Operant conditioning is but one way to manage the classroom and maintain the learning environment. Advocates of humanistic theories stress that it is important to know the individual student, and know how to meet the needs of the individual. They talk about having a humane, just environment where students do not feel threatened. For the teacher, this would imply that the teacher works with the students to develop ways that the classroom will function, and to invite the students into the learning process as they feel comfortable in the classroom. Of course, the classroom has to be a place where it is physically, emotionally, and cognitively safe for the student to express him-/herself.

Most textbooks on classroom management give advice to teachers to establish rules and be flexible, bending at times, but not breaking them. Teachers who have been found to be good classroom managers tend to be rather eclectic in their management. They have rules and consequences for misbehavior. They teach the students the behaviors that are expected. They monitor behavior, stopping misbehavior. They are able to effectively present a lesson, and to make sure students feel responsible for their work. That is, they take actions in advance, so that they are less likely to have a situation emerge that they had not planned on, one which they may feel compelled to react to. They also tend to have a high level of interaction with their students. Good managers may never sit at their desks over the course of the entire day. They are likely to have been walking about, working with individual students, showing concern for student learning, monitoring small groups, using "teachable moments" to help a group of students grasp a particular concept, and moving close to students who have a hard time controlling their own behavior. Teachers who become really adept at these behaviors keep the learning flowing in the room. They are not stopping to think, "I have to move toward Warren who is acting up." They are already there because they thought, and acted. "When it is individual work time, Warren tends to lose concentration about five minutes into the session. It is just about that time, so time to move close to cue him to continue with his work."

The problem with observing management in action, especially good management, is that it is an endless loop of a variety of behaviors. Focusing on just one is difficult. This is where the clinical supervision model can be applied to help understand the management processes used and provide a focal point for the behavior.

Reflective Questions:
- Based on what you know about classroom discipline, how would you expand or change the observation form?
- Based on what you know about classroom discipline, what other objective observations of the application of this idea might you develop?

Form C5P: **Teacher** **Use** **of** **Behavior** **Modification** **with** **a** **Student**

School:_____ Room:_____ Teacher:_____

Grade Level____ Subject Matter:_____ Number of Students:_____

Date:_____Start Time:_____ Finish Time:_____Total Observation Time:_____

Room Set-up/Special Information:_____

Part 1: Interview with the teacher:

1. We are focusing on a student who is having problems with inappropriate behavior in the classroom. What is the problem behavior?

2. What observable behavior would you like to have occur instead?

3. What do you know that the student's likes? What will the student do work for to obtain?

4. What do you know that the student's dislikes? What will the student try to avoid?

5. There are typically four options for dealing with the behavior. You can give the student something he/she likes when he/she engages in the desired behavior. You can take away something the student does hot like when he/she engages in the desired behavior. You can also punish the student for engaging in the behavior you want to change. In punishment, you either give the student something he/she dislikes, or take away something he/she likes. Which of the four possible choices for reinforcement or punishment did you choose? Why?

Part 2: Observation of the teacher-student interaction

1. The problem behavior occurs a total of _____ times (keep track).

2. When the problem behavior occurs, the teacher tell the student:

3. When the problem behavior occurs, the teacher (describe teacher behavior):

4. When the problem behavior occurs, and the teacher reacts, the student (describe student reaction to teacher's reaction):

5. When the desired, appropriate behavior occurs, the teacher tells the student:

6. When the desired, appropriate behavior occurs, the teacher (describe teacher behavior):

7. When the desired, appropriate behavior occurs, and the teacher reacts, the student (describe student reaction to teacher's reaction):

8. The desired behavior occurs a total of _____times (keep track).

INVOLVING PARENTS AND CARE-GIVERS IN THE CLASSROOM COMMUNITY

In recent years there has been a surge in the use of the word "community" in relation to education. Educators that seek to have the students understand and feel that they are part of a larger environment may use the word "community" in a variety of contexts. Some educators talk about making each classroom function as a community. Some educators talk about the school as a community. Some educators talk about the school as part of the community, while others reverse that and talk about the community as part of the school. Some expand that to talk about the learners, their classroom, and the school being part of the global community. Whatever the context for the word, the idea is that the classroom is nolonger a closed, segregated place that students enter in the morning and leave in the afternoon, having little or no contact with the outside world.

While schools have usually relied on parents for various help with the schooling process, including monitoring field trips, making treats, helping with homework, etc., in recent years both educators and parents have come to expect the schools to provide different opportunities for parents. Some schools have reached out in the direction of seeking parent help for the classroom, as aides, mentors, etc. Other schools have reached out in the direction of providing classes for parents, providing day care centers, using part of their buildings as community centers, or even providing care centers for the elderly. The challenge is for teachers and students to find and use the possible linkages in the classroom.

In our society, many students come from families that are not based on the "biological father with biological mother and biological siblings" concept. There are split families, step-families, adopted families, foster families, relatives as parents, friends of parents as parents, one parent, older sibling acting as parent, and other versions of families. Many teachers are aware that generically using the term "parent" in the classroom may cause emotional pains or consternation among their students. To avoid these issues, teachers may use a term that reflects the sociodynamics of the living situations of their students and refer to the adult that the student lives with as a "care-giver." Some teachers who use this term in the classroom discover that their students share more important information with them, because the student assumes that the teacher is less judgmental when he/she uses this term. One teacher told me that students started approaching her and telling her about jailed parents, parents who were forbidden by the courts to see their kids because of abuse, parents who had abandoned the students to relatives, etc. The teacher said she was shocked to learn all these things, but also now had a new appreciation for what some students had experienced, and the emotionality they brought to some classroom situations. She also understood why threats to contact parents didn't work for managing the classroom, and why many parents rarely had contact with the school.

Yet, in most circumstances, involving the parent/care-giver in the classroom is an important way to enhance student learning. If the care-giver is aware of the curriculum, the care-giver can provide resources, materials, time, and support for the student at home. The care-giver may also have resources to share with the teacher or the class. If the care-giver feels that he/she is valued by the school, he/she is more likely to want to be a part of the school. With this, the care-giver is likely to volunteer for some school activities, come in and give presentations to the students, link the classroom to the care-giver's job, etc. Even if the care-giver works the same hours that the school is in session, the care-giver may still provide valuable interactions with the school. The care-

Form C5Q: Parental/Care-taker Questionnaire

My Name is:_____ My student's name is_____

The date is:_____ My student is in grade:_____ The teacher is:_____

As the parent/care-taker of this student, you have a lot of information which is important for the teacher to know. Please share those things you would like the teacher to know.

1. The time that you get to spend with the student is important, and may vary by your schedule and your student's schedule.

    A. During the average weekday night, how much time do you get to spend with your student?

    B. What do you get to do during that time?

2.   A. What are the activities that you and your child get to do together?

    B. What does your child particularly like to do?

    C. What does your child not like to do?

3.   A. When you teach your child something, what works? How do you think that your child best learns?

4.   A. What type of homework is easy for your child?

    B. What type of homework is difficult?

    C. What can the teacher do to make the difficult learning easier?

5.   A. What do you expect your child to achieve in school?

    B. What grades?

    C. What would you like him/her to do once he/she is done with school?

6.   A. Do you have time to provide some help for the teacher and the school? If so, what can you offer?

giver may be in a position to get donations for the school, or provide substantial help in getting information about the school out to others, etc.

In many schools, although there is some sort of parent-teacher organization, it is up to the classroom teacher, and the students, to make care-givers aware of the opportunities that the school offers for interaction, and to find out what the care-giver is willing and able to do. Most schools try to involve their parents in two ways, one is getting the parent to be involved directly with his/her child. The second is getting the parent involved with the school. Form C5Q is an example of a form one school used early in the school year to start interactions with the care-givers.

Reflective Questions:
- Based on what you know about involving others in the classroom, how would you expand or change the observation form?
- Based on what you know about involving others in the classroom, what other objective observations of the application of this idea might you develop?

OBSERVING THE APPLICATION OF PRINCIPLES FOR TEACHING IN CLASSROOMS: LEARNER-CENTERED CLASSROOMS

In recent years the term "learner-centered" has been emerging in the educational psychology literature. The exact meaning of the term has depended upon the author, and the context. In the late 1980's and early 1990's, the American Psychological Association Presidential Task Force on Psychology in Education held a series of conferences and working sessions that resulted in the clarification of the concept and development of guidelines for teaching, based on psychological principles derived from educational research. This group drew on the results of hundreds of observational and other studies of teaching and learning processes. The principles which were developed integrate research and practice, reflecting conventional and scientific wisdom. They are intended to apply to all learners, and should be applicable to any age level student. The present concern is the extent to which learners experience the principles in action in their classrooms and their schools. The principles are:

---

1. The Nature of the Learning Process. Learning is a natural process of pursuing personally meaningful goals that is active, volitional, and both internally and socially mediated; it is a process of discovering and constructing personal and shared meaning from information and experience, filtered through each individual's unique perceptions, thought, and feelings--as well as through negotiations with others.
2. Goals of the Learning Process. The learner seeks to create meaningful, coherent representations of knowledge regardless of the quantity and quality of data available.
3. The Construction of Knowledge. The learner links new information with existing and future-oriented knowledge in uniquely meaningful ways.
4. Higher-Order Thinking. Higher-order strategies for "thinking about thinking and learning"--for overseeing and monitoring mental operations--facilitate creative and critical thinking and the development of expertise.
5. Motivational Influences on Learning. The depth and breadth of understanding constructed, and what and how much is learned and remembered, if influenced by (a) self-awareness and beliefs about personal control, competence, and ability; (b) clarity and saliency of personal and social values, interests, and goals; (c) personal expectations for success or failure; (d) affect, emotion, and general states of mind; and (e) the resulting motivation to learn.

---

6. Intrinsic Motivation to Learn. Individual are naturally curious and enjoy learning, but intense negative cognitions and emotions (e.g., insecurity, worrying about failure, being self-conscious or shy, fearing punishment or verbal ridiculing or stigmatizing labels) thwart this enthusiasm.
7. Characteristics of Motivation -- Enhancing Learning Tasks. Curiosity, creativity, and higher-order thinking are stimulated by relevant, authentic learning tasks of optimal difficulty, challenge, and novelty for each learner.
8. Developmental Constraints and Opportunities. Individuals progress through stages of physical, intellectual, emotional, and social development that are a function of unique genetic and environmental factors.
9. Social and Cultural Diversity. Learning is facilitated by social interactions and communication with others in flexible, diverse (in age, culture, family background, etc.). and adaptive instructional settings.
10. Social Acceptance, Self-Esteem, and Learning. Learning and self-esteem are heightened when individual are in respectful and caring relationships with others who see their potential, genuinely appreciate their unique talents, and accept them as individuals.
11. Individual and Cultural Differences in Learning. Although basic principles of learning, motivation, and effective instruction may apply to all learners (regardless of ethnicity, race, gender, physical ability, religion, or socioeconomic status), learners have different capabilities and preferences for learning mode and strategies. These differences are a function of both environment (what is learned and communicated in different cultures or other social groups) and heredity (what occurs naturally as a function of genes). Learning is most effective when differences in learners; linguistic, cultural, and social backgrounds are taken into account.
12. Cognitive and social filters. Personal thoughts, beliefs, and understandings resulting from prior learning and unique interpretations become the individual's basis for constructing reality and interpreting life experiences.

Observing all the principles in action is a difficult process. Instead of trying to observe that all twelve principles occur in a classroom, the observer should focus on one principle at a time and determine if the subject will be the student, the teacher, or the teacher-student interaction. If you think it this way, many of the observational processes and forms in this text already can be applied to observe these principles in action. Additionally, hundreds of other potential observations may be developed. For instance, think of the observations related to:

- the opportunities for teacher and peer interactions
- the ways students are encouraged to link prior knowledge and new information
- the types of content presented and the processes used to facilitate acquisition of the content
- the questions the teacher asks
- the feedback the teacher gives
- the learning strategies that are taught and promoted
- the problem solving that is taught and used
- the ways students are encouraged to interact in the classroom
- the ways moods of students are handled
- the types of assessments provided
- the types of materials and activities used
- the use of physical space and facilities
- the accommodations to differences made by teachers and students
- the technologies used
- the supports given to students

- the individualizations made for students in the classroom
- the types of student choices available
- the student groupings that are used

As you become more and more skilled as an observer, you should be able to determine other observations which will provide you information as to which principles are being applied, and the extent to which they are being applied in the classroom.

Reflective Questions:
- Based on what you know about learner-centered classrooms, what objective observations of the application of this idea might you develop?

APPLYING THE CLINICAL SUPERVISION MODEL TO OBSERVE STAFF AND COLLEAGUES

Many principals, superintendents, college department chairs, and college deans use the clinical supervision model when they observe their staff. The clinical supervision model (e.g., Stallings & Kaskowitz, 1972; Showers, 1984) for observation typically includes a three part process. First, the supervisor and the teacher meet to prepare for the observation. To prepare for the meeting, the teacher has usually filled out a form to indicate the processes the teacher is using in instructing the classroom, and the major problems the teacher feels he/she is having. At that meeting, there is discussion about what has been going on in the class, and what the teacher would like to learn as a result of the observation. That is, what does the teacher feel should be the defined behavior that is observed? The supervisor and the teacher then agree as to what the objective observation will involve, what process of observation will be used, if the supervisor will act only as an objective observer or also be involved in class processes (Warning: It is easy to lose objectivity if you get involved!), when and how long the observation will occur, and how the results will be shared.

Second, the supervisor engages in the observation. To prepare, the supervisor has read the literature related to the concerns the teacher has, and has prepared the observation sheet(s). Skilled observers will sometimes prepare two or three different ways to observe the particular behavior so that they can choose which is most appropriate given the actual classroom circumstances. Typically, the supervisor will introduce him-/herself to the class, and explain that he/she is focusing on the teacher, not the students. Most supervisors will also make sure that someone else is "in charge" of the school while they observe, so that they are not interrupted unless it is an emergency.

Third, the supervisor and the teacher will meet within a few days of the observation. The supervisor will have prepared a copy of the observation for the teacher, and will also have a reflective comments sheet, if the nature of the supervision is to also provide feedback for the teacher to develop his/her skills. The teacher and the supervisor will discuss the results of the observation. The teacher may ask for clarification, or may express surprise that he/she engaged in a particular aspect of the observed behavior. The teacher may be pleased with the observation, and move to reflective thinking about how the behavior could be further enhanced or applied, or may be displeased. If the teacher is displeased, the supervisor may set-up another observation, and go back to the first step. The supervisor may also use this displeasure to build reflective skills, asking the teacher to focus on why he/she is displeased, and what changes need to be made not only in the observation process, but also in the instructional process. Is the teacher able to verbalize the skills that are part of the instructional process that are observable? Is the teacher able to understand the difference between good, detailed, objective observation, and subjective/overall impressions observation? I have known many supervisors and peer observers of teachers who report that the observed spent lots of time pointing to wall decorations and how nice the book covers were that the students made, and were so busy trying to keep students "looking like they were learning," that no time was spent on actual instruction.

Although the clinical supervision model was designed to be used in a supervisory situation, it can easily to applied in the classroom for teachers to observe each other and help themselves identify instructional processes and ways to further their own development (Willerman et al, 1991). Throughout this book, there have been examples of teacher observing each other, and of supervisors observing teachers. The specific strategies for using this model were not explained earlier because the average observer needs to have spent time observing before he/she can begin to effectively use the model. Too often, teachers and administrators assume that with a few hours of training or practice, or simply because they have already spent so many hours in classrooms, they can use the model. To effectively use the model, the observer needs to be an astute observer who is familiar with a wide variety of instructional practices, and who is willing and able to suspend judgment to help another person learn and grow. Because this model takes more time and effort than simply coming into a classroom and observing, it is typically best used when the teacher is having a particular problem which involves teacher-student interactions. Forms C5R, C5S, and C5T are examples of pre- and post-observation process forms (adapted from Willerman et al, 1991), which may be used when a clinical supervision model is applied.

Reflective Questions:
- Based on what you know about the clinical supervision model, what objective observations of the application of this idea might you develop?

Form C5R: Getting ready for the Preconference Meeting for Clinical Supervision Observation: To Be Completed by the Teacher who is to be Observed

To prepare for the preconference, the teacher who is going to be observed needs to conceptualize and clarify the classroom behaviors that are of a concern. The teacher should complete this worksheet prior to the preconference, so that the teacher can be specific at the preconference, and so that the supervisor/peer coach can best help determine how the observation may occur.

1. Describe your teaching strategies. What are the things you typically do in a classroom?

2. How has your teaching been working for you? Are things going well?

3. What are two or three problems you have been experiencing in the classroom?

4. What have been the ways you have tried to deal with these problems? Have the results been successful or created more concerns?

5. Can the problems be observed in the classroom? Can the ways that you deal with the problems be observed?

6. What goal do you have for dealing with the problems?

7. What kind of information about the problem would be useful for you?

8. If it was up to you, how would you collect this information?

9. What other information about your classroom would be useful for you?

Form C5S: The Preconference Meeting: Getting Ready for the Observation

Use this form at the preconference meeting. As you complete the form, make sure that there is agreement between the teacher who is going to be observed and the observer. If there is disagreement, this needs to be noted, and wherever possible, additional time should be taken to develop consensus.

Teacher's Name_____ Observer's Name_____

Agreed Date, Time, and Place of Observation_____

1. The current teaching strategies used by the teacher are:

2. The current student behaviors are:

3. The desired student behaviors are:

4. The lesson objectives are:

5. The instructional processes the teacher will use are:

6. The problem that the teacher would like help observing is:

7. The teacher and the observer have defined the observable behavior as:

8. The way that information/data will be collected will be:

9. The special information the observer should know is:

10. The information obtained during this observation is confidential and will be used for the purpose of:

11. We are in agreement concerning the above items, except for the following:

_____   _____   _____
Teacher's signature   Observer's signature   Date

Form C5T: The Post-Conference Meeting: Reflecting on the Information Collected

Use this form at the post-conference meeting. As you complete the form, make sure that there is agreement between the teacher who was observed and the observer. If there is disagreement, this needs to be noted, and wherever possible, additional time should be taken to develop consensus.

Teacher's Name_____ Observer's Name_____

1. The observer should provide a copy of the data or information obtained to the teacher, if this has not already been done.

2. What is the objective summary of the data/information from the observation?

3. Were the lesson objectives achieved? Why or why not? What happened?

4. Did the problem the teacher was concerned about occur? Why or why not? What happened?

5. What does the data/information tell us about the problem, teacher-student interaction, teaching strategies, and student behavior?

6. How is the teacher going to use this information?

7. Will this information be shared with anyone else? If so, with whom, and how?

8. Where will this information be stored?

9. Will there be another observation? If so, another pre-conference form should be completed.

11. We are in agreement concerning the above items, except for the following:

_____   _____   _____
Teacher's signature   Observer's signature   Date

REVIEW QUESTIONS:

1. What are the different types of cooperative learning?
2. What are the different types of peer tutoring?
3. What are some of the various labels that students may have in the classroom?
4. What are some of the ways that teachers can develop creativity in their students?
5. What are some of the ways that teachers may promote gender and ethnic equity in the classrooms?
6. What are some of the ways that teachers may build multicultural awareness in the classroom?
7. What are some ways that teachers use technology in the classroom?
8. What are some of the ways that teachers may assess the student learning?
9. How can a teacher resolve a classroom conflict?
10. What does it mean when a teacher is a learner-centered manager?
11. What are some of the ways that schools and teachers promote interaction with parents?
12. When is the model of clinical supervision likely to be used in classroom observing?

DISCUSSION QUESTIONS:

1. Why is it important that teacher-student interactions be observed in the classroom?
2. Compare and contrast the ways that teachers interact with students who have been given various labels in the classroom. Do you expect teachers to interact differently with students who have different labels? Why, or why not?
3. Why is it important for a teacher to know and use a variety of instructional strategies in the classroom?
4. What are some other types of teacher-student interactions, not yet covered in this text, which might lend themselves to objective observation? What would those observations entail?

CHAPTER 6

BUILDING REFLECTIVE SKILLS
AND MAKING DECISIONS
BASED ON OBSERVATIONS

LEARNING OBJECTIVES:

After you read this chapter, you should know:

1. appropriate and inappropriate ways to use the observation forms in the classroom
2. the process for compiling data obtained during observations
3. the process for making decisions based on the data you obtain
4. ways to think about modifying the observation forms for your use
5. ways to think about building observation forms for your use
6. some common ways that the observation forms are misused.

After you read this chapter, you should be able to:

1. collect, compile, and analyze data from an objective observation
2. make decisions based on an accumulation of information from observations
3. modify observation forms for your own use in the classroom
4. develop new observation forms for your own use in the classroom.

INTRODUCTION

Throughout this text, the focus has been on concise, planned, well-defined objective observations of classroom behavior, with the goal of gaining objective information about the student, the teacher, the instructional processes, the teacher-student interactions, and other aspects of the classroom. Each theory and model that was discussed was briefly presented, and an idea or two was presented for observing some application of this in the classroom. Some observational processes involved various coding systems, some checklists, some verbatim records, some interviews, some anecdotal records, etc. None of these processes were meant to be presented as the only possible way to observe the theory or model. Rather, they were meant to be examples which you could then think about, decide how to change, or decide to reject and develop something else. The idea is to know and comprehend the theory well-enough that you can not only think about its application, but analyze how it might best be observed, and then synthesize that information into the appropriate observational process.

Each chapter has had reflective questions for you. Although the questions may seem redundant, they were designed for the purpose of getting you to start to reflect, to start to think about the use of the forms, think about what might work given your situation, and revise the forms to meet your needs. If the reflective questions seemed difficult for you, be patient. As you learn more about the theories, and observe in various classrooms, the connections should become easier for you. As you move from novice to expert, you may be able to conceptualize observation forms that are more advanced, and require you to have multiple focuses.

In the beginning of this text, the issue of reliability and validity in observing was also introduced. As you start to think about how to appropriately use objective observations for decision making, you need to make sure that you have valid, reliable data. Without this, you will risk making incorrect decisions.

RATIONALE FOR USING OBJECTIVE OBSERVATIONS FOR DECISION MAKING

We make decisions about students, teachers, and classrooms every day. Sometimes before we are even in a classroom we use our background knowledge to make decisions. Any decisions which are based on hearsay, rumors, intuition, or the like are most likely faulty decisions. To effectively make decisions related to classrooms, we need to be professional, and not have our attitudes and feelings interfering with the objective reality of the situation.

The first forms you were introduced to asked you to process your feelings prior to observation. It is also important to process your feelings after you observe. This may be at the end of an hour of observation, a day of observation, a few days, etc. The idea is that prior to your trying to make rational, appropriate decisions, you become aware of any feelings that the observation generated in you. Form C6A can be used to help you become aware of your feelings. When you have completed it, you can use this information to help you build your decisions in an effective way.

This text introduced you to Steve, Danielle, Fran, Alton, Selma, Geri, Nell, Juan, and Miguel. All of them had different needs for classroom observation. Each of them developed and/or applied objective observations based on their needs. What was missing from the brief descriptions of the forms or the observations they did, was discussion of the conclusions they may reach and the decisions they may make as a result of the observations.

It is misuse of any observational processes to use it once or twice, and then jump to conclusions. Rather, observations need to occur multiple times, preferably in multiple places (more than one classroom, or with more than one teacher, or more than one group of students). Observations are enhanced even further if reliability and validity are established with multiple observers conducting multiple observations. It is wrong to assume that anyone else would agree 100% with what you observed one time, much less more than once. It is also wrong to assume that any one observation is representative of what normally occurs in a classroom. Even if you have been observing in a classroom for some hours, it is likely that the class is different by your being there. The students and the teacher are likely to be a bit more anxious, reserved, concerned about your presence, etc. This impacts on what you observe in the students' behaviors, the teacher's behavior, and the teacher-student interactions. Therefore, you need to be cautious in drawing any conclusions about what you observed.

Some of the observation forms had a place for you to summarize your notes, or to add notes. In doing so, you may have provided information about what you saw in a way that drew conclusions about that particular observation. That is the starting point for

Form C6A: Getting in Touch With Your Feelings After Your Observation

1. What were your impressions of the observation? How did the observation go?

2. Did the observation meet your expectations? Why or why not?

3. What did you feel while you were observing? Did anything you saw make you smile, laugh, feel happy, feel sad, feel angry? If so, what was it?

4. At any point, did you find your feelings getting in the way of your observing? Why? What happened?

5. What do you feel now that you are done observing?

6. How do you think that your feelings may have affected your ability to be build reliable and valid, objective observations?

making decisions, drawing conclusions about each observation, and then drawing conclusions across the observations that you make.

In the chapter on observing students in the classroom, we looked at possible observations of student physical development, cognitive development, intelligence, various learning styles, social and affective development, personality development, language development, moral development, place in ecological systems, and needs. In any observation of a student, the student should be observed over time, and in different places as he/she interacts with various students and teachers. The consistency of the observed behavior should be noted. Additionally, inconsistencies are important because they also provide information about the malleability of the development or raise concerns about the reliability and validity of the observations. While an observer may be tempted to try to use a different form to focus on a different behavior each time a student is observed, and thusly try to get some overall picture of the student, no one-shot observation should be considered valid. There are too many issues which arise when one does that. Rather, if the observer seeks to get some sort of overall picture of the various developmental characteristics of the student, the observer should use the forms multiple times in multiple places. The problem becomes doing this in a short period of time, before the student further develops and changes his/her behavior in the classroom.

In the chapter on observing teachers in the classroom, observations of the teacher's own development, and the way the teacher applies developmental theories and models in the classroom were explored. Similar to the observations of students, no one observation of a teacher should be used to make decisions. Rather, multiple observations using the same observation form should be completed before any conclusions are drawn and any decisions made. Also, it is helpful to see the teacher at different times of the day and with different students. Unlike the student observations, the concern typically is not on describing development at one point in time, and therefore, observations are typically extended over a longer period of time.

The same holds true for observing instructional processes and teacher-student interaction. Typically, observing across time and settings will provide more complete information on which to draw conclusions and make decisions. It would not be prudent to try to observe cooperative learning in action, and because a different strategy of instruction is used at that time, conclude that cooperative learning never happens. It also would not be prudent to observe cooperative learning in the classroom, and then conclude that that is the only instructional strategy used.

When observing strategies of instruction and the teacher-student interactions that are related to these, the observer needs to be careful to maintain the focus of the observation. If the teacher is using cooperative learning as a method to reach at-risk, special needs, and gifted students, it may be tempting to change your focus, or add to the data you are collecting. The problem is that if you change the focus of your observation, you really should start a whole new observation form, and redefine the behavior that you are observing. Of course, once you do that, you should again collect multiple samples over multiple time periods before you try to draw any conclusions and make any decisions.

Assuming that you have collected good, objective information, what do you do with it? How do you use it to make decisions? To start with, you compile the information you obtained over the multiple times you observed the same behavior. You sum the information, noting totals of numbers of times for each observation, and across observations. You may want to total the number of minutes you observed, so that you can mathematically determine the number of minutes between each occurrence, or the number of occurrences per minutes.

Instead of being concerned about totaling and looking at occurrences and time, you may be interested in what behaviors were seen, and which ones weren't. You may be interested in the sequence of events, and if the sequence remained the same. You may also be concerned about which type of instructional method was used when, or where. You may use your compilation to develop an overall description of the characteristic or behavior. You may use your compilation to develop questions about what you didn't observe, or what was missing in your own forms and observational processes. You may also use your compilation to help you develop ideas for new forms and new observations.

Once you have compiled your information, you are in a position to determine what you have. Is it significant? Does it provide you with new, important information? Does is answer your questions? Does it give you enough to think about? Does it give you information on which to base decisions?

When Steve observed his own teaching through coding videotapes, he was able to compile the information, and then decide if he wanted to try to change one of the things he was doing in the classroom. Note the word *one*. One change at a time is a good starting point. Trying to change too much at once is generally difficult and overwhelming! If Steve did make a change, he could then videotape and see if he did indeed change his behavior, and the effects of the change. That is, if he did something differently, did that lead to different reactions in the students.

When Danielle, Geri, Nell and Juan observed other teachers, they could collect information to share with the teachers. By applying the clinical supervision model in a peer coaching situation, they could share what they learned, without making judgments. Sharing the information then allows the observed teacher to determine what, if any, modifications may be appropriate in the classroom. Note that the observer is not telling the observed what to do, but rather, providing the objective information so that the observed can then use it to draw his/her own conclusions, and make decisions.

When Miguel observed teachers, he also collected information he could share. In using the clinical supervision model, he also is supposed to provide the objective information so that the observed can then use it to draw his/her own conclusions and make decisions. However, as a principal, Miguel also had the responsibility to supervise, and provide written evaluations in his teachers' files. He had to also draw conclusions and make decisions. In these cases, good supervisors try to withhold their drawing conclusions and making decisions until after they have had the post-conference meeting. They can use the post-conference meeting to gather more information, and to help them decide if they have enough information to move ahead to drawing conclusions, or they can decide that they need more information, and thus begin another round of pre-conference meetings and observations.

When Fran, Alton, and Selma observed teachers, they collected information for their own purposes. When they compiled their information, they could draw their own conclusions. While it is tempting for those conclusions to become judgments, judging is dangerous. In reality, it does little good to judge any observed teacher. Judging leads to a loss of objectivity. It may give a false sense of security, or a sense that we might do better. Judging also becomes dangerous when we have made judgments and then find ourselves back observing the same teacher or the same students. Under these circumstances it is very difficult to regain our objectivity, or to even find observations which we can try to objectively make. Instead, Fran, Alton, and Selma may enhance their own learning if they reflect on the conclusions and think about how they might apply this information to their own situations and teaching. Such reflection is likely to result in their making more selective decisions when it comes to their own teaching.

When Fran, Alton, and Selma were done observing, some of the teachers in whose rooms they were observing asked for information about what they had observed. While each pre-service teacher reminded the observed teachers that the information they had obtained was for their own learning, they also wanted to provide some sort of information back to the teachers. They used Form C6B to provide that information, answering the questions in an objective manner, and also providing a way to thank the teachers for allowing them into their classrooms. Note that they showed the completed form to their instructors before they shared it with the teachers. This way they were able to get some feedback from their instructors as to the appropriateness of their summative information prior to sharing it.

MODIFYING AND BUILDING YOUR OWN FORMS FOR PRACTICE

When you have been observing for several hours, and have good comprehension of the theories and models of education that are applied in the observations, you should find it becoming easier to modify the forms in this text for your own use. You may find that knowing a theory well, and knowing the different observation strategies, helps you to think about and plan your observations. The better you know a theory, the more likely you are to spend some time in the classroom deciding what works best to observe the application of the theory, and what possible problems might be encountered with the observation.

One of the problems that novice observers typically encounter is that they decide that a particular form doesn't meet their needs, so they start to try to modify it, or build another one. The problem is that they have not had many hours observing, and typically then find it difficult to know how to modify or build a form that really applies the theory in an objective manner. They may start to make modifications that lose their objectivity. They may start to make modifications that lose the focus of the observation, and nolonger apply the theory. They may even try to build a form that is inappropriate for classroom use because it violates confidentiality or becomes experimental in nature.

Novice observers may or may not have good theory background. Exposure to a theory by reading a text that covers the theory in a couple of pages of print is just that, exposure. It is typically not providing enough in-depth information for the observer to really develop a good theoretical background. Good theoretical backgrounds are always growing. However, to be able to develop observation forms based on theory, typically the observer should have read the original authored works related to the theory, a good cross-sampling of various applications, and any challenges to the theory. With this type of background, the observer is in position to make informed decisions about the application of this theory to objective classroom observation.

Good observers rarely make major modifications to forms, or build new observation forms in isolation. Throughout this text there were examples of teachers modifying forms based on observations they made, and based on input from others. Pre-service teachers who are observing may link up with peers and practice using forms and comparing notes. In-service teachers may both use a form on a video, and then talk through modifications. Supervisors may also compare notes with another supervisor. In many schools, the clinical supervision model and some form of peer observation is in

Form C6B: Feedback to the Teacher In Whose Room I Observed

My Name is:_____ Today's date is:_____

The teacher in whose room I observed is _____

The dates and time that I observed include: _____

_____

     I want to thank you for taking all the time and making all the efforts you did to welcome me into your classroom to observe. I hope that you will accept my thanks, and also pass my thanks along to your students.

     You have asked for feedback on what I observed. While most of the information was related to specific items that my instructor chose to help me become a better observer, and really is best left at that, there are some things I can tell you.

     Please remember that this information should not be used to draw conclusions or to make decisions. I am just learning how to observe. You may want to use this information to then develop your own observations. If you like, I can share copies of my blank observation forms with you.

Related to the students:

1. For _____minutes, I observed your students. I was observing their individual differences in development.

2. When I was observing, I especially was trying to apply the theory(ies) of:

3. I looked specifically at the behaviors of:

4. After observing these students, I compiled some summative information. The information that I obtained, and that my instructor agrees that I should give you is:

Related to the teacher:

1. For _____minutes, I observed you as you were teaching.

2. When I was observing, I especially was trying to apply the theory(ies) of:

3. I looked specifically at the behaviors of:

4. After observing the teacher, I compiled some summative information. The information that I obtained, and that my instructor agrees that I should give you is:

place. Using this model allows the teachers to talk with one another, and to help each other make modifications, get feedback, build forms, etc. The other value of the model is that meetings are confidential, and teachers should feel free to make modifications and try them out without fears of retribution or causes of alarm from their supervisors.

One of the problems that I often encounter is that those who build forms lose their objectivity in the building. They ask the wrong questions. They ask things like, "what is the teacher doing wrong," or "why is so-and-so a good teacher?" They already have decided what they are going to see before they begin! While these are pretty straight forward examples, there also are more subtle ones, like, "what is the teacher doing that gets students to like him/her?" This kind of observation starts with an assumption, that the teacher is liked, and that alone brings subjectivity into the observation.

One of the reasons that teachers often build their own observation forms is because they want to gather data on a particular phenomena or theory as it is applied in their classrooms. While they may start with some "off the cuff" observations to build their ideas, typically, they have a purpose for the data, and the method of collection is designed to gather the needed information. For example, a teacher is concerned about the out-of-seat behaviors of one student. These behaviors are disturbing to others, and distracting to the teacher. The teacher designs a form to track that student's behavior. The data that is collected can then be summarized to share with the student, the student's care-giver, and other professionals in a staffing.

Reflective Questions:
- Based on what you know about modifying and building your own forms for observation, and any attempts you have made, what other recommendations do you have for someone who is using observational forms?

CONTEXTS FOR MISUSE OF THE FORMS

It was stated earlier that it is important to use the observation forms in a fair, ethical manner. It is not appropriate to collect information on someone for the purpose of trying to prove your point, or to show that someone is not doing something correctly. It is also not appropriate to continue to use a form that does not adequately work with a classroom situation, or to use a form out of the context for which it was designed.

I have had some pre-service and in-service teachers, who are also parents, try to use the forms on their children at home. The forms in this text were not designed to be used at home. Even though some of the forms focus on the individual differences among students, these differences are applied in the classroom, not the home. If you want to use any of the forms at home, you need to know and apply the theories to make the appropriate modifications.

I have also had various parents argue that they should be able to use the forms in the classroom to observe students and parents. Confidentiality is one issue here. The other is that this is an inappropriate use of the form. Without the requisite background knowledge of the theory which is being applied, the observer is likely to misapply the form, and to engage in subjective observations. Parents who are knowledgeable about educational theories and models may be able to use some of the forms, but the general rule of thumb is that unless they are trained observers, it is best to refrain from using the forms.

In a recent discussion with a politician, the elected official was quick to expound on all that was wrong with the schools of today. As I listened to the list, I asked how many of these things this person had observed first hand in the schools. When the quick reply was "well, most of them," I had to pursue this and ask the specific ways that the official had engaged in classroom observation. I asked what processes were used, what the defined objective behavior was, what kind of data was collected over what time period, and what the calculated reliability and validity of the observation was. I quickly found that all of the official's "data" was impressions from brief, planned visits. I explained that such observations can easily provide misinformation, and offered to help the official develop the appropriate observation forms the next time that he really wanted to know what was going on in the schools. This official was not misusing the forms, only but he was misusing the idea of observation.

The observation forms are also misused when the observer seeks only to become familiar with classrooms of today. Typically, going in with a defined objective observation will limit the overall familiarity that the observer may be striving to achieve. Under this circumstance, it is better for the observer to simply go in and note things that the observer was unfamiliar with, or make some general notes while engaging in the process of looking and learning.

Remember, anyone can misuse any of these forms, it is up to you to try to use them appropriately, and to share what you have learned in an ethical manner. The next chapter of this text contains copies of the various forms that occur earlier. They are provided here so that you can more easily compare them, choose among them, and think about the differences in knowledge and skills that they require.

Reflective Questions:
- Based on what you know about classrooms, what other misuse of the forms can you think of? How can you protect the integrity of the process?

EXAMPLES OF DECISION-MAKING BASED ON OBSERVATIONS: THE CASES

How Steve Used Observation to Help Him Make Decisions for the Classroom:

When we first met Steve Whilder, he had a number of issues that he was concerned about. Among these were the use of advisor-advisee programs, how team-teaching was going to work, how inclusion of special education students was going to work, and how to mentor Danielle Poke. Steve knew he should make one change at a time in his room, with his teaching. He also knew that one change may well impact other areas or concerns.

To learn about the advisor-advisee programs, Steve interviewed Danielle, and he read about various ways the programs can be set-up and put into action. He then developed an observation sheet for the classroom, and revised the interview form he used with Danielle. He visited another school where the program was running. He interviewed the teachers, and he observed the program in action in the classroom on three occasions. One of the teachers was also kind enough to audiotape the sessions, and after any confidential information was deleted, the tapes were forwarded to Steve. Steve now had three sources of information from which he could compile data. He learned how long program sessions typically last, what topics are involved, how the sessions are conducted, what the typical learning objectives are, and how to link the sessions to the rest of the curriculum. He also learned how to use the sessions to help students cope with immediate problems in their daily lives. As a result of compiling this data, Steve went back to Danielle and again interviewed her. This time, he sought to confirm or disconfirm the data. When Danielle agreed with him, he then used the data to make decisions. He provided the rest of the teachers with his information. They all used this as they met to set-up the program. They also decided that since they were all novices at this, they would purchase materials to help them. Armed with the data, they were able to convince the administration to immediately purchase materials to help them start up and run the program.

Steve also had used the videotapes of his room to code various information and gather data for decision making. By charting the student-student interactions, and the teacher-student interactions in his room at various times, over a few weeks, Steve was able to gather enough information to give him a picture of the interactions that occurred among his regular education students, among his special education students, and as students interacted with the special education teacher and with him. Steve charted the frequency of the interactions over the weeks he observed. He was surprised that once the special needs students were integrated into the room, there were no real changes in the number and types of interactions. The special needs students were interacting with all students at the same rate as the regular education students. Additionally, they were interacting with him at the same rate as the regular education students. It seemed to him that the students knew how to use him as a resource, and how to use the special education teacher, and they were proceeding to do so. He also noticed that the regular education students were also asking questions of the special education teacher. Armed with this information, Steve felt that he could now encourage more self-regulated behavior in all of his students, and start to teach his students how to use other instructional grouping patterns and learning strategies in the classroom. Instead of relying so heavily on cooperative learning, he could now try more peer tutoring and reciprocal learning groups.

Team-teaching was another issue for Steve. He didn't hold high hopes for him to have the time to implement this effectively. One of his colleagues pointed out that since he already teamed in the planning meetings, the actual teaching as a team would be easy. Steve's team made the goal that by the end of the first semester they would have at least two integrated lessons in each unit, and at least one of these lessons would be team-taught. They also decided that at the end of the semester they would look at how well they did at meeting their goal, and then determine the goals for the next semester. Steve's team had worked out a data collection in which each kept track of the number of lessons that they integrated with someone else, and the time it took to plan these lessons. They also each kept track of the number of times that they team-taught, and how long each teaching session lasted for a particular date. At the end of the semester, as they sat down to compare information, Steve realized that they had been engaged in collecting objective information through self-observation. He was surprised at the instances in which one teacher had recorded data, but the other had not. This didn't show good reliability. He also learned that teachers had been teaming at least once a week, and among them, an average of twelve lessons a week were integrated with at least one other subject area. However, it was taking the teachers an additional three hours a week to lesson plan. As the team considered this, they decided that their main goal was to have everyone collecting objective data! Keeping the other goals intact, they could then continue to try to develop these lessons without feeling overwhelmed or adding more hours to their work week.

Steve and Danielle engaged in a variety of information-sharing sessions. He also shared videotapes of his room with her, and invited her in to observe him. He shared his objective observation forms with her, and together they also revised and build forms. As he shared his interests and concerns, Danielle started to share some of hers. He was able to observe her, and give her information which could help her teaching, without being threatening, and without Danielle fearing that the administration would know every little thing. The observations became a focal point for Steve to mentor Danielle, and for her to feel that she also was providing input.

How Danielle Used Observation to Help Her Make Decisions for the Classroom:

Danielle had begun the school year anxious to teach and have her own room. She was pleased to be working in a middle school, and felt that she could handle the work load just fine. Her concern had been on mentoring. She had wondered why she had to be mentored and how mentoring would work. She was surprised to learn that this was not painful, and not time-consuming. Every time they met, Steve had some tid bit about paperwork for the school, or upcoming events that helped Danielle plan. Additionally, he didn't tell her what to do. He shared his own concerns, and allowed her a chance to share hers. In a short time, Danielle learned how Steve's observations of himself was changing some of his thinking, and hers. As issues came up, she learned to approach them objectively, and to think about how to observe them. She also learned to go back to the literature, the theories, the research, and figure out what might be going on in the situation.

Danielle started to welcome the videotaping. At first she found it very difficult to watch herself teach. She would think about what she looked like on camera, how silly a gesture was, etc. In time, she came to ignore those things and focus on the observations she planned. She and Steve compared notes on what they learned, and Danielle found herself thinking through various teaching processes and the various ways she reacted. She even videotaped her team teaching, so she could learn if under that situation students were getting more, less, or the same amount of teacher contact as in regular lessons. As the school year continued, Danielle's supervisor complimented her on her management, and her professionalism in dealing with classroom situations. She shared her compliment with Steve, thanking him, and asking if he would be willing to continue mentoring her the following year.

How Geri Used Observation to Help Her Make Decisions for the Classroom:

Geri had set-out observing in her early childhood center with the goal of finding out what the teachers were doing, determining where they needed inservicing, providing inservices, and then seeing if the inservices changed the teaching. However, as Geri got into observing, she realized that she had anticipated doing far more than she could. She could not use observation to identify every behavior the teachers were engaged in. She couldn't conclude from the observations what teachers did and did not know. She had to rethink the observations. She started much smaller. She looked at teacher-student interactions, charting the number of, and length of verbal interactions that were one-to-one. She then conducted more observations in which she charted the language used by the teachers and by the students. Some of the observed students were those labeled "at-risk," and some were not. She compiled this data. She learned that teachers had about twice as much one-to-one interaction time with the "at-risk" students as with those not labeled that way. The teachers also were engaging in less dynamic language use with the "at-risk" students. That is, they didn't use as many different words, their sentences were shorter, and they spoke slower, leading to a longer verbal exchange. Now the one-to-one interactions took on new meaning. She couldn't assume that just because there seemed to be more interactions that the students were getting the same content in the interactions.

Geri shared her information with the teachers. They set-up inservices on language learning, and on some general strategies for dealing with "at-risk" students. The teachers agreed to try to make one change at a time, and they all agreed to try to build the vocabulary of the "at-risk" students by raising their levels when they spoke one-on-one to them. Geri was able to then wait a few weeks, and go back to observe. She knew that the teachers now were aware of what she was coding, and therefore may purposely be engaging in the desired behaviors. However, if they were even just making changes for the observation, they were changes, and that was a good starting point for Geri. She again compiled her data, and shared it with the teachers. As a result, they made the decision to start to schedule one-on -one sessions in which they purposely met with and worked on the language skills of the at-risk students.

How Nell Used Observation to Help Her Make Decisions for the Classroom:

In Nell's eight years of teaching, she had only been exposed to the clinical supervision model for observation once. However, as she was searching the literature to learn how to give her colleagues feedback on what she observed, she repeatedly found this model referenced and used in various peer coaching formats. She decided to use this model as she planned and conducted her observations. Prior to the pre-conference meetings, Nell informed the teachers that she was interested in instructional techniques as a focus for the observations. She was giving this a broad definition, and she was interested to see what ideas the teachers had.

Nell was surprised when most teachers began the pre-conference with no concerns about their teaching. They said that Nell was welcome to get her hours of observation done, but they really didn't need feedback from her. Nell decided that the teachers may be concerned about what information was going to the principal, or how she would supply feedback. Nell made copies of several different forms related to instruction. None of them focused specifically on what the teacher said, or solely on what the teacher did. She also provided a sample feedback sheet for each form. She went back to the teachers and told them that they should pick out which form they wanted used. Now, the teachers could see what information was gathered with each form, and they easily chose the forms they wanted used in their classes.

As many teachers chose the same form, Nell was able to compile data which compared the grade levels and subject areas of the curriculum as they related to the instructional techniques, particularly the types and numbers of questions asked by teachers and by students. Nell shared this information, without any teacher names attached, with the teachers she observed. Nell concluded that her 25 hours of observation had not provided enough time for her to gather enough reliable data to draw conclusions about what instructional techniques needed to be used in the classroom (which had been her principal's goal). Rather, she reported that many different techniques were being used, and the teachers needed to know more about what they were doing that was working. Nell proposed that the entire school start using peer coaching as a means to build trust and share techniques.

How Juan Used Observation to Help Him Make Decisions for the Classroom:

Juan had been given inservices on peer coaching, and forms for observing the ways that teachers met student individual differences in the classroom. As Juan thought about it, peer coaches were supposed to work on issues the teachers individually brought to the coaching situation, not on pre-determined areas of concern from the administration. He wondered why the initial focus had been the same across the board. Juan collected the requested data, met with his peers, and began the process of deciding what objective observations would be used next. Juan's administration asked for reports on the process. A few months into the school year, Juan was surprised to see the administration issue a report to the school board requesting money for teacher training. The administration had compiled information from the observations and drawn its own conclusions, making its own decisions.

Juan continued with the process. His group focused on two other issues, and observed each other. They also engaged in some video exchanges to allow them to continue to gather information without taking time to be in each other's classrooms. Juan's hesitations about the process were relieved, and he started to expand on his ideas for how he could use objective observations to help his teaching. By the end of the school year, Juan reported that he had learned some things about his teaching, and the next year would make some changes in his methods based on what he had learned. However, he wanted time to think about how to implement the changes, and to practice them before he began them on a new group of students.

How Miguel Used Observation to Help Him Make Decisions for the School:

Miguel also applied a clinical supervision model to his observational processes. He made it clear to the teachers that he was observing that none of the information he obtained in his first observations would be put in their files. Rather, they were for his decision-making. As he focused on observing instructional methods, he quickly learned the necessity of a good interview to clarify what the teacher typically did, and what the teacher planned on the day of observation. Miguel learned that only a handful of teachers actually did what they normally do when they were being observed. Most reported developing something special for the observation. In some rooms, students even told him that they had "practiced" the lesson already so that they could do well when they were observed. Miguel encountered the serious problem of the observations not being naturally occurring and real.

Miguel also encountered the problem that if he really wanted to compare the techniques of teachers who had been taking classes, attending inservices and keeping current in the field, with those of teachers who were not seeking to continue their education, he had to use the same observation form at various times with the same group of teachers. Based on the literature and working with his superintendent, he made revisions in existing forms so that he could observe specific instructional techniques that were used in the classrooms. As he compiled his data, he remembered that not all the data was accurate, and he was careful to try to not draw too many conclusions from the data he obtained. He did decide that when he had observed, all teachers had used a variety of techniques. He also decided that he needed to have a more specific focus for upcoming observations, and at least part of that focus should be determined by the individual teacher.

Reflecting on the Cases:

Most of the cases have a couple of things in common. The observers learned the importance of good, objective, well-defined observations for their decision making. They also learned that observation takes time and energy, and cooperation. They learned that good observation raised more questions for them, and it was not so easy to jump to conclusions once they had begun observing.

Some of the cases engaged in various types of clinical supervision and peer coaching. They learned how to use the model, and how to make the model work for them. They also learned that the process can easily be integrated into what they do, and used repeatedly to help them with their own learning.

Hopefully, all of the cases presented learned the importance of developing observations based on theory as it is applied to practice. They should have learned that observing is a skill that is built in time. As they become better at the skill, they should be able to expand upon what they think about observing, and develop the forms they need for the observations.

Finally, whether they were in-service or pre-service teachers, they should have learned that observation involves cooperation. Without a cooperative observee, there cannot be a good observation. Without a cooperative classroom, there cannot be a good observation. If the observation is flawed, the observer will be hard-pressed to draw any conclusions and make any decisions. Therefore, it is always in the interest of the observer to take the time to gain the cooperation of those that are being observed!

REVIEW QUESTIONS:

1. What are some of the ways that the observation forms can be used appropriately in the classroom?
2. What are some of the ways that the observation forms can be used inappropriately in the classroom?
3. What is the process for compiling data and making decisions based on observations?
4. What are some of the ways to think about modifying the observation forms?
5. What are some of the ways to think about building observation forms for your use?
6. What are some common ways that the observation forms are misused?

DISCUSSION QUESTIONS:

1. Why is it important to use the observation forms appropriately?
2. Why is it important to be able to modify the observation forms?
3. Why is it important to be able to build your own observation forms?
4. Why should you guard confidentiality when you use observation forms and compile the results of your observations?

CHAPTER 7

A COMPILATION OF THE
OBJECTIVE OBSERVATION FORMS

INTRODUCTION

The various observation forms that are presented throughout the text are compiled in this chapter. These forms are usually blank, allowing you to fill in the various aspects that you are observing, and to define the behaviors or characteristics that you are observing. The forms are designed so that you can copy them and use them, share them, and encourage others to use them when they are observing you.

Please remember when you are using the forms that if you want to be able to compile information as a result of your observations, and if you want to be able to make decisions based on the information that you have obtained, it is usually better that you repeatedly use one form than use a variety of forms once each. It is also helpful for you to remember that you can always develop your own coding systems and keys for the defined behaviors. The nature of putting this text into print did not provide opportunities to present you examples of completed hand-coded systems, and examples of more complex coding systems which can be done by hand. Some observers like to use arrows, or draw lines to show interactions. Some like to draw circles around particular items to denote events or groupings. Some like to circle numbers or circle letters, or the like to denote particular actions on the part of the teacher or the students. It is up to you. As you practice using the forms, I have no doubt that you will find ways to expand upon them, and ways to make them useful for you. That is, afterall, the intent of providing these for you.

Once you have been using the forms, and have developed some defined objective observation that works particularly well, feel free to forward information about it to me. I will, if you give me permission, share it in the next edition of this text.

Form C2A: Preparing for the School Visit

My Name:_____ Date:_____

Part 1:

1. What do I know about the school?
2. What is my philosophy of education?
3. Why do I want to visit the school?
4. What do I hope to learn by being an observer?
5. Do I want to see one teacher or several?
6. Do I want to see one group or students or several?
7. What grade level(s) and subject(s) am I interested in observing?
8. What days and times do I have available?
9. How many hours do I plan on being there each time? In all?
10. Do I have any relatives, friends, colleagues, acquaintances at the school?
11. Do I have any special needs for the school/school official to be aware of?
12. Am I also going to visit another school?

Part 2:

1. What are your policies for visitors and observers?
2. Where is the school located?
3. Where do visitors park?
4. What door should I use?
5. Where is the place I should check in when I arrive?
6. What are the hours that classes are in session?
7. Are they any days the school will be closed or there will be special events that I am not to be there?
8. How is the school organized? Are there grades? Are there teams? Is there departmentalization? Are there combined grades? What grade levels does the school serve?
9. What are the arrangements for special education? Is inclusion used? Are there special education rooms?
10. Does the school have a dress code for teachers? For students? What is the typical dress for teachers? Are there any kinds of clothes or colors that I should avoid?
11. What are the typical student characteristics? Anything I should know before I come in?
12. What is the school motto?
13. What is the average number of students per room? Do the students stay with the same teacher all day? Do the students have recess? Where do the students eat lunch?
14. Is there a teacher break room or work room for observers to sit and write-up notes?
15. Are there any special things that I should know about the school that I have not asked about?

Form C2B: My Memories and Feelings About School

Part 1: Free-write:

What comes to mind when I think of school? What are my best memories? What are my worse memories? What do I feel when I think about these things?

Part 2: Specific questions:

1. How many schools did I attend as I was growing up? Which was my favorite? Why?

2. What were the names of my teachers? What teachers don't I remember? Why do I remember some names and not others? What do I think and feel about the teachers that I remember?

3. Who was my favorite teacher? Why? What did I learn from this teacher?

4. Who was my least liked teacher? Why? What did I learn from this teacher?

5. What was my favorite school subject? Why?

6. What was my least liked school subject? Why?

7. What did I feel about the school office/disciplinarian? When was I sent for discipline? Why?

8. Why did I miss school? What happened when I missed school?

9. What interests did I have with my peers that the school met? What clubs did I participate in?

10. What after-school or out-of-school activities was I involved with?

11. The one word I would use to describe my feelings about school is:

Part 3: Free write:

What do I think I might feel when I am in school observing? What events may trigger feelings or memories? Are there any things that may impact my being a good observer?

Form C2C: While I Visit the School:

Part 1: Just before I enter the school:

What are my thoughts and feelings?

What are my predictions of what I will find when I look around?

Part 2: In the school:

What are my thoughts and feelings?

How is this school similar to the schools I went to?

How is this school different from the schools I went to?

Part 3: Now that I have spent some time looking around:

What do I expect of a good teacher at this school? Is this expectation different from what I would normally expect of a good teacher? If so, how, and why?

What do I expect of a teacher who is having problems? is this expectation different form what I would normally expect? If so, how, and why?

How do the classroom set-ups differ from what I expected?

What do I expect of a well-disciplined student at this school? Is this expectation different from what I would normally expect of a well-disciplined student? If so, how, and why?

What do I expect a teacher to do if a student does not behave appropriately in this school? Is this expectation different from what I would normally expect? If so, how, and why?

What are my other thoughts and feelings?

Form C2D Coding Counting System

School:_____ Room:_____ Teacher:_____

Grade Level____ Subject Matter:_____ Number of Students:_____

Date:_____Start Time:_____ Finish Time:_____Total Observation Time:_____

Room Set-up/Special Information:_____

Definition of Observation:_____

Interval (time span =)	Count of: (behavior =)
1	
2	
3	
4	
5	
6	
7	
8	
9	
10	
11	
12	
13	
14	
15	

Form C2D2: Revised Coding Form for Counting System for Four Items

School:_____ Room:_____ Teacher:_____

Grade Level____ Subject Matter:_____ Number of Students:_____

Date:_____Start Time:_____ Finish Time:_____Total Observation Time:_____

Room Set-up/Special Information:_____

Definition of Observation:_____

Interval (time span =)	Count of: (behavior =)			
	Computer #1	Computer #2	Computer #3	Computer #4
1				
2				
3				
4				
5				
6				
7				
8				
9				
10				
11				
12				
13				
14				
15				
16				
17				
18				
19				
20				

Form C2E: Sign System Coding for Specified Behaviors

School:_____ Room:_____ Teacher:_____

Grade Level_____ Subject Matter:_____ Number of Students:_____

Date:_____Start Time:_____ Finish Time:_____Total Observation Time:_____

Room Set-up/Special Information:_____

Definition of Observation:_____

Five-Minute					Intervals					Behaviors
1	2	3	4	5	6	7	8	9	10	
										T criticizes a student (S)
										T criticizes S in public
										T judges S
										T judges S in public
										T embarrasses S (public)
										T assigns/has small grp tasks
										T assigns/has individual task
										T uses different tasks/group
										T references S learning styles

Form C2F: Example of an Event System Frequency Count

School:_____ Room:_____ Teacher:_____

Grade Level_____ Subject Matter:_____ Number of Students:_____

Date:_____Start Time:_____ Finish Time:_____Total Observation Time:_____

Room Set-up/Special Information:_____

Definition of Observation:_____

Behavioral Event	Frequency of Event to Small Group	Frequency of Event to Individual Ss
Affirmation		
Praise		
Provides information		
Gives assessment		
Explains		
Cues		
Responds to a S		

Form C2G: Symbol Coding Frequency-Sequence Event Recording

School:_____ Room:_____ Teacher:_____

Grade Level____ Subject Matter:_____ Number of Students:_____

Date:_____Start Time:_____ Finish Time:_____Total Observation Time:_____

Room Set-up/Special Information:_____

Definition of Observation:_____

Key:	Affirmation = A	Praise = +	Provides information = >	
	Gives assessment = ^	Explains = !	Cues = //	Responds to a S = <

Event #	Code:	Note: (to whom?)
1		
2		
3		
4		
5		
6		
7		
8		
9		
10		
11		
12		
13		
14		
15		
16		
17		
18		

Form C2H: Duration Recording (with Frequency Count)

School:_____ Room:_____ Teacher:_____

Grade Level_____ Subject Matter:_____ Number of Students:_____

Date:_____Start Time:_____ Finish Time:_____Total Observation Time:_____

Room Set-up/Special Information:_____

Definition of Observation:_____

This recording is done in # of seconds the behavior occurs.

Event #	S1 hands	S2 moves
1		
2		
3		
4		
5		
6		
7		
8		
9		
10		
11		
12		
13		
14		

Form C2l: Duration Recording, with Frequency, and Event Noting

School:_____ Room:_____ Teacher:_____

Grade Level____ Subject Matter:_____ Number of Students:_____

Date:_____Start Time:_____ Finish Time:_____Total Observation Time:_____

Room Set-up/Special Information:_____

Definition of Observation:_____

This duration recording is done in # of seconds the behavior occurs.
The event noting key uses T for teacher and S for another student in the classroom.

Event #	S1 hands	Cue S1	S2 moves	Cue S2
1				
2				
3				
4				
5				
6				
7				
8				
9				
10				
11				
12				
13				
14				

Form C2J: Checklist of Classroom Management

School:_____ Room:_____ Teacher:_____

Grade Level_____ Subject Matter:_____ Number of Students:_____

Date:_____Start Time:_____ Finish Time:_____Total Observation Time:_____

Room Set-up/Special Information:_____

Definition of Observation:_____

___ Teacher states his/her expectations for behavior.
___ Teacher explains what work is supposed to be done.
___ Teacher holds students' accountable for their behaviors.
___ Students follow teacher expectations for behavior.
___ Students do the required work.
___ Students are seen working on school-related tasks.
___ Students follow school rules.
___ Teacher tells students that they are important.
___ Students praise each other.
___ Teacher has students work in small groups.
___ Teacher has students work individually.
___ Students follow established routines.
___ Teacher shows respect for students and their property.
___ Students show respect for teachers.
___ Students show respect for each other and their property.
___ Students are allowed to talk with each other.
___ Students work together to get a group task done.
___ Students say they are responsible for their own learning.
___ Teacher has consequence for misbehavior.
___ Student misbehavior is given consequences.
___ Teacher tells students they should cooperate.
___ Teacher deals with interruptions.
___ Students return to tasks after interruptions.
___ Teachers gives directions.
___ Students follow directions.
___ Teacher sets noise level for tasks.
___ Students function at or below the set noise level for tasks.
___ Teacher has students participate in the classroom tasks and activities.
___ Students volunteer to participate in the classroom tasks and activities.
___ Teacher encourages students to be creative.
___ Teacher encourages the students to problem solve.
___ Teacher encourages the students to think about their behavior.
___ Students serve as resources for each other.
___ Students move from task to task without teacher oversight.
___ Students encourage each other to behave per classroom rules and expectations.

Form C3A: Partial Classroom Schematic

School:_____ Room:_____ Teacher:_____

Grade Level____ Subject Matter:_____ Number of Students:_____

Date:_____Start Time:_____ Finish Time:_____Total Observation Time:_____

Room Set-up/Special Information:_____

Definition of Observation:_____

Key:

Boards

Door

Demonstration Table		Work/Demo Table

B o a r d s	Table of:		Table of:		Table of:
	Table of:		Table of:		Table of:
	Desk of:	Desk of:	Desk of:	Desk of:	Desk of:

Reading area

	Work Table

Resource Table

Teacher's Desk

Storage Cabinets, and Charts

Form C3B: Some Indicators of Cognitive Development Applying Piaget's Theory

School:_____ Room:_____ Teacher:_____

Grade Level____ Subject Matter:_____ Number of Students:_____

Date:_____Start Time:_____ Finish Time:_____Total Observation Time:_____

Room Set-up/Special Information:_____

Definition of Observation:_____

___simple reflexive moves
___imitations centered on own body
___retrieves partially hidden objects
___retrieves hidden object from first place hidden
___searches in many places for hidden object
___engages in deferred imitation
___unaware of other's viewpoints
___inanimate objects have lifelike qualities
___judges based on current perceptions
___centers on one aspect of a situation
___focuses on present, not past and future
___cannot go backward through a series of steps
___wrong linking of events as cause and effect
___cannot group objects into categories
___knows mass stays same as shape changes
___understands relations of distance and time
___coordinates several features of a task
___arranges items in logical series
___can work backwards through a problem
___can infer relationships among objects
___can group objects into categories
___tests hypothesis in an orderly manner
___evaluates abstract verbal statements

Form C3D: Some Possible Intelligence Considerations Based on Typical School Definitions of Intelligence

School:_____ Room:_____ Teacher:_____

Grade Level____ Subject Matter:_____ Number of Students:_____

Date:_____Start Time:_____ Finish Time:_____Total Observation Time:_____

Room Set-up/Special Information:_____

Definition of Observation:_____

Student is able to:
___decode and recognize written words
___correctly spell words orally
___correctly spell words in writing
___listen to spoken prose
___write prose
___speak prose
___listen to a passage and supply deleted words
___read a passage and supply deleted words
___use vocabulary correctly when responding orally
___use vocabulary correctly when responding in writing
___listen to material and immediately recall it verbally
___listen to material and immediately recall it in writing
___use symbols as abbreviations for words
___after studying, recall material that is not required
___after studying, recall material that is required
___listen to a foreign language and repeat the words
___listen to a passage and respond verbally to provide information
___read a passage and respond verbally to provide information
___listen to a passage and respond in writing to provide information
___read a passage and respond in writing to provide information
___listen to a passage and respond verbally to comprehension questions
___read a passage and respond verbally to comprehension questions
___listen to a passage and respond in writing to comprehension questions
___read a passage and respond in writing to comprehension questions
___listen to a passage and discuss how concepts are similar and different
___read a passage and discuss how concepts are similar and different
___listen to a passage and respond in writing how concepts are similar and different
___read a passage and respond in writing how concepts are similar and different
___listen to a problem and do the mathematical calculations without paper
___read a problem and do the mathematical calculations without paper
___do mathematical calculations with the help of a calculator
___listen to and then repeat sequences of words or numbers forward
___listen to and then repeat sequences backwards
___construct a pattern from something that is presented visually
___construct a pattern from something that is presented auditorily
___look at an incomplete picture and identify what is missing
___listen to an incomplete passage and identify what is missing
___look at a set of pictures and place them in sequence
___listen to a set of sentences and place them in sequence
___look at a set of pieces and put them together to form an object
___compare different groups of items presented visually and indicate what they have in common
___work from the beginning to the end of a task, staying with the sequence needed
___work through a task, not necessarily using the generally recognized sequence

___interact appropriately with other
___physically reproduce movements of others
___sustain conversation
___determine what to study
___complete required tasks
___attend to details
___think about things in a new way
___ask for help when needed
___organize a learning task
___make supplementary material useful
___correctly paraphrase
___choose among learning tasks

Form C3E: Learning Styles Adapted from Kolb's Model:

School:_____ Room:_____ Teacher:_____

Grade Level____ Subject Matter:_____ Number of Students:_____

Date:_____Start Time:_____ Finish Time:_____Total Observation Time:_____

Room Set-up/Special Information:_____

Definition of Observation:_____

Directions: For the student you are observing, place a check next to the item which describes what you see happen in the classroom. At the bottom, make any notes that help explain or provide examples of the decisions you made.

Converger
___likes active experimentation
___uses hypothetical-deductive reasoning
___likes learning where there is one correct answer
___does not challenge ideas
___likes to work alone with things
___does not show emotion
___likes to problem solve
___likes technical tasks

Diverger
___likes to think about things instead of experiment with them
___likes brainstorming
___likes to consider multiples perspectives
___is imaginative
___is interested in various cultural dimensions, especially the humanities
___shows emotion
___is oriented toward feelings
___is open-minded

Assimilator
___uses inductive reasoning
___likes to create models and designs
___questions the facts if they don't seem to fit
___likes to follow a plan for learning
___is interested in math and quantitative tasks
___likes to work alone when thinking
___is good at designing experiments
___does not like to make decisions

Accommodator
___likes active experimenting in a trial-and-error manner
___is usually busy
___takes risks, tries new experiences
___likes to interact with others
___often relies on others for analysis
___is able to push his/her ideas on others
___adapts to new situations well
___uses trial and error to solve problems

Notes:

Form C3F: Learning Style Descriptors Adapted from Dunn and Dunn

School:_____ Room:_____ Teacher:_____

Grade Level____ Subject Matter:_____ Number of Students:_____

Date:_____Start Time:_____ Finish Time:_____Total Observation Time:_____

Room Set-up/Special Information:_____

Definition of Observation:_____

Directions: For each behavior or characteristic, place the number that best describes the placement on the continuum scale:
> 1= not observed as a concern
> 2= observed as a minor concern, happens once in awhile
> 3= observed as a concern, happens a few times in class
> 4 =observed as a major concern, happens frequently in class

TIME:
___Student asks what time it is/is seen looking at the clock/is seen looking at his/her watch
___Student asks how much time is allotted for a task
___Student does more work when challenged to "beat the clock"

SCHEDULE:
___Student works on a task over a short interval of time, gets it all done at once
___Student works on a task over a long interval of time, does part now and part later
___Student works on a variety of tasks at once

AMOUNT OF SOUND:
___Student works when there is total quiet
___Student creates noise when there is total quiet
___Student works when there is conversation
___Student works when there are many noisy disruptions
___Student wears ear plugs when working

TYPE OF SOUND:
___Student hums when he/she works
___Student listens to music when he/she works
___Student sings when he/she works
___Student taps out beats when he/she works

TYPE OF GROUP WORK:
___When given choice, student chooses to work alone
___When given choice, student chooses to work in small groups
___When given choice, student chooses to work when whole class is involved

AMOUNT OF PRESSURE AND MOTIVATION:
___Student works when others tell him/her to
___Student works when has own set goals and deadlines
___Student works when others set goals and deadlines
___Student works when given public recognition
___Student works when given external rewards

PLACE:
___Student works in the normal classroom
___Student works at the computer
___Student works in the library
___Student does homework
___Student homework completed, seatwork not completed
___Student seatwork completed, homework not completed

PHYSICAL ENVIRONMENT AND CONDITIONS:
___When given choice, student sits at desk
___When given choice, student sits at table
___When given choice, student sits on the floor
___When given choice, student stands
___When given choice, student sits near window or light
___When given choice, student sits away from window or light
___When given choice, student wears sunglasses
___Student wears heavy clothes even in warm weather
___Student wears light clothes, even in cold weather

TYPE OF ASSIGNMENTS:
___When given choice, student chooses self-directed tasks
___When given choice, student chooses teacher-assigned tasks
___Student works when has work contract
___When given choice, student chooses peer-directed tasks

PERCEPTUAL STRENGTHS AND STYLES:
___Student chooses visual materials to learn
___Student chooses aural materials to learn
___Student chooses printed materials to learn
___Student chooses hands-on/tactile materials to learn
___Student chooses a variety of different kinds of materials to learn

STRUCTURE AND EVALUATION:
___Student chooses a strict structure for the class work
___Student chooses a flexible structure for the class work
___Student self-starts on tasks
___Student inquires as to how well he/she is learning
___Student develops a time-line to complete an ongoing task
___Student does all he/she can on a task at one time

Form C3G: Cognitive Tempo in the Classroom

School:_____ Room:_____ Teacher:_____

Grade Level____ Subject Matter:_____ Number of Students:_____

Date:_____Start Time:_____ Finish Time:_____Total Observation Time:_____

Room Set-up/Special Information:_____

Definition of Observation:_____

Response #	Student							
	#1 Time	#1 Error	#2 Time	#2 Error	#3 Time	#3 Error	#4 Time	#4 Error
1								
2								
3								
4								
5								
6								
7								
8								
9								
10								

Form C3H: Social, Affective Learning Style Differences

School:_____ Room:_____ Teacher:_____

Grade Level____ Subject Matter:_____ Number of Students:_____

Date:_____Start Time:_____ Finish Time:_____Total Observation Time:_____

Room Set-up/Special Information:_____

Definition of Observation:_____

Student Characteristics

Participant _____ **Avoidant**_____

___engages in learning course content
___attends class regularly
___assumes responsibility for learning
___participates in class
___completes required work

___does not engage in learning course content
___misses class
___assumes no responsibility
___does not participate
___does not complete required work

Collaborative _____ **Competitive**

___shares with others
___is cooperative
___enjoys working with others
___interacts with others in class
___is not concerned about winning

___competes, does not share
___tries to do better than others
___enjoys competing
___"shows off" to others
___tries to win

Independent _____ **Dependent**_____

___creates own structure
___works on own without supervision
___will work to learn what is needed
___listens to others
___confident
___curious

___relies on teacher for structure
___needs supervisor to tell what to do
___learns minimum that is required
___listens to teacher only
___lacks confidence
___lacks intellectual curiosity

FORM C3I: A Modified Checklist of Indicators of a Student's Psychosocial Development Applying Erikson's Theory

School:_____ Room:_____ Teacher:_____

Grade Level____ Subject Matter:_____ Number of Students:_____

Date:_____Start Time:_____ Finish Time:_____Total Observation Time:_____

Room Set-up/Special Information:_____

Definition of Observation:_____

Student behavior
- [ ] Allows contact with others
- [ ] Initiates contact with others
- [ ] Allows others near his/her desk
- [ ] Allows others near his/her body
- [ ] Says "No" to some task choices
- [ ] Moves away from others
- [ ] Tries to learn show skills through counting, recitation, etc.
- [ ] Scolds self aloud
- [ ] Shakes head as engages in tasks
- [ ] Refuses to choose a task when given a choice
- [ ] Asks adults for confirmation it is okay to try a task
- [ ] Asks adults if tasks are accomplished appropriately or correctly
- [ ] Initiates play by self with the toy _____ for _____ seconds/minutes
- [ ] Chooses the task of _____, and is seen engaging in this task·
- [ ] Tries a task and stays with it for _____ seconds/minutes
- [ ] Imitates a modeled behavior of _____ for _____seconds
- [ ] Initiates play with others for ____ seconds/minutes
- [ ] Plays with others for ____seconds/minutes
- [ ] Works with others on a task for ____seconds/minutes
- [ ] Work with students in a small group for ____seconds/minutes
- [ ] Cooperates/works with the teacher
- [ ] Refuses to engage in tasks
- [ ] Says aloud is not smart enough to do the task
- [ ] Asks other students for help when engaged in a task
- [ ] Asks teacher for help when engaged in a task
- [ ] Complies with teacher request of _____ for ____seconds/minutes
- [ ] Complies with student request of _____ for ____seconds/minutes
- [ ] Works on a task by self for ____seconds/minutes
- [ ] Comes back to a task when given free time in the class
- [ ] Cleans up after self when completes a task or task time is over
- [ ] Cleans up after self and others when done with small group activity
- [ ] Tells others why task is important
- [ ] Tells others own vocational goals
- [ ] Tells others why learning is important
- [ ] Tells others who they are, what they feel, what they believe
- [ ] Expresses opinions as own in front of peers in classroom
- [ ] Expresses own opinions in front of teacher in classroom
- [ ] Labels friends as such in front of others in classroom
- [ ] Labels close friends/special relationships as such in front of others in classroom
- [ ] Says aloud does not know what will do in the future

Form C3J: Personality Differences as Observed in the Classroom

School:_____ Room:_____ Teacher:_____

Grade Level____ Subject Matter:_____ Number of Students:_____

Date:_____Start Time:_____ Finish Time:_____Total Observation Time:_____

Room Set-up/Special Information:_____

Definition of Observation:_____

The Individual Student:

Surgency

Talkative | **Silent**
___engages in discussion in class | ___engages in discussion only when called upon
___is seen initiating conversation with peers | ___is not seen initiating conservation with peers
___talks out during classtime | ___is silent during classtime
___talks to teacher during class | ___does not talk to teacher during class

Social | **Reclusive**
___is seen initiating contact with others | ___is not seen initiating contact with others
___engages others in work/play | ___works/plays alone
___shares with others | ___does not share with others
___enjoys working with others | ___enjoys working alone
___interacts with others during class | ___interacts with others only when forced to do so
___energetic | ___easily fatigued

Adventurous | **Cautious**
___tries new learning tasks | ___stays with known tasks
___looks to outside world | ___looks inward
___takes chances | ___does not take chances
___moves around the classroom | ___stays in seat or assigned area
___tries out new ideas in class | ___only does assigned work
___speaks mind/ideas | ___keeps ideas to self

Agreeableness

Good natured | **Irritable**
___interacts with others in class | ___complains about others
___jokes with others | ___finds nothing funny
___does not complain, goes with the flow | ___complains about things in the room

Mild | **Headstrong**
___listens to others | ___listens to teacher only
___accepts more than one way of thinking | ___believes own way of thinking is correct
___accepts differences with others | ___believes differences are wrong

Cooperative | **Negativistic**
___shares with others | ___does not share
___presents things positively | ___presents things in negative manner
___finds ways to deal with problems | ___believes problems can't be solved

Conscientiousness

Responsible / Undependable

___engages in learning course content	___does not engage in learning course content
___assumes responsibility for learning	___assumes no responsibility
___participates in class	___does not participate
___completes required work	___does not complete required work
___can be relied upon for leadership	___cannot be relied upon for leadership

Persevering / Quitting

___attends class regularly	___misses class
___works on own without supervision	___needs supervisor to tell what to do
___will work to learn what is needed	___learns minimum that is required
___continues to work on a task until done	___works on task only during assigned time
___refuses to give up on a complicated task	___gives up on a complicated task

Tidy / Carelessness

___cleans up after self	___leaves work area messy
___offers to help clean up room	___does not offer to help clean up room
___carefully erases mistakes	___papers contain smudges and dirty erasures
___papers are handed-in that are clearn	___papers are handed-in that are dirty

Emotional Stability

Calm / Anxious

___calm, relaxed	___restless, tense
___normal rate of speech	___increased rate of speech
___focused attention	___easily distracted
___does not seem threatened	___threatened easily

Composed / Excitable

___confident	___lacks confidence
___emotions are appropriate to situation	___shows emotions inappropriately
___thinks before acts	___immediately reacts in situations

Poised / Nervous

___secure	___insecure
___performs well on tasks	___performs based on others approval
___self-assured, self-confident	___questions self, lacks confidence
___mature	___immature, childish

Intellect

Intellectual / Nonreflective

___curious	___lacks intellectual curiosity
___engages in thinking tasks	___does not think about how to do tasks
___presents alternative ways to do tasks	___does tasks with direction
___accepts new ideas	___rejects new ideas
___tolerates ranges of answers	___looks for right and wrong answers only

Imaginative / Simple

___creates own structure	___relies on teacher for structure
___elaborates	___does not elaborate
___flexible	___inflexible

Artistic / Insensitive

___expands on learning	___does only what is required
___creates designs on worksheets	___not seen doodling, designing
___likes to show work to others	___does not show work to others

Form C3K: Categorizing Student Personality on Introversion/Extroversion

School:_____ Room:_____ Teacher:_____

Grade Level_____ Subject Matter:_____ Number of Students:_____

Date:_____Start Time:_____ Finish Time:_____Total Observation Time:_____

Room Set-up/Special Information:_____

Definition of Observation:_____

Directions: Check all those that are observed as applying to the individual student:

Student name:_____

Extroverts tend to:

___perform complex motor sequences
___be conditioned by positive experiences
___use short-term retention skills
___seek affiliation
___tolerate frustration
___be impulsive
___be friendly, sociable
___take risks
___be energetic
___enjoy numerous tasks at once
___focus on stimuli
___be influenced by others
___be aggressive
___enjoy change
___like disorder
___go with the moment

Introverts tend to:

___read instead of doing motor activities
___be conditioned by negative experiences
___use long-term retention skills
___seek academic achievement
___be intolerant of frustration
___be reflective
___avoid friendship/social situations
___avoid risks
___tire easily
___work on one thing at a time
___ignore interruptions
___use personal values as guides
___shrug from confrontation
___enjoy stability
___like order
___plan ahead

Form C3O: Observing the Humanistic Needs of Students Adapted from Maslow's Theory

School:_____ Room:_____ Teacher:_____

Grade Level____ Subject Matter:_____ Number of Students:_____

Date:_____Start Time:_____ Finish Time:_____Total Observation Time:_____

Room Set-up/Special Information:_____

Definition of Observation: Physiological, safety and security, love and belongingness, self-esteem, self-actualization observed in students.

Checklist part:

☐Student is dressed in weather-appropriate attire
☐Student's clothes are clean
☐Student is bathed, groomed
☐Student has food for meals and snacks
☐Student has no visible bruises, injuries
☐Student has own desk or workspace in classroom
☐Student moves around classroom appropriate to activities
☐Student expresses work-related emotions in the classroom
☐Student cooperates with other students and with the teacher
☐Student raises hand to ask or respond to questions
☐Student praises others for good work
☐Student shows own work to others

Interview part:

1. What things need to be in a classroom so that you feel safe? Are those things in this classroom?

2. What things need to be in a classroom so that you feel that you are part of the classroom? Are those things present in this classroom?

3. Tell me what you know about how you learn. Are the things you need to help your learning provided in this classroom?

4. Tell me what you need to feel good about your self, to feel important. Are the things you need to help you feel good about yourself provided in this classroom?

Form C4A: Physical Behaviors of a Teacher

School:_____ Room:_____ Teacher:_____

Grade Level_____ Subject Matter:_____ Number of Students:_____

Date:_____Start Time:_____ Finish Time:_____Total Observation Time:_____

Room Set-up/Special Information:_____

Definition of Observation:_____

Five-minute Interval	Position of Teacher	# of Students Interacting With	Description of Teacher Physical activity
1			
2			
3			
4			
5			
6			
7			
8			
9			
10			

Form C4B: Observation for Broad Piagetian Theory Applications in the Classroom

School:_____ Room:_____ Teacher:_____

Grade Level____ Subject Matter:_____ Number of Students:_____

Date:_____Start Time:_____ Finish Time:_____Total Observation Time:_____

Room Set-up/Special Information:_____

Definition of Observation:_____

Directions: Check those teacher (T) behaviors that are observed:

___T allows baby simple reflexive moves
___T provides chances for imitations
___T partially hides objects as baby watches
___T allows child to retrieve hidden object
___T allows child to search in many places for hidden object
___T provides for child to engage in deferred imitation
___T allows for child to have own views, even when wrong
___T provides interactions with inanimate objects
___T has child practice making judgments
___T provides various situations for child to learn
___T focuses on present, but also tries to build past and future
___T provides chances to practice a series of steps
___T provides chances to learn cause and effect
___T provides various objects of different groups
___T provides hands on opportunities to work with mass and shapes
___T provides problems with distance and time
___T gives tasks with multiple features
___T gives problems requiring sequencing
___T gives multiple step problems
___T provides objects that have relationships
___T provides objects that can be grouped
___T provides chances to test hypothesis
___T provides opportunities for discussion/reflection

Note: Describe any behaviors of the teacher that further provide evidence of meeting this theory.

Form C4C: Checklist for Teacher Behaviors that Support Student Information Processing

School:_____ Room:_____ Teacher:_____

Grade Level_____ Subject Matter:_____ Number of Students:_____

Date:_____Start Time:_____ Finish Time:_____Total Observation Time:_____

Room Set-up/Special Information:_____

Definition of Observation:_____

___T has students prepare for a new task
___T tells students what kind of learning they will be engaging in
___T tells students what the objectives of the learning are
___T cues students to the task, tells them to pay attention
___T tells students what prior knowledge they will need to use for this task
___T tells students why this learning/task is important
___T tells students how the information is organized
___T tells students how they will be tested to show they have acquired/can use the information
___T provides learning task which involves more than one sense/modality
___T provides information at a pace that students have time to work with the information
___T groups individual bits of data into a chunk
___T provides that no more than five chunks have to be worked with at a time
___T provides information chunks within a conceptual framework
___T shows students more than one way to put the information together
___T allows time for the students to process the information
___T refers to prior learning as it connects to new learning
___T uses familiar terms when explaining the information
___T focuses students on salient information/task cues
___T tells students to ignore extraneous stimuli
___T has students practice the new infprmation
___T provides specific links of the new information to previous learned information
___T asks students questions about their learning
___T tells students to think about what they are learning
___T tells students how to use this information in practice
___T tells students how to use this information in future work
___T provides visual information in accompaniment with aural information
___T labels pictures, graphs, and other visual stimuli
___T associates specific new items with specific familiar items as part of the place method mnemonic device
___T provides an image for linking new items together as part of the link method mnemonic device
___T associates specific new items with familiar pegs as part of the peg method mnemonic device
___T uses a keyword to link items that are to be associated as part of the keyword method mnemonic device
___T uses imagery to associate new items
___T points out the main idea
___T tells students if part of their learning is more important than other parts
___T points out common misconceptions and shows how and why they are incorrect
___T asks adjunct questions about the learning
___T cues students to take notes, underline, draw pictures, etc.
___T provides review of material
___T provides for further learning practice
___T works individually with students on their learning
___T has students work in small groups or individually
___T questions student learning
___T allows three to five seconds after asking a question before seeking a response
___T monitors student practice/work

Form C4D: Vygotskian Strategies in the Classroom

School:_____ Room:_____ Teacher:_____

Grade Level____ Subject Matter:_____ Number of Students:_____

Date:_____Start Time:_____ Finish Time:_____Total Observation Time:_____

Room Set-up/Special Information:_____

Definition of Observation:_____

Scaffolding:
___T uses direct instruction for students who indicate that they do not know how to proceed
___T demonstrates task performance while verbalizing aloud the thinking that guides it
___T simplifies the task by reducing the task to steps
___T provides prompt or dues that help student move on with the task
___T provides questions that focus on the reasons for errors
___T encourages alternative strategy use
___T provides feedback to let students know how well they are learning
___T withdraws support as students show they can work on the task alone

Intersubjectivity:
___T and student discuss how to proceed with task
___T and student negotiate how the learning will occur
___T and student negotiate how to proceed with finishing the task
___T helps students discuss how to proceed with task
___T helps students negotiate how the learning will occur
___T helps students negotiate how to proceed with finishing the task

Cooperative learning:
___T assigns students to mixed ability groups
___T assigns groups to work on tasks
___T holds individuals and the group accountable for the learning
___T has different groups working on different learning
___T monitors group interactions

Reciprocal Teaching:
___T forms collaborative learning groups
___T monitors groups members as they read a passage
___T, or a student monitored by the T, asks questions about the content of the passage
___T, or the student monitored by the T, manages the group as they pose answers, raise additional questions
___T, or the student monitored by the T, summarizes the passage
___T, or the student monitored by the T, leads discussion to achieve consensus on the summary
___T, or the student monitored by the T, helps the group clarify ideas that are ambiguous
___T, or the student monitored by the T, encourages the group to predict upcoming content

Form C4E: Teacher Behaviors Related to Student Classroom Intellectual Skills

School:_____ Room:_____ Teacher:_____

Grade Level____ Subject Matter:_____ Number of Students:_____

Date:_____Start Time:_____ Finish Time:_____Total Observation Time:_____

Room Set-up/Special Information:_____

Definition of Observation:_____

Teacher provides classroom opportunities for the student to:

___decode and recognize written words
___correctly spell words orally
___correctly spell words in writing
___listen to spoken prose
___write prose
___speak prose
___listen to a passage and supply deleted words
___read a passage and supply deleted words
___use vocabulary correctly when responding orally
___use vocabulary correctly when responding in writing
___listen to material and immediately recall it verbally
___listen to material and immediately recall it in writing
___use symbols as abbreviations for words
___after studying, recall material that is not required
___after studying, recall material that is required
___listen to a foreign language and repeat the words
___listen to a passage and respond verbally to provide information
___read a passage and respond verbally to provide information
___listen to a passage and respond in writing to provide information
___read a passage and respond in writing to provide information
___listen to a passage and respond verbally to comprehension questions
___read a passage and respond verbally to comprehension questions
___listen to a passage and respond in writing to comprehension questions
___read a passage and respond in writing to comprehension questions
___listen to a passage and discuss how concepts are similar and different
___read a passage and discuss how concepts are similar and different
___listen to a passage and respond in writing how concepts are similar and different
___read a passage and respond in writing how concepts are similar and different
___listen to a problem and do the mathematical calculations without paper
___read a problem and do the mathematical calculations without paper
___do mathematical calculations with the help of a calculator
___listen to and then repeat sequences of words or numbers forward
___listen to and then repeat sequences backwards
___construct a pattern from something that is presented visually
___construct a pattern from something that is presented auditorily
___look at an incomplete picture and identify what is missing
___listen to an incomplete passage and identify what is missing
___look at a set of pictures and place them in sequence
___listen to a set of sentences and place them in sequence
___look at a set of pieces and put them together to form an object
___compare different groups of items presented visually and indicate what they have in common
___work from the beginning to the end of a task, staying with the sequence needed
___work through a task, not necessarily using the generally recognized sequence

___interact appropriately with others
___physically reproduce movements of others
___sustain conversation
___determine what to study
___complete required tasks
___attend to details
___think about things in a new way
___ask for help when needed
___organize a learning task
___make supplementary material useful
___correctly paraphrase
___choose among learning tasks

Form C4F: Teacher's Use of Learning Styles: Field Dependence and Field Independence

School:_____ Room:_____ Teacher:_____

Grade Level____ Subject Matter:_____ Number of Students:_____

Date:_____Start Time:_____ Finish Time:_____Total Observation Time:_____

Room Set-up/Special Information:_____

Definition of Observation:_____

Teacher provides opportunity for students to:

Field Dependent
___engage in global thinking
___follow a given structure
___be externally directed
___attend to social information
___resolve conflict
___be social
___affiliate with others
___have friends
___work with a provided hypothesis
___work with facts
___be influenced by the format
___use others decisions
___be sensitive to others
___use stress for learning

Field Independent
___engage in analytic thinking
___generate own structure
___be internally directed
___be inattentive to social information
___think things through philosophically
___be distant in social relations
___work alone
___have acquaintances
___generate own hypothesis
___work with concepts
___generate own format
___use own decisions
___be insensitive to others
___ignore external stress for learning

Form C4G: Teacher's Use of Learning Styles Adapted from Kolb's Model:

School:_____ Room:_____ Teacher:_____

Grade Level____ Subject Matter:_____ Number of Students:_____

Date:_____ Start Time:_____ Finish Time:_____Total Observation Time:_____

Room Set-up/Special Information:_____

Definition of Observation:_____

Teacher provides opportunities for students to:
___engage in active experimentation
___use hypothetical-deductive reasoning
___engage in learning where there is one correct answer
___challenge ideas
___work alone with things
___show emotion
___think about things instead of experiment with them
___brainstorm
___consider multiples perspectives
___be imaginative
___explore various cultural dimensions, especially the humanities
___show emotion
___use inductive reasoning
___create models and designs
___question the facts if they don't seem to fit
___follow a plan for learning
___work alone when thinking
___actively experiment in a trial-and-error manner
___take risks, try new experiences
___interact with others
___share analysis with others
___share ideas on others

Notes:

Form C4H: Teacher's Use of Learning Style Descriptors Adapted from Dunn and Dunn

School:_____ Room:_____ Teacher:_____

Grade Level____ Subject Matter:_____ Number of Students:_____

Date:_____Start Time:_____ Finish Time:_____Total Observation Time:_____

Room Set-up/Special Information:_____

Definition of Observation:_____

TIME:
___Teacher allows for the task to be completed with different time frames
___Teacher tells students how much time is allotted for a task
___Teacher allows students to challenge themselves to "beat the clock"

SCHEDULE:
___Teacher allows students to work on a task over a short interval of time, get it all done at once
___Teacher allows student to work on a task over a long interval of time, do part now and part later
___Teacher allows students to work on a variety of tasks at once

AMOUNT OF SOUND:
___Teacher provides a place for students to work in quiet
___Teacher provides a place for students to work where there is noise.
___Teacher allows students to work and converse.
___Teacher allows students to wear ear plugs when working

TYPE OF SOUND:
___Teacher allows students to hum when working
___Teacher allows students to listen to music when working
___Teacher allows students to sing to selves when working
___Teacher allows students to tap out beats when working

TYPE OF GROUP WORK:
___Teacher gives students choice to work alone
___Teacher gives students choice to work in small groups
___Teacher gives students choice to work in large groups

AMOUNT OF PRESSURE AND MOTIVATION:
___Teacher tells students when to work
___Teacher tells students to set their own goals and deadlines
___Teacher tells students to help each other set goals and deadlines
___Teacher gives students public recognition
___Teacher gives students external rewards

PLACE:
___Teacher has students work in normal classroom
___Teacher has students work at the computer
___Teacher has students work in the library
___Teacher assigns students homework
___Teacher assigns students seatwork
___Teacher has some students do seatwork but not homework
___Teacher has some students do homework but not seatwork

PHYSICAL ENVIRONMENT AND CONDITIONS:
___Teacher gives students choice to sit at desk
___Teacher gives students choice to sit at table
___Teacher gives students choice to sit on the floor
___Teacher gives students choice to stand
___Teacher gives students choice to sit near window or light
___Teacher gives students choice to sit away from window or light
___Teacher gives students choice of clothing to wear

TYPE OF ASSIGNMENTS:
___Teacher gives students choices of tasks
___Teacher gives students choices of self-directed tasks
___Teacher gives students work contract
___Teacher gives students choices of peer-directed tasks

PERCEPTUAL STRENGTHS AND STYLES:
___Teacher gives students choice of visual materials for learning
___Teacher gives students choice of aural materials for learning
___Teacher gives students choice of printed materials for learning
___Teacher gives students choice of hands-on/tactile materials for learning
___Teacher gives students choice of different kinds of materials for learning

STRUCTURE AND EVALUATION:
___Teacher gives student choice of structure for the class work
___Teacher allows students to self-start on tasks
___Teacher allows students to inquire as to how well they are learning
___Teacher allows students to develop a time-line to complete an ongoing task
___Teacher allows students to do all they can on a task at one time

Form C4I: Teacher's Use of Cognitive Tempo in the Classroom

School:_____ Room:_____ Teacher:_____

Grade Level_____ Subject Matter:_____ Number of Students:_____

Date:_____Start Time:_____ Finish Time:_____Total Observation Time:_____

Room Set-up/Special Information:_____

Definition of Observation:_____

Teacher Question #	Amount of Seconds Before Seeks Respondent	Hand Was Raised? Yes/No	Amount of Seconds Before Seeks Respondent Again	Hand Was Raised? Yes/No
1				
2				
3				
4				
5				
6				
7				
8				
9				
10				

Form C3J: Teacher Dealing with Student Social, Affective Learning Style Differences

School:_____ Room:_____ Teacher:_____

Grade Level____ Subject Matter:_____ Number of Students:_____

Date:_____Start Time:_____ Finish Time:_____Total Observation Time:_____

Room Set-up/Special Information:_____

Definition of Observation:_____

Teacher provides opportunities for students to:

Participant_____ **Avoidant**_____

___engage in learning course content   ___avoid engaging in learning course content
___attend class regularly   ___miss class
___assume responsibility for learning   ___not take responsibility
___participate in class   ___not participate
___complete required work   ___not complete required work

Collaborative_____ **Competitive**_____

___share with others   ___compete
___be cooperative   ___try to do better than others
___work with others   ___work alone
___interact with others in class   ___"show off" to others
___focus on participating, not winning   ___try to win

Independent_____ **Dependent**_____

___create own structure   ___rely on teacher for structure
___work on own without supervision   ___have a supervisor tell them what to do
___work to learn what is needed   ___learn the minimum that is required
___listen to others   ___listen to the teacher only
___be confident   ___be unsure of self
___be curious   ___lack intellectual curiosity

Form C4K: **Teacher Application of a Modified Checklist of Indicators of a Student's Psychosocial Development Using Erikson's Theory**

School:_____ Room:_____ Teacher:_____

Grade Level_____ Subject Matter:_____ Number of Students:_____

Date:_____ Start Time:_____ Finish Time:_____ Total Observation Time:_____

Room Set-up/Special Information:_____

Definition of Observation:_____

Teacher provides opportunities for students to:
- [ ] Have contact with others
- [ ] Initiate contact with others
- [ ] Have others near his/her desk
- [ ] Have others near his/her body
- [ ] Say "No" to some task choices
- [ ] Move away from others
- [ ] Try to learn show skills through counting, recitation, etc.
- [ ] Scold self aloud
- [ ] Shake head as engages in tasks
- [ ] Refuse to choose a task when given a choice
- [ ] Ask adults for confirmation it is okay to try a task
- [ ] Ask adults if tasks are accomplished appropriately or correctly
- [ ] Initiate play by self with the toy _____ for _____ seconds/minutes
- [ ] Choose the task of _____
- [ ] Try a task and stay with it for _____ seconds/minutes
- [ ] Imitate a modeled behavior of _____ for _____seconds
- [ ] Initiate play with others for _____ seconds/minutes
- [ ] Play with others for _____seconds/minutes
- [ ] Work with others on a task for _____seconds/minutes
- [ ] Work in a small group for _____seconds/minutes
- [ ] Cooperate/work with the teacher
- [ ] Refuse to engage in tasks
- [ ] Say aloud is not smart enough to do the task
- [ ] Ask other students for help when engaged in a task
- [ ] Ask teacher for help when engaged in a task
- [ ] Comply with teacher request of _____ for _____seconds/minutes
- [ ] Comply with student request of _____ for _____seconds/minutes
- [ ] Work on a task by self for _____seconds/minutes
- [ ] Come back to a task when given free time in the class
- [ ] Clean up after self when completes a task or task time is over
- [ ] Clean up after self and others when done with small group activity
- [ ] Tell others why task is important
- [ ] Tell others own vocational goals
- [ ] Tell others why learning is important
- [ ] Tell others who they are, what they feel, what they believe
- [ ] Express opinions as own in front of peers in classroom
- [ ] Express own opinions in front of teacher in classroom
- [ ] Label friends as such in front of others in classroom
- [ ] Label close friends/special relationships as such in front of others in classroom
- [ ] Say aloud does not know what will do in the future

Form C4L: Teacher Application of Personality Differences as Seen in the Classroom

School:_____ Room:_____ Teacher:_____

Grade Level____ Subject Matter:_____ Number of Students:_____

Date:_____Start Time:_____ Finish Time:_____Total Observation Time:_____

Room Set-up/Special Information:_____

Definition of Observation:_____

Teacher provides opportunities for the individual student to:

Surgency

Talkative | **Silent**
___engage in discussion in class | ___engage in discussion only when called upon
___initiate conversation with peers | ___initiate conservation with peers
___talk out during classtime | ___be silent during classtime
___talk to teacher during class | ___not talk to teacher during class

Social | **Reclusive**
___initiate contact with others | ___not initiate contact with others
___engage others in work/play | ___not engage others in work/play
___share with others | ___not share with others
___work with others | ___work alone
___interact with others during class | ___interact with others only when forced to do so
___be energetic | ___be fatigued

Adventurous | **Cautious**
___try new learning tasks | ___stay with known tasks
___look to outside world | ___look inward
___take chances | ___not take chances
___move around the classroom | ___stay in seat or assigned area
___try out new ideas in class | ___only do assigned work
___speak mind/ideas | ___keep ideas to self

Agreeableness

Good natured | **Irritable**
___interact with others in class | ___complain about others
___joke with others | ___find nothing funny
___not complain, goes with the flow | ___complain about things in the room

Mild | **Headstrong**
___listen to others | ___listen to teacher only
___accept more than one way of thinking | ___believe own way of thinking is correct
___accept differences with others | ___believe differences are wrong

Cooperative | **Negativistic**
___share with others | ___not share
___present things positively | ___present things in negative manner
___finds ways to deal with problems | ___believe problems can't be solved

Conscientiousness

Responsible / **Undependable**

___engage in learning course content	___not engage in learning course content
___assume responsibility for learning	___assume no responsibility
___participate in class	___not participate
___complete required work	___not complete required work
___be relied upon for leadership	___not be relied upon for leadership

Persevering / **Quitting**

___attend class regularly	___miss class
___work on own without supervision	___need supervisor to tell what to do
___work to learn what is needed	___learn minimum that is required
___continue to work on a task until done	___work on task only during assigned time
___refuse to give up on a complicated task	___give up on a complicated task

Tidy / **Carelessness**

___clean up after self	___leave work area messy
___offer to help clean up room	___not offer to help clean up room
___carefully erase mistakes	___have papers contain smudges and dirty erasures
___hand-in papers that are clean	___hand-in papers that are dirty

Emotional Stability

Calm / **Anxious**

___be calm, relaxed	___be restless, tense
___talk at a normal rate of speech	___talk at an increased rate of speech
___focus attention	___be easily distracted
___not seem threatened	___be easily threatened

Composed / **Excitable**

___be confident	___lack confidence
___show emotions appropriate to situation	___show emotions inappropriately
___think before acts	___immediately react in situations

Poised / **Nervous**

___be secure	___be insecure
___perform well on tasks	___perform based on others approval
___be self-assured, self-confident	___question self, lack confidence
___be mature	___be immature, childish

Intellect

Intellectual / **Nonreflective**

___be curious	___lack intellectual curiosity
___engage in thinking tasks	___not think about how to do tasks
___present alternative ways to do tasks	___do tasks with direction
___accept new ideas	___reject new ideas
___tolerate ranges of answers	___look for right and wrong answers only

Imaginative / **Simple**

___create own structure	___rely on teacher for structure
___elaborate	___not elaborate
___be flexible	___be inflexible

Artistic / **Insensitive**

___expand on learnings	___do only what is required
___create designs on worksheets	___not engage in doodling, designing
___show work to others	___not show work to others

Form C4M: Teacher Application of Introversion/Extroversion in the Classroom

School:_____ Room:_____ Teacher:_____

Grade Level____ Subject Matter:_____ Number of Students:_____

Date:_____Start Time:_____ Finish Time:_____Total Observation Time:_____

Room Set-up/Special Information:_____

Definition of Observation:_____

Teacher provides student opportunities to:

Be Extroverts:_____ **Be Introverts:**

___perform complex motor sequences   ___read instead of doing motor activities
___be conditioned by positive experiences   ___be conditioned by negative experiences
___use short-term retention skills   ___use long-term retention skills
___seek affiliation   ___seek academic achievement
___tolerate frustration   ___be intolerant of frustration
___be impulsive   ___be reflective
___be friendly, sociable   ___avoid friendship/social situations
___take risks   ___avoid risks
___be energetic   ___tire easily
___enjoy numerous tasks at once   ___work on one thing at a time
___focus on stimuli   ___ignore interruptions
___be influenced by others   ___use personal values as guides
___be aggressive   ___shrug from confrontation
___enjoy change   ___enjoy stability
___like disorder   ___like order
___go with the moment   ___plan ahead

Form C4N: Teacher Language Development in the Classroom

School:_____ Room:_____ Teacher:_____

Grade Level____ Subject Matter:_____ Number of Students:_____

Date:_____Start Time:_____ Finish Time:_____Total Observation Time:_____

Room Set-up/Special Information:_____

Definition of Observation:_____

Teacher does the following:
___uses adult language, not baby talk
___engages in vocal exchanges with students
___encourages proper pronunciation of works
___gives students new words to learn
___takes turns in conversations with students
___uses proper grammar
___adjusts speech with social expectations
___gives students words to learn that have multiple meanings
___uses multi-syllabic words
___uses passive voice and other complex grammatical structures
___uses words which have abstract meanings
___uses referential language
___has students make up stories and conversations
___uses visual aids to supplement printed materials
___allows students to use dialect
___allows students to use vernacular
___allows students to use native language
___gives feedback to students about their language development
___praises students for attempting to use language
___explains grammar
___explains irregularities in language

Copyright © 1997 by Allyn and Bacon

Form C4O: **Teacher** **Social** **Development** **in** **the** **Classroom**

School:_____ Room:_____ Teacher:_____

Grade Level____ Subject Matter:_____ Number of Students:_____

Date:_____Start Time:_____ Finish Time:_____Total Observation Time:_____

Room Set-up/Special Information:_____

Definition of Observation:_____

Teacher provides students the opportunity to:
___engage in play activities with other students
___give help to each other
___receive help from each other
___practice taking turns
___seek help from other students
___tease others appropriately
___practice kindness to other students
___practice fairness to other students
___practice giving consideration to other students' needs
___practice giving consideration to other students' opinions
___provide encouragement to other students
___provide praise to each other
___play games that have rules
___learn how to play games with rules
___explain how to play games to others
___practice self-control with others
___engage in play activities
___interact with various groups of students
___develop friendships with age mates
___develop friendships with both genders
___practice using emotions
___practice imitating appropriate behaviors
___accept strengths and weaknesses of peers
___choose to conform or not conform to peer demands
___respond negatively to direct peer pressures
___practice modeling peer behaviors
___engage in rough-and-tumble play
___interpret other people's thoughts and feelings
___respond to other people's thoughts and feelings
___practice taking other people's perspectives
___practice third party thinking and feeling

Form C4P: Interview for Teacher Development of Morals in the Classroom

School:_____ Room:_____ Teacher:_____

Grade Level_____ Subject Matter:_____ Number of Students:_____

Date:_____Start Time:_____ Finish Time:_____Total Observation Time:_____

Room Set-up/Special Information:_____

Definition of Observation:_____

> **Directions:** This is a structured interview. Use the questions below. Write down the responses for each question. Try not to show emotion as you ask the questions or listen to the answers.

1. Tell me what you know about the state laws regarding your teaching about morals in the classroom.

2. Tell me about how you run your classroom. What are the classroom rules? What are the rewards for following the rules? What are the consequences for not following the rules?

3. What vocabulary do you use with the students to explain the rules and procedures in the classroom?

4. What responsibilities do your students typically have on a day-to-day basis?

5. What, if any, responsibilities do your students get to earn?

6. What do you tell a student that you are giving consequences or punishments? Please give me an example.

7. What are your procedures for special disciplinary issues?

8. Tell me what you teach about the social order, and what societal behaviors are considered normal. Please give me an example.

9. Tell me how you handle the concept of teaching moral development in the classroom.

10. Tell me what you teach your students about justice and ethics.

11. Please tell me anything else I should know about moral development in your classroom.

Form C4Q: Applying Bronfenbrenner's Model to Teachers

School:_____ Room:_____ Teacher:_____

Grade Level____ Subject Matter:_____ Number of Students:_____

Date:_____Start Time:_____ Finish Time:_____Total Observation Time:_____

Room Set-up/Special Information:_____

Definition of Observation:_____

Directions: Record the interactions of one teacher with other teachers. While this is an anecdotal record, make sure you are as objective as possible.

Date	Time	Interacted with whom?	Description of the nature of the interaction	Length of interaction

Form C4R: **Teacher** **Report** **of** **Meeting** **the** **Humanistic** **Needs** **of** **Students** **as** **Adapted** **from** **Maslow's** **Theory**

School:_____ Room:_____ Teacher:_____

Grade Level_____ Subject Matter:_____ Number of Students:_____

Date:_____ Start Time:_____ Finish Time:_____Total Observation Time:_____

Room Set-up/Special Information:_____

1. Please describe how you determine the humanistic needs of your students.

2. Please describe how you determine what student needs are important to meet in your classroom.

3. Please describe how you try to meet the important student needs in your classroom.

4. Please describe how you deal with students having different needs.

Form C4S: Teacher Modeling Behaviors in the Classroom per Social Learning Theory

School:_____ Room:_____ Teacher:_____

Grade Level_____ Subject Matter:_____ Number of Students:_____

Date:_____Start Time:_____ Finish Time:_____Total Observation Time:_____

Room Set-up/Special Information:_____

Definition of Observation:_____

Behavior Modeled:_____
____Teacher tells students to pay attention/watch
____Teacher performs/models the behavior of _____
____Teacher has a student perform/model the behavior
____Teacher has the class students perform/practice the behavior
____Teacher provides the reinforcement of _____for students who successfully model the
behavior.

Behavior Modeled:_____
____Teacher tells students to pay attention/watch
____Teacher performs/models the behavior of _____
____Teacher has a student perform/model the behavior
____Teacher has the class students perform/practice the behavior
____Teacher provides the reinforcement of _____for students who successfully model the
behavior.

Behavior Modeled:_____
____Teacher tells students to pay attention/watch
____Teacher performs/models the behavior of _____
____Teacher has a student perform/model the behavior
____Teacher has the class students perform/practice the behavior
____Teacher provides the reinforcement of _____for students who successfully model the
behavior.

Behavior Modeled:_____
____Teacher tells students to pay attention/watch
____Teacher performs/models the behavior of _____
____Teacher has a student perform/model the behavior
____Teacher has the class students perform/practice the behavior
____Teacher provides the reinforcement of _____for students who successfully model the
behavior.

Form C4T: Teacher Use of Locus of Control and Self-Regulation Theories in the Classroom

School:_____ Room:_____ Teacher:_____

Grade Level____ Subject Matter:_____ Number of Students:_____

Date:_____Start Time:_____ Finish Time:_____Total Observation Time:_____

Room Set-up/Special Information:_____

Definition of Observation:_____

Incident #	# minutes teacher does task	# minutes teacher has students do task	Teacher verbalization about responsibility for student successes and failures (who is to blame?)

Form C5A: Student-Teacher Interaction During Cooperative Learning Session

School:_____ Room:_____ Teacher:_____

Grade Level_____ Subject Matter:_____ Number of Students:_____

Date:_____Start Time:_____ Finish Time:_____Total Observation Time:_____

Room Set-up/Special Information:_____

Definition of Observation:_____

Key:	@ = student who has assigned role to interact with teacher as contact
	# = student who has assigned role as manager
	% = student who has assigned role as writer
	* = student who has assigned role as encourager
	< = student interaction with teacher
	> = teacher interaction with student
	] = teacher interacts with whole team
	} = teacher interacts with whole class
	1, 2, 3... = order of interaction

Directions: Draw the classroom, and use the key above to engage in keeping track of the student-teacher interactions during cooperative learning among one or more groups of students.

Form C5B-example: Who Initiates Student-Teacher Contacts

School:_____ Room:_____ Teacher:_____

Grade Level_____ Subject Matter:_____ Number of Students:_____

Date:_____Start Time:_____ Finish Time:_____Total Observation Time:_____

Room Set-up/Special Information:_____

Definition of Observation:_____

key:	R< = student who is tutor initiates contact with teacher
	E< = student who is tutee initiates contact with teacher
	#< = both students initiate contact with teacher
	>R = teacher initiates contact with student who is tutor
	>E = teacher initiates contact with student who is tutee
	># = teacher initiates contact with both students
	1, 2, 3...= actual number of tasks completed for each group

Directions: Draw the classroom below. Using the key above, keep track of the student and teacher initiated contacts during peer tutoring.

Form C5C: Teacher and At-Risk Student Interactions

School:_____ Room:_____ Teacher:_____

Grade Level_____ Subject Matter:_____ Number of Students:_____

Date:_____Start Time:_____ Finish Time:_____Total Observation Time:_____

Room Set-up/Special Information:_____

Definition of Observation:_____

Time	Student Verbalization	Student Behavior	Teacher Verbalization	Teacher Behavior

Form C5D: Teacher and Special Needs Student Interactions

School:_____ Room:_____ Teacher:_____

Grade Level____ Subject Matter:_____ Number of Students:_____

Date:_____Start Time:_____ Finish Time:_____Total Observation Time:_____

Room Set-up/Special Information:_____

Definition of Observation:_____

Student Name: Special Need:	
Teacher:	Student responds by:
says to student:	
indicates that the learning task for the student is modified by:	
indicates that the learning assessment for the student is modified by:	
references study skills and learning strategies for the student:	
provides routine for the student of:	
focuses on student's abilities by:	

Form C5E: Teacher and Gifted Student Interactions

School:_____ Room:_____ Teacher:_____

Grade Level____ Subject Matter:_____ Number of Students:_____

Date:_____Start Time:_____ Finish Time:_____Total Observation Time:_____

Room Set-up/Special Information:_____

Definition of Observation:_____

In this school, gifted is defined as:_____

Student Name: _____ Special gift:_____	
Teacher:	Student responds by:
says to student:	
indicates that the learning task for the student is modified by:	
indicates that the learning assessment for the student is modified by:	
references the student's giftedness by:	
provides special opportunities for the student by:	
focuses on student's abilities by:	

Form C5F: Creative Student Interactions with the Teacher

School:_____ Room:_____ Teacher:_____

Grade Level____ Subject Matter:_____ Number of Students:_____

Date:_____Start Time:_____ Finish Time:_____Total Observation Time:_____

Room Set-up/Special Information:_____

Definition of Observation:_____

Student Name: Student:	Teacher responds by:
indicates his/her choice of learning tasks by:	
engages on working on a learning task by:	
changes to other approaches to learn by:	
focuses on evaluation by:	
develops new, unique solution of:	
otherwise evidences creativity by:	

Form C5G: Teacher-Student Interactions Related to Gender Equity in the Classroom

School:_____ Room:_____ Teacher:_____

Grade Level____ Subject Matter:_____ Number of Students:_____

Date:_____Start Time:_____ Finish Time:_____Total Observation Time:_____

Room Set-up/Special Information:_____

Definition of Observation:_____

Directions: For the first part, keep track of the number of times that the teacher says something related to, or uses the phrases, by putting a slash on the line prior to the item. Immediately following the item, make any specific notes for clarification or examples. For the second part, look at the task materials and test, and count the number of instances, again noting them with slashes on the line prior to the item. Note examples after the item.

Part One: Teacher verbalizations: Number of times teacher says:
_____"boys and girls"
_____"girls and boys"
_____boys can..
_____girls can...
_____calls on goys
_____calls on girls
_____something related to luck
_____how the teacher likes
_____boys clothes/dress are...
_____girls clothes/dress are...
_____girls can do what boys do
_____girls and boys/boys and girls are to work together
_____girls and boys/boys and girls can cry, have other emotions
_____boys and girls/girls and boys have same tasks to do
_____boys should put forth effort
_____girls should put forth effort
_____boys have ability
_____girls have ability
_____the task is hard for boys
_____the task is hard for girls

Part Two: Analysis of Materials and Tests: Number of times:
_____"he" appears in text
_____"she" appears in text
_____male examples
_____female examples
_____females in traditional male roles
_____males in traditional female roles
_____males in traditional male roles
_____females in traditional female roles

Form C5H: Observing Touching Behaviors in the Classroom

School:_____ Room:_____ Teacher:_____

Grade Level_____ Subject Matter:_____ Number of Students:_____

Date:_____Start Time:_____ Finish Time:_____Total Observation Time:_____

Room Set-up/Special Information:_____

Definition of Observation:_____

Person who initiates touching	Person who receives touch	Reaction of receiver	Permission to touch requested?

Form C5I: Structured Interview with a Teacher Related to Cultural Interactions

School:_____ Room:_____ Teacher:_____

Grade Level____ Subject Matter:_____ Number of Students:_____

Date:_____ Room Set-up/Special Information:_____

Please respond to the following questions. Please be honest in your answers.

1. What culture(s) do you participate in, practice the beliefs of, and feel you are a part of?
2. What are the predominant cultural practices that you engage in in the classroom?
3. What language(s) do you speak?
4. What language (s) do your students speak?
5. A student speaks his/her non-English native language in your classroom. What is your response?
6. What specific things do you do to help students learn English in your classroom?
7. How do your students define success? How do you define success for your students? What do you do in the classroom to compare the differences in definitions?
8. What do you do when students lack the resources they need for learning in your classroom?
9. What behaviors do your students engage in that you do not think are part of the dominate/majority culture? How do you react when they do these things?
10. How do your students show respect, and to whom do they show it? How do you show you respect them?
11. How do your students show their feelings, and to whom do they show them? How do you show your feelings?
12. How do your students show that they know the answer, and to whom do they show this? How do you acknowledge this in the classroom?
13. How do your students show that they are thinking, and to whom do they show this? How do you acknowledge this in the classroom?
14. How do your students socialize with others in the classroom? What socializing do you have in your classroom? How do you socialize with your students?
15. What work do you have students do individually? What work do you have students do in groups? What do you tell students about the differences between individual and group accountability?
16. What interactions do you have with parents of your students? Please describe some typical interactions.

Form C5J: Multicultural Education Integrated into a Lesson

School:_____ Room:_____ Teacher:_____

Grade Level_____ Subject Matter:_____ Number of Students:_____

Date:_____Start Time:_____ Finish Time:_____Total Observation Time:_____

Room Set-up/Special Information:_____

Definition of Observation:_____

___ethnic content and perspectives are incorporated into the lesson
___instructional materials treat racial and ethnic differences and groups realistically
___instructional materials treat racial and ethnic differences sensitively
___resources for learning are representative of various racial, ethnic, and cultural groups
___classroom decorations reflect various racial, ethnic, and cultural groups
___instructional processes accommodate ethnic and cultural differences in learning styles
___instructional processes accommodate ethnic and cultural differences in behaviors
___instructional materials respect the dignity and worth of students as individuals
___instructional materials respect the dignity and worth of students as members of various groups
___instructional processes provide opportunities for students to develop a better sense of self
___instructional materials provide support for students to strengthen their self concepts
___instructional materials allow the student to examine the diversity across and within groups
___instructional materials provide the student the opportunity to explore the similarities and differences of groups within U.S. society
___instructional processes provide students opportunities to develop decision-making abilities
___instructional processes provide students opportunities to develop social participation skills
___instructional processes provide students opportunities to distinguish facts from opinions in various cultures
___instructional processes provide students opportunities to develop skills in obtaining and using information from various cultures
___instructional processes allow those students for whom English is a second language a chance to clarify and develop their vocabulary
___assessment processes take into account ethnic and cultural differences among students

Form C5K: Teacher and Student Interactions with Technology in a Classroom

School:_____ Room:_____ Teacher:_____

Grade Level____ Subject Matter:_____ Number of Students:_____

Date:_____Start Time:_____ Finish Time:_____Total Observation Time:_____

Room Set-up/Special Information:_____

Definition of Observation:_____

1.   The classroom technology that is visible is:

2.   The teacher uses the technology by:

3.   The number of minutes that the teacher uses technology is:

4.   The student uses the technology by:

5.   The number of minutes that the student uses technology is:

6.   The teacher interacts with the student related to technology by:

7.   The teacher and the student(s) use technology together by:

8.   An example of what the teacher says about technology is:

9.   Examples of what the students say about technology are:

Form C5L: Teacher Motivational Techniques and The Associated Student Outcomes

School:_____ Room:_____ Teacher:_____

Grade Level____ Subject Matter:_____ Number of Students:_____

Date:_____Start Time:_____ Finish Time:_____Total Observation Time:_____

Room Set-up/Special Information:_____

Definition of Observation:_____

Teacher:
___designs learning task that is challenging
___designs learning task that can be completed with a reasonable amount of effort
___divides difficult tasks into subgoals that are achievable without requiring excessive effort
___provides diverse opportunities for students to demonstrate mastery
___differentiates tasks across students and over time
___adapts instruction to students' knowledge and experience
___designs tasks for exploration and experimentation
___defines success in terms of mastery and personal improvement
___designs tasks where students have an equal opportunity to be involved, and if the task is competitive, students have an equal chance to win
___provides clear and frequent feedback conveying developing competence.
___provides rewards contingent on effort, improvement, and good performance
___avoids unnecessary differential treatment of high and low achievers
___focuses on effort and strategy as primary causes of failure
___uses rewards only when necessary
___emphasizes the informational purpose of rewards
___provides substantive, informative evaluation that is based on mastery rather than on social norms
___treats errors and mistakes as a normal part of learning

Student:
___says/indicates expects to succeed
___says/indicates is academically competent
___says/indicates rewards on contingent on behavior
___says/indicates has ability to produce behavior upon which rewards are contingent
___says/indicates that poor outcomes are attributable to low effort or poor strategy
___approaches tasks without teacher reprimand to do so
___seeks help for task work
___persists when encounters difficulty
___takes pride in success
___says/indicates feelings of mastery
___says/indicates enjoys the task
___selects challenging tasks
___uses effective problem-solving strategies

Form C5M: **Questionnaire** **for** **Students:** **Assessing** **Student** **Learning**

School:_____ Room:_____ Teacher:_____

Grade Level_____ Your Name:_____

Today's Date_____ Person who helped with this form?_____

You are given a task to do, something to learn.
    What kind of task would you like it to be?
        What should the teacher give you do to?
    What kind of task do you do best?
        Did you ever tell the teacher that this is how you do best?
    Would you like to work on this task alone, or would you like help?
        If you want help, who would you like to help you?
    Should the teacher give you homework for this task?
        If you have homework, do you do it?
        If you have homework, what do you think about when you do it?
    Do you want to be graded for your work?
    Do you want to earn the grade alone or with others?
    What do you think a good grade is?
        What do you think when you earn a good grade?
        What do you think when you earn a grade that is not so good?

After you do the task, the teacher says that you have to show that you know how to do the task, that you learned the skill.
    If it was up to you, how would you show the teacher that you learned the task?
    If the teacher let you do this task, and you did well, why would you have done well?
    What would you say to yourself?
    If the teacher let you do this task, and instead of doing well you did poorly, why would you have done poorly?
        What would you say to yourself?
    Would you like to take a test?
        If so, what kind of test?
        If not, why not?
    Would you like to do something in front of others to show that you learned?
        If so, what would you like to do?
        If not, why not?

Pretend for a minute that the teacher says that you have to put away your books and take a hard test.
    What do you think about?
    If you start taking the test and you know the material, what do you think about?
    If you continue taking the test and it gets hard, and you don't know the material, what do you think about?

Pretend for a minute that your care-givers, your parents, relatives, or others who care about you, are coming to school to see your work.
    Who is most likely to come?
    What work are you going to show them? Why?
    What work are you not going to show them? Why?
    What will they say about the work that you show them?
    What will they tell the teacher about your work?

Form C5N: Student and Teacher Response Sheet for Portfolio Work

Student Completes This Part:

My Name Is:_____ Room #_____

Today's Date is:_____. My teacher is _____

This work is called:_____Grade_____

In completing this work I learned:

I want to put this in my portfolio because:

I did this work with the help of:

I would like to learn more about:

_____

Teacher response:

Date:_____ Room #_____Name_____

I have read the work. I think that the student learned:

The student should be proud of:

I would like the student to learn to:

Form C5O: Student Conflict Resolution Worksheet

My name is:_____My conflict is with _____

1. My problem is: OR: I need: (Use an "I" message)

2. Tell your problem to the person you have a conflict with. Make sure you use "I" messages.

3. Now, listen to the other person, what does the other person need? Write down what you think you heard the other person needs.

4. Once you have agreement that each of you has a clear understanding of the other person's needs, brainstorm possible solutions. Write down the possible solutions here.

5. For each solution you wrote in #4, write down a possible consequence after it. Then, discuss these, and choose the best solution. The solution we choose is:

6. Now, describe how you are going to implement the solution. Determine who is going to do what and by when.

Form C5P: Teacher Use of Behavior Modification with a Student

School:_____ Room:_____ Teacher:_____

Grade Level____ Subject Matter:_____ Number of Students:_____

Date:_____Start Time:_____ Finish Time:_____Total Observation Time:_____

Room Set-up/Special Information:_____

Part 1: Interview with the teacher:

1. We are focusing on a student who is having problems with inappropriate behavior in the classroom. What is the problem behavior?

2. What observable behavior would you like to have occur instead?

3. What do you know that the student's likes? What will the student do work for to obtain?

4. What do you know that the student's dislikes? What will the student try to avoid?

5. There are typically four options for dealing with the behavior. You can give the student something he/she likes when he/she engages in the desired behavior. You can take away something the student does not like when he/she engages in the desired behavior. You can also punish the student for engaging in the behavior you want to change. In punishment, you either give the student something he/she dislikes, or take away something he/she likes. Which of the four possible choices for reinforcement or punishment did you choose? Why?

Part 2: Observation of the teacher-student interaction

1. The problem behavior occurs a total of _____ times (keep track).

2. When the problem behavior occurs, the teacher tell the student:

3. When the problem behavior occurs, the teacher (describe teacher behavior):

4. When the problem behavior occurs, and the teacher reacts, the student (describe student reaction to teacher's reaction):

5. When the desired, appropriate behavior occurs, the teacher tells the student:

6. When the desired, appropriate behavior occurs, the teacher (describe teacher behavior):

7. When the desired, appropriate behavior occurs, and the teacher reacts, the student (describe student reaction to teacher's reaction):

8. The desired behavior occurs a total of _____times (keep track).

Form C5Q: Parental/Care-taker Questionnaire

My Name is:_____ My student's name is_____

The date is:_____ My student is in grade:_____ The teacher is:_____

As the parent/care-taker of this student, you have a lot of information which is important for the teacher to know. Please share those things you would like the teacher to know.

1. The time that you get to spend with the student is important, and may vary by your schedule and your student's schedule.

    A. During the average weekday night, how much time do you get to spend with your student?

    B. What do you get to do during that time?

2.   A. What are the activities that you and your child get to do together?

    B. What does your child particularly like to do?

    C. What does your child not like to do?

3.   A. When you teach your child something, what works? How do you think that your child best learns?

4.   A. What type of homework is easy for your child?

    B. What type of homework is difficult?

    C. What can the teacher do to make the difficult learning easier?

5.   A. What do you expect your child to achieve in school?

    B. What grades?

    C. What would you like him/her to do once he/she is done with school?

6.   A. Do you have time to provide some help for the teacher and the school? If so, what can you offer?

Form C5R: Getting ready for the Preconference Meeting for Clinical Supervision Observation: To Be Completed by the Teacher who is to be Observed

To prepare for the preconference, the teacher who is going to be observed needs to conceptualize and clarify the classroom behaviors that are of a concern. The teacher should complete this worksheet prior to the preconference, so that the teacher can be specific at the preconference, and so that the supervisor/peer coach can best help determine how the observation may occur.

1. Describe your teaching strategies. What are the things you typically do in a classroom?

2. How has your teaching been working for you? Are things going well?

3. What are two or three problems you have been experiencing in the classroom?

4. What have been the ways you have tried to deal with these problems? Have the results been successful or created more concerns?

5. Can the problems be observed in the classroom? Can the ways that you deal with the problems be observed?

6. What goal do you have for dealing with the problems?

7. What kind of information about the problem would be useful for you?

8. If it was up to you, how would you collect this information?

9. What other information about your classroom would be useful for you?

Form C5S: The Preconference Meeting: Getting Ready for the Observation

Use this form at the preconference meeting. As you complete the form, make sure that there is agreement between the teacher who is going to be observed and the observer. If there is disagreement, this needs to be noted, and wherever possible, additional time should be taken to develop consensus.

Teacher's Name_____ Observer's Name_____

Agreed Date, Time, and Place of Observation_____

1. The current teaching strategies used by the teacher are:

2. The current student behaviors are:

3. The desired student behaviors are:

4. The lesson objectives are:

5. The instructional processes the teacher will use are:

6. The problem that the teacher would like help observing is:

7. The teacher and the observer have defined the observable behavior as:

8. The way that information/data will be collected will be:

9. The special information the observer should know is:

10. The information obtained during this observation is confidential and will be used for the purpose of:

11. We are in agreement concerning the above items, except for the following:

_____   _____   _____
Teacher's signature   Observer's signature   Date

Form C5T: The Post-Conference Meeting: Reflecting on the Information Collected

Use this form at the post-conference meeting. As you complete the form, make sure that there is agreement between the teacher who was observed and the observer. If there is disagreement, this needs to be noted, and wherever possible, additional time should be taken to develop consensus.

Teacher's Name_____ Observer's Name_____

1. The observer should provide a copy of the data or information obtained to the teacher, if this has not already been done.

2. What is the objective summary of the data/information from the observation?

3. Were the lesson objectives achieved? Why or why not? What happened?

4. Did the problem the teacher was concerned about occur? Why or why not? What happened?

5. What does the data/information tell us about the problem, teacher-student interaction, teaching strategies, and student behavior?

6. How is the teacher going to use this information?

7. Will this information be shared with anyone else? If so, with whom, and how?

8. Where will this information be stored?

9. Will there be another observation? If so, another pre-conference form should be completed.

11. We are in agreement concerning the above items, except for the following:

_____ _____ _____

Teacher's signature   Observer's signature   Date

Form C6A: Getting in Touch With Your Feelings After Your Observation

1. What were your impressions of the observation? How did the observation go?

2. Did the observation meet your expectations? Why or why not?

3. What did you feel while you were observing? Did anything you saw make you smile, laugh, feel happy, feel sad, feel angry? If so, what was it?

4. At any point, did you find your feelings getting in the way of your observing? Why? What happened?

5. What do you feel now that you are done observing?

6. How do you think that your feelings may have affected your ability to be build reliable and valid, objective observations?

Form C6B: Feedback to the Teacher In Whose Room I Observed

My Name is:_____ Today's date is:_____

The teacher in whose room I observed is _____

The dates and time that I observed include: _____

_____

     I want to thank you for taking all the time and making all the efforts you did to welcome me into your classroom to observe. I hope that you will accept my thanks, and also pass my thanks along to your students.

     You have asked for feedback on what I observed. While most of the information was related to specific items that my instructor chose to help me become a better observer, and really is best left at that, there are some things I can tell you.

     Please remember that this information should not be used to draw conclusions or to make decisions. I am just learning how to observe. You may want to use this information to then develop your own observations. If you like, I can share copies of my blank observation forms with you.

Related to the students:

1. For _____minutes, I observed your students. I was observing their individual differences in development.

2. When I was observing, I especially was trying to apply the theory(ies) of:

3. I looked specifically at the behaviors of:

4. After observing these students, I compiled some summative information. The information that I obtained, and that my instructor agrees that I should give you is:

Related to the teacher:

1. For _____minutes, I observed you as you were teaching.

2. When I was observing, I especially was trying to apply the theory(ies) of:

3. I looked specifically at the behaviors of:

4. After observing the teacher, I compiled some summative information. The information that I obtained, and that my instructor agrees that I should give you is:

238

REFERENCES

Alberti, R.E. & Emmons, M.L. (1991). *Your perfect right: A guide to assertive living, 6th ed.* San Luis Obispo, CA: Impact Publishers.

Anderson, V., & Roit, M. (1994). Linking reading comprehension instruction to language development for language-minority students. Center for the Study of Reading Technical Report No. 603. Illinois University Urbana, ERIC Document #376740

Aronson, E., Blaney, N., Stephan, C., Sikes, J., & Snapp, M. (1978). *The jigsaw classroom.* Beverly Hills, CA: Sage.

Bandura, A. (1986). *Social foundations of thought and action.* Englewood Cliffs, NJ: Prentice-Hall.

Banks, J.A. (1994). *Multiethnic education.* Needham Heights, MA: Allyn & Bacon.

Beckstead, S. & Goetz, L. (1990). EASI 2. Social Interaction Scale, V. 6. U.S. Department of Education, Washington, D.C. EDD00001/ ERIC Document #365049

Bronfenbrenner, U. (1989). Ecological system theory. In R. Vasta (Ed.), *Annals of child development* (Vol.6, p 187-251). Greenwich, CT: JAI Press.

Butera, G., et.al. (1994). Classroom behaviors of students in rural mainstreamed settings: A comparison of students with disabilities and their normative peers. Paper presented at the Annual National Conference of the American Council on Rural Special Education. 14th, Austin, TX, March. ERIC Document #369605

Dunn, R., & Dunn, K. (1978). *Teaching students through their individual learning styles.* Englewood Cliffs, NJ: Prentice-Hall.

Eisenberg, N. (1982). The development of reasoning regarding prosocial behavior. In N. Eisenberg (Ed.), *The development of prosocial behavior* (p 219-249). New York: Academic Press.

Eisenberg, N., Martin, C.L., & Fabes, R.A. (1996). Gender development and gender effects. In D. Berliner & R. Calfee (Eds.), *Handbook of educational psychology.* (p 358-396) New York: Macmillan.

Erikson, E.H. (1950). *Childhood and society.* New York: Norton.

Eysenck, H.J. (1960). *The structure of human personality.* London: Methuen.

Good, T., & Brophy, J. (1990). *Educational psychology: A realistic approach, 4th ed.* New York: NY: Longman

Good, T., & Brophy, J. (1995). *Contemporary educational psychology, 5th ed.* New York: Longman

Gordon, T. (1975). *Parent effectiveness training.* New York: New American Library.

Grasha, A.F., & Reichmann, S.W. (1975). *Student learning styles questionaire.* Cincinatti, OH: University of Cincinatti Faculty Research Center.

Guilford, J. (1959). Three faces of intellect. *American Psychologist, 14,* 469-79.

Hocker, J., & Wilmot, W.W. (1991). *Interpersonal conflict.* Dubuque, IA: Wm. C. Brown.

Johnson, D.W., & Johnson, R.T. (1987). *Learning together and alone: Cooperative, competitive, and individualistic learning, 2nd ed.* Englewood Cliffs, NJ: Prentice Hall.

Johnson, D.W., & Johnson, R.T. (1994). *Learning together and alone: Cooperative, competitive, and individualistic learning, 4th ed.* Needham Heights, MA: Allyn & Bacon.

Jones, M.G. (1989) Gender issues in teacher education. *Journal of Teacher Education, 40(1),* 33-38.

Kagan, J. (1965). Impulsive and reflective children: significance of conceptual tempo. In J. Krumboltz (Ed.), *Learning and the educational process.* (P1330161). Chicago: Rand McNally

Kagan, S. (1985). Dimensions of cooperative classroom structures. In R. Slavin, S.Sharan, S. Kagan, R. Hertz-Lazarowitz, C. Webb, & R. Schmuck (Eds.). *Learning to cooperate, cooperating to learn.* (P 67-96). New York: Plenum Press.

Kohlberg, L. (1976). Moral stages and moralization: The cognitive-developmental approach. In T. Lickona (Ed.), *Moral development and behavior: Theory, research, and social issues* (p. 31-53). New York: Holt

Kolb, D.A., Rubin, I.M., & McIntyre, J.M. (1971). *Organizational psychology.* Englewood Cliffs, NJ: Prentice-Hall.

Lisi, P. W. (1982) *The relationship betwen professional development of teachers and student time-on-task.* Doctoral dissertation, University of Wisconsin, Program on student diversity and school processes. ERIC Document 268518

Maslow, A. (1962). *Toward a psychology of being.* Princeton, NJ: Van Nostrand.

McCrae, R.R. (1989). Why I advocate the five-factor model: Joint factor analysis of the NEO-PI with other instruments. In D.M. Buss & N. Cantor (Eds.), *Personality psychology: Recent trends and emerging directions.* (P 237-245). New York: Springer-Verlag.

McIntosh, R, et.al. (1994). Observation of students with learning disabilities in general education classrooms. *Exceptional Children, 60(3),* 249-61.

Mitchell, J. & Williams, S.E. (1993). Expert/novice differences in teaching with technology. Paper presented at the Annual Meeting of the American Educational Research Association, Atlanta, GA, April.

Nielsen, R. S. (1988) Improving teacher questioning. *Illinois School Research and Development, 24(3),* 94-101.

Olweus, D. (1984). Development of stable aggressive reaction patterns in males. In R.Blanchard & C.Blanchard (Eds.), *Advances in the study of aggression* (Vol.1). New York: Academic Press.

Piaget, J. (1928). *Judgment and reasoning in the child.* New York: Harcourt, Brace & World. (Original work published 1926).

Rotter, J.B. (1966). Generalized expectancies for internal versus external control of reinforcement. *Psychological Monographs: General and Applied. 80(1),* 1-28.

Secada, W., & Lightfoot, T. (1993). Symbols and political context of bilingual education in the United States. In M. Arias & U. Casanova (Eds.), *Bilingual education: Politics, practice, and research,* 92nd Yearbook of the National Society for the Study of Education (Part II), (p 36-64). Chicago: University of Chicago Press.

Selman, R.L. (1981). The child as a friendship philosopher. In S. R. Asher & J.M. Gottman (Eds.), *The development of friendships* (p 242-272). New York: Cambridge University Press.

Sharan, S. & Hera-Lazarowitz, R. (1980). A group-investigation method of cooperative learning in the classroom. In S. Sharan, P. Hare, C.D. Webb, & R. Hertz-Lazarowitz (Eds.), *Cooperation in education* (p 14-46). Provo, UT: Brigham Young University Press.

Showers, B. (1984) *Peer coaching: A strategy for facilitating transfer of training.* Eugene, OR: Center for Educational Policy and Management.

Shrock, S. A., & Stepp, S. L. (1991) The role of the child microcomputer expert in an elementary classroom: A theme emerging from a naturalistic study. *Journal of Research on Computing in Education, 23(4),* 545-59.

Skinner, B.F. (1938). *The behavior of organisms: An experimental analysis.* New York: Appleton-Century-Crofts.

Skinner, B.F. (1968). *The technology of teaching.* New York: Appleton-Century-Croft.

Skinner, B.F. (1969). *Contingencies of reinforcement.* Englewood Cliffs, NJ: Prentice Hall.

Slavin, R.E. (1980). Effects of student teams and peer tutoring on academic achievement and time-on-task. *Journal of Experimental Education, 48,* 252-257.

Stacy, K. (1992). Mathematical problem solving in groups: Are two heads better than one? *Journal of Mathematical Behavior, 11(3),* 261-275.

Stallings, J. & Kaskowitz, D. (1972) *Follow through classroom observation evaluation.* Menlo Park, CA: SRI International.

Stipek, D. J. (1996). Motivation and instruction. In D. Berliner & R. Calfee (Eds.), *Handbook of educational psychology.* (p 85-113) New York: Macmillan.

Vygotsky, L.S. (1928)(1962 translation). *Thought and language.* Cambridge, MA: MIT Press

Walker, V., & Brokaw, L. (1995). *Becoming aware, 6th ed.* Dubuque, IA: Kendall Hunt.

Webb, N.M., & Palinscar, A.S. (1996). Group processes in the classroom. In D. Berliner & R. Calfee (Eds.), *Handbook of educational psychology.* (p 841-873) New York: Macmillan.

Weisz, J.R., et.al. (1995). A multimethod study of problem-behavior among Thai and American Children in School: Teacher reports versus direct observations. *Child Development, 66 (2),* 402-15.

Willerman, M., McNeely, S.L., & Koffman, E.C. (1991) *Teacher helping teachers: Peer observation and assistance.* New York: Praeger.

Witkin, H., Moore, C., Goodenough, D., & Cox, P. (1977). Field dependent and field independent cognitive styles and their educational implications. *Review of Educational Research, 47,* 1-64.

INDEX